Sec sci 13 00 24124 RM

PUBLIC PURITY,
PRIVATE SHAME

RONALD PEARSALL

PUBLIC PURITY, PRIVATE SHAME

VICTORIAN SEXUAL HYPOCRISY EXPOSED

WEIDENFELD AND NICOLSON
LONDON

ISBN 0 297 77122 1

Setting by
TRI-AM Photoset Ltd
Bridge Foot, Warrington
Printed in Great Britain by
Morrison & Gibb Ltd., London and Edinburgh

CONTENTS

INTRODUCTION

I T is ill-advised for us to throw too many stones at the Victorians on account of their hypocrisy over sex, impertinent for us to look back in hindsight and tell them how they should have straightened themselves out. That they failed to live up to their expectations is undeniable, but they did have ideals; they thought what they did was for the best.

Their morality, or at least the morality ordered by the dominant middle classes, rested on the belief that if one could not be virtuous one could at least be respectable. Respectability was the armour one put on to differentiate oneself from the naked irresponsibility of the immoral and the licentious. There were gaps left in the armour for natural functions.

There was some doubt about such natural functions. It was necessary to propagate the race, but there was no need to make a fuss about it and it had to be done within a strict framework – marriage. The family was the basis of respectable life, and anything that threatened it was outlawed; it was a microcosm of the state, and while it flourished there would be no abatement in the rate of progress.

With the decline of religion, marriage became a civil institution instead of a Christian compact, though appearances were kept up. Attempts to formulate some alternative to marriage that would fit in with the immense changes in life were doomed to failure. 'The English will never abolish marriage,' decided Bernard Shaw. 'They never abolish things; but they circumvent them more unscrupulously than any other nation.'

The importance of marriage and the family to the understanding of the Victorians cannot be overestimated; they were the stable features in a sea of change. It was understood that it was the principal aim of women to get married, and a woman who remained unmarried was, by definition, a failure; although a spinster really means a woman who spins, it became a term of obloquy. As soon as she married, a woman lost her rights as an individual. She could not make a will, she could not own property, and even her own earnings belonged to her husband. These unfairnesses were gradually done away with as the nineteenth century moved towards its close, and with women's awareness that if they pushed strong enough they could be individuals, beholden to no man, what we understand as Victorianism began to come apart at the seams.

Marriage involved sexual intercourse; it was sad but true. It was woman's place to accept it uncomplainingly without a great show of enthusiasm, and many did this, though some were perverse enough to enjoy it. Some were aberrated enough to look outside marriage for such pleasure, finding it in other men, other women, and, the prime sin, themselves. It was man's duty to remain abstinent until he married. Unfortunately there was no ready definition of abstinence, and some doctors had the temerity to maintain that there was no such thing; was masturbation abstinence? Few would answer the question, for it was the undiscussed topic (theoretically).

The effort to live up to an ideal could lead to all kinds of troubles, social, psychological and physiological, for both men and women. Most could not. They thought that they were vicious, evil, weak, perverted – and unique. Men were more fortunate than women, especially if they were of the class that went to a boarding school where masturbation and homosexuality were rife. Only fortunate in one sense, for they were told by clergymen and masters that if they persisted they would go blind or mad or, preferably, both. Women were confused; often totally uninformed, they found their wedding night a frightening experience, an experience that some of them never forgot, or forgave.

But men and women had to keep up a pose; they had to be hypocrites to survive in a world that was full of eyes and ears. They engendered more hypocrites, sons and daughters who could not be told the real facts of life but had to find them out for themselves. It was a gigantic failure of communication at a time when communication had reached a sophistication that would have been undreamt of a century before. One could find out everything about anything – provided that it did not concern the relation of the sexes, or sex itself.

A conspiracy of silence never works for long, and gradually men and women found that their anxieties and fears were shared by others, and that their, as they thought, perverse pleasures were not special to them alone. Women discovered that other women enjoyed sex, disliked children, wanted careers for themselves. This could be dangerous; this could upset the institution of the family.

The family had to be protected, and danger to it squashed. This meant that birth control, called Neo-Malthusianism because birth control was an obscene term, must be suppressed, and its literature banned. This was also economically necessary; the classes who would use birth control were precisely those who were best qualified to proliferate. The lower classes should not learn about birth control either, for if they did so there would be no great pool of unemployed, on which it was believed a capitalist economy depended. A working man with a wife and two children, instead of five or six, would be a man who might get above himself.

The family had to be protected by making divorce all but impossible. Although a divorce act was passed in 1857, it was still immensely expensive to get a divorce. There were never more than a thousand a year up to the end of the nineteenth century. There were mixed feelings about whether prostitutes were a threat to the family; there were a lot of them (up to 80,000 in London alone), and it was found that the men who made most use of them were not licentious youngsters or perverts, but respectable married men, who probably loved their wives but wanted a bit of excitement, were bored with an unresponsive partner, or felt the seven-year itch. A reformer who fulminated against prostitution was not wholly appreciated; prostitutes were openly regarded as the guardians of a nation's virtue.

Extra-marital sex was all right for a man, disgraceful for a woman; a woman could not divorce a husband for adultery, but a man could divorce a wife. Most often he did not; he was allowed by law to chastise her, which could mean a legal thrashing. A man could take a mistress – if he did it quietly and kept up the pretence of living a respectable married life. The cardinal sin was to be found out; this was true of all sexual diversions. Hypocrisy was not only overlooked – it was approved.

The key to the future well-being of the institution of marriage lay in the children, and especially the purity of the daughters. Chastity was essential, and chastity meant physical virginity; suitors did not want a damaged packet. Daughters could not be put under glass domes like wax flowers, but the next best thing was to keep them in a state of suspended antisepsis. Books were censored so that daughters would not be contaminated; opera had to be vetted in case there was a ballet (in which people showed their legs); going out alone was strictly prohibited; a staunch etiquette was rigorously enforced. They had to be fresh for their sacrificial rites, modest and decent.

It was not only difficult – it was impossible. There were servants, saucy young men who did not obey the rules, newspapers which dotted the i's on such matters as divorce cases (Queen Victoria demanded that divorce reportage be stopped, but failed in her attempt), and the girl's own curiosity and sense of adventure. A chaperone who was not left stranded in a crowded shopping arcade while her charge slid away was a chaperone not yet born.

If they failed with their daughters, parents failed with their sons. And they failed with themselves. They tried to live an impossible life according to rules imposed by people who if they knew the facts of life tried to hide them for the good of society. The doctors told lies about every aspect of sex, and the clergy backed them up. If brought to book, they maintained that it was for the best; they ignored the guilt, shame, and worry inflicted on millions of men and women who merely wanted to live their lives according to the rules.

There were some who did not worry about respectability, decency, modesty, and the other middle-class shibboleths. These were mostly at the top and the bottom of society; the aristocracy ignored the rules, the lower classes did not know about them. And there were the outsiders, the Bohemians who clicked their fingers at the establishment, the homosexuals, male and female, who made their own arrangements, largely left alone if they pretended to be 'normal', the professional bachelors who were contemptuous of marriage, and the girls who supported Women's Rights, emancipation, and the rest of it (though most of them eventually got married and fell into line).

Some pretence at being other than one is is a necessary factor in advanced societies. And the Victorians belonged to an incredibly advanced society. They were hypocritical about sex, but their motives were not contemptible. What will the twenty-first century say about our hypocrisies? Perhaps it is better not to speculate about this. We have our guilt and shame, too.

1

THE CULT OF ABSTINENCE

THE celebration of sexual abstinence was dear to the hearts of many Victorians. Unlike chastity, abstinence is a negative quality; it was unproductive, literally and figuratively, a somewhat mean concept considered to be good for society and for oneself. Many of those who promoted it were well-meaning, if muddled, while others were arrant hypocrites who urged abstinence on the young without for a moment considering it for themselves.

Those who took a lead from the church found themselves confused. True, the church regarded manifestations of the sexual impulse as unnecessary and evil, yet marriage was approved as proper and moral, even though it was the satisfaction of the impulse under licence. The Christian church was historically split on the question of sex; Luther's revolt against Catholicism was part due to its rigid insistence on sexual abstinence.

The medical profession was also divided, and doctors who should have known better made wild pronouncements. It was in England that the virtues of abstinence were most often broadcast, and J. F. Scott in his book *Sexual Instinct* pointed out the number of geniuses who have lived chastely as bachelors. However, his choice was unfortunate, as he selected Jesus, Newton, Beethoven, and Kant as 'men of vigour and mental acumen'. Although the church would have gone along with Scott in his choice of Jesus, there is no doubt that both Newton and Kant led distorted unsatisfactory lives, and probably would have done whether they were married or single. Tradition had elevated Beethoven as a man of singular purity, and ignored the fact that Beethoven had not been chaste and that his deafness was most likely the result of syphilis contracted when young. There was nothing particularly commendable about abstinence after a liberal sowing of wild oats.

Sir James Paget coupled sexual intercourse with theft or lying, and in his *Syphilis and the Nervous System* (1892), Sir William Gowers asserted that 'no man ever yet was in the slightest degree or way the worse for continence or better for incontinence. From the latter all are worse morally; a clear majority are worse physically; and in no small number the result is, and ever will be, utter physical shipwreck on one of the many rocks, sharp, jagged-edged, which beset the way, or on one of the many beds of festering slime which no care can possibly avoid'. An interesting passage which tells us more about Sir William Gowers than about syphilis and the nervous system.

Most doctors hedged their bets, answering yes to a spot question as to whether sexual abstinence was harmless but anxious to provide riders. The happiest were those who declared that abstinence was impossible, and that to draw a line between sexual intercourse and masturbation was absurd as the end was the same – the release of sexual tension. This was supposing that masturbation was as universal as many believed. But even those who did not think that this was the case pointed out that abstinence apparently excluded involuntary emissions at night.

As with the clergy, doctors often committed themselves to a contradiction. Those who advocated abstinence were the last to criticise marriage. They were merely falling in line, telling the middle classes what they wanted to hear; doctors provided a service, and as the middle classes were those who took greatest advantage of them it was to the doctors' interest not to alienate them by seeming to encourage promiscuity, which, though not logical, was seen as the opposite of continence and abstinence. Doctors preferred continence to abstinence, as it was much easier for a layman to see continence as a good word, and incontinence, used almost exclusively as a synonym for bed-wetting, as a bad word.

The most thoughtful medical men realised that it was not a simple matter at all, and everyone's opinion on what constituted abstinence was different. To some, abstinence meant not going with prostitutes before marriage. Iwan Bloch, one of the most prolific writers on sexual topics, advocated abstention during early life and temporary abstention in adult life. His reasons were interesting; energy would be conserved and transformed, and the abstainer would realise that there were other things in life than sex. This notion, sublimation, provided a reason for abstinence, and it was eagerly seized by propagandists who could thus seem to make abstinence not only respectable but laudable. They could argue that Scott's quartet of Jesus, Kant, Beethoven, and Newton were abstinent (disputed) not because they were great men, but great men because they were abstinent.

Freud naturally gave the matter of abstinence attention. The sexual instinct was so powerful that keeping it under control was a full-time job. Subjugation through sublimation could succeed with a minority; others could become neurotic or come to grief. Adele Schreiber, a psychologist whose *Mutterschutz* continued the Freudian argument, thought that the wrong question was being asked. Happy love and marriage was the healthy life, 'and its complete absence cannot fail to lead to severe psychic depression, even if no direct physiological disturbances can be demonstrated'.

In all nineteenth-century medical matters there was always a pro, a neutral, and a con. Even such a useful invention as the stethoscope had the three camps battling it out. So it is not surprising that there were some doctors who considered that it was their duty to recommend sexual intercourse to a patient who felt it his moral duty to remain celibate. There were not many of these doctors in Britain, but in Europe Gyurkovechky, Nystrom, and Marcuse said just this; one, Lederer, went further. It was a physician's duty to advise a wife whose husband was impotent to go out and have intercourse with another man. 'Whether,' he wrote, 'she does so with her husband's consent is no affair of the physician's, for he is not the guardian of morality, but the guardian of health.'

This brave venture, therefore, was not suited to Britain, for whatever else they were, doctors deemed themselves guardians of morality. Two of the loudest voices in praise of abstinence were those of Sir James Paget and Dr William Acton. Paget (1814-99) was at one time, by his own assessment, the highest paid surgeon in London, with an income of more than £10,000 a year. He progressed through a series of medical jobs, such as curator of a medical museum, contributor to the *Penny Cyclopaedia* and the biographical dictionary published by the Society for the Diffusion of Useful Knowledge, demonstrator of morbid anatomy, and surgeon to the Finsbury Dispensary. He was well over forty before his income was greater than his expenditure. He was a hard worker who sneered at the attempt to give workers a ten-hour day when he himself rarely did less than twelve, contemptuous of many others in the profession, taciturn, and seemingly cold. His two favourite proverbs were 'Never alter a plan once made' and John Hunter's advice to his pupils, 'Don't think, try; be patient, be accurate'.

A man of great application and perseverance, Paget knew his role in society. He knew best. In the 1863 address at the opening of the winter session of his hospital he told his audience 'to do your duty with all your might'. He went on to talk about experience:

> Experience is of no natural growth in us; it is not commensurate with age. After about thirty, wise men may grow wiser, but unwise men rarely grow wise. Therefore there are many old men with no experience at all . . . That which will most harass you in your practice will be the apparent success of dishonesty. You must be prepared for it; for it will not cease in your time, if indeed it ever does. In our department of social life, as in all others, the supply of rogues is duly proportioned to that of fools.

It is worth quoting these maxims, because they show the man. Contemptuous of cleverness, short with fools, feared by young doctors, held in awe by older men, he knew his own mind, did not hesitate to pontificate on matters that were not within his jurisdiction, and never dreamed that he was not right. Young men should be abstinent for otherwise they would catch syphilis, turn to thieving, be liars, or go mad. That was the programme he had prepared for them. They could overcome temptation by 'work, lifelong work . . . there is no success without it, no happiness without it'.

Occasionally he had doubts, but not often. Writing to his wife in July 1863 he wrote, 'I am ashamed and angry with myself that I can so little enjoy what kind people take so much trouble to make agreeable . . . but I could not enjoy myself, and sat with a feeling of kid gloves in my stomach, and white neckcloth round my brains'. In 1867 he was in attendance on the Princess of Wales (later Queen Alexandra) at Wiesbaden. Crustily he wrote to his brother:

> There are crowds here who have nothing to cure but what might be cured by moderate self-denial, or borne with moderate patience. But they like the place and the gossip, and the idleness that they need not apologise for, and the occasions of making

acquaintance with those who would not know them in England.

Paget was typical of a kind of man that flourished in the nineteenth century, illustrating the victory of self-help and effort, but unwilling and unable to be flexible, reluctant to realise that people were different, and yet conscious that he himself was subject to the failings about which he was indignant. A significant passage arises in a letter he wrote to his wife in 1858:

> I see and do nothing but my work, and at the day's end am glad to feel how many evils of thought and word one is saved from by having one's mind so occupied, and by having no temptation to think and talk of other men's affairs and characters . . . I am every day the more sure that the more *things* are thought of to the exclusion of *persons*, the less is the sin and folly and waste of thoughts.

There is ambiguity here, the guarded use of language – 'evils of thought', 'sin and folly and waste of thoughts' – and the reader becomes aware that Sir James Paget was not all of a piece, that the image that he had strenuously built up was cracking, and that he was being activated by forbidden thoughts. It is interesting to compare this passage with one from a letter written by John Ruskin to Mrs Cowper in January 1870, where sexual repression is breaking:

> My mind is getting so mixed up now of desire for revenge – and a kind of hatred which the love is changing into – that my whole life is getting distorted and I don't well understand anything, besides a shame and anger at myself – increasing day by day – which checks me and lowers me fatally.

Another characteristic of men who fulminated against sexual incontinence and promiscuity was petulance. *They* had practised abstinence, they had kept themselves pure until their wedding night, they had been obliged to wait until they could afford to marry and renounce abstinence – so why should not others? Paget was paying off family debts until he was forty-eight which kept him from climbing up in his profession as rapidly as he would have liked. Lack of money kept him from marriage until he was thirty; he was engaged more than seven years. Did he lapse during those years, with the consequent anger at self becoming directed at others?

Whatever else Paget might have advised, he would never have suggested patients suffering from sexual problems go out and take a woman, or for neurotic women to take a man. He considered that he had to follow a rule of conduct, come what may. A permissive doctor has to consider the social implications; in Victorian times this meant being an accessory to the patient catching venereal disease (syphilis was almost uncurable, and the mercury treatment could be as bad as the disease) or of some unfortunate woman having a baby (birth control was haphazard and not altogether efficient).

The traditional way of working off sexual energy was to exercise, or take cold baths. Patients so advised could find that it could work against them, for they found that some kinds of exercise excited them. Bicycling being one of the great outdoor exercises of the last part of the nineteenth century, many women attempting to work off their randiness by cycling found that the action of the saddle against their sexual parts contributed to the orgasm that they were anxious to prevent.

In his *Dictionary of Domestic Medicine* (1856), Spencer Thomson wrote: 'The use of cold as a hygienic agent . . . is invaluable . . . When used to subdue certain forms of excited and inflammatory action, the temperature must of course be suited to the case, but ice-cold is most generally useful.' Cold baths were widely used in the lunatic asylums for subduing the sexually disturbed; the top of the bath was fitted with a wooden board with a hole for the head, so that the bather had his cold bath whether he or she liked it or not. Mr Hooper of Pall Mall devised vulcanised cushions that could be filled with ice-cold water. Cold baths were included in the regimen of the public schools that went in for manliness.

The ascetics of old had known that cold contracted the skin and deadened sexual feelings. Heat was widely believed to encourage such feelings. Hot climates, a close atmosphere, heavy bed-clothing, hot baths, all stimulated the skin and with it the senses. Another encouragement to lewd thoughts that might lead to lewd deeds was tight-lacing and constricted clothing; the opponents of knicker-wearing used this as one of their arguments. The author of the pornographic *Mysteries of Verbena House* (1882) claimed: 'The greatest enemy to a woman's chastity is *contact*. Let her wear her things loose, and she may keep her blood cool. Nuns – Continental ones at least – don't wear drawers.'

More dangers to abstinence lay in food and drink, especially alcoholic drinks, erotic reading, and thinking about 'objects which keep the genital organs in a sort of permanent turgescence and excitation'. The sure-fire formula for ending abstinence was the wearing of 'tight corsets while reading French novels'. Mental exercise was widely advocated as a way of calming sexual excitement. One bewildered lady wrote 'I have tried mechanical mental work such as solving arithmetical or algebraic problems, but it does no good; in fact it seems only to increase the excitement'. Havelock Ellis records this without comment, and goes on to say that it is easier to avoid rousing the sexual impulses than to silence them when they are once aroused.

The effort to be abstinent could be psychically crippling. 'I may say,' one woman wrote to Havelock Ellis, 'that it is the most passionate desire of my heart to be freed from this bondage, that I may relax the terrible years-long tension of resistance, and be happy in my own way. If I had this affliction once a month, once a week, even twice a week, to stand against it would be child's play. I should scorn to resort to unnatural means [i.e. masturbation] however moderately. But self-control itself has its revenges, and I sometimes feel as if it is no longer to be borne.' Another correspondent wrote: 'If I had only had three weeks' happiness I would not quarrel with Fate, but to have one's whole life so absolutely empty is horrible.'

The propagandists of abstinence had a lot to answer for. They were a power in the schools. It might be supposed that physical exercise and compulsory games at school were to develop the body and improve health. Not so. In his *Sexualpedagogik*, Konrad Höller stated that the aim was: 'not the development of the active and passive strength of the body and its skill, but the establishment and fortification of the authority of the will over the body and its needs, so much given up to indolence. He who has learnt to endure and overcome, for the sake of a definite aim, hunger and thirst and fatigue [what physical exercises did Höller have in mind, for God's sake?] will be better able to withstand sexual impulses and the temptation to gratify them.'

It was natural for those concerned with the running of schools to have their prejudices confirmed, and it was easier to enforce exercises and games than to face the undeniable fact that children at the age of puberty did not take philosophically to abstinence. Höller and his like also gave backing to those schools which went in for a Spartan regime, which favoured cold baths and hard mattresses, and produced ten ruddy-faced footballers to every candidate for Oxford or Cambridge. The abstinence-mongers were contemptuous of the tendency in progressive education to foster intellectual superiority. Of this, William Acton wrote in *The Functions and Disorders of the Reproductive Organs* (1857):

> For, as any one may observe, it is not the strong athletic boy, fond of healthy exercise, who thus early shows marks of sexual desire, but your puny exotic, whose intellectual education has been fostered at the expense of his physical development.

Acton went on to say that although he did not wish to keep boys and girls from improper books, there were inherent dangers.

> He reads in them of the pleasures, nothing of the penalties, of sexual indulgence. He is not intuitively aware that, if the sexual desires are excited, it will require greater power of will to master them than falls to the lot of most lads; that if indulged in, the man will and must pay the penalty for the errors of the boy; that for one that escapes, ten will suffer; that an awful risk attends abnormal substitutes for sexual intercourse; and that self-indulgence, long pursued, tends ultimately, if carried far enough, to early death or self-destruction.

Acton was a Cassandra crying woe, calling doom on those who did not cower under his instructions to be abstinent at all costs. Born in 1813, the son of a clergyman, Acton was apprenticed to the Resident Apothecary at St Bartholomew's Hospital, where he remained until 1836, then going to Paris and specialising in diseases of the urinary and generative organs. Back in England in 1840, he began practice as a surgeon, wrote highly regarded text books on his subject, and turned his attention to the social factors that led to venereal diseases.

He became an expert on prostitution, and unlike most of the self-styled pundits on this explosive subject he knew a lot about it. He was a realist, and scorned 'the dull stupidity that shuts its eyes to well-known evils'. Prostitution should, as on the continent, be controlled; prostitution was reprehensible, but human nature being what it was, it would continue to flourish. A clean healthy prostitute was better than a dirty diseased one; periodical examination could make a visit to a prostitute naughty but not self-destructive. Acton was not a man to be taken in by stereotypes. He thought for himself. It was traditional that a prostitute's life was short and brutish, and vile disease and a pauper's grave was all that she could anticipate. From his researches, Acton found that this was the exception; 'no other class of females is so free from general disease', he wrote. Prostitutes had iron constitutions, and far from sinking them at the bottom of the social pile the trade could elevate them in a way that would have been impossible by taking the path of virtue. To make middle-class women even more uneasy, he claimed that many working-class women went through prostitution as a stage, and emerged little harmed by their experiences. Furthermore, 'the better inclined class of prostitutes become the wedded wives of men in every grade of society, from the peerage to the stable'.

In the same way as he would have liked to have controlled prostitutes, lining them up and organising them, he would have liked to have controlled small boys – bed-wetters, dirty talkers, and all. He knew it was difficult; he knew what boarding schools were like, and how easily the young were 'contaminated'. Persuasion was wasted; the lads had to be frightened, just as prostitutes who did not guard against infection should be summarily deposited in gaol. Acton did not point out the advantages (if any) of continence, only the disadvantages of what he considered the worst kind of incontinence, masturbation:

> The frame is stunted and weak, the muscles undeveloped, the eye is sunken and heavy, the complexion is sallow, pasty, or covered with spots of acne, the hands are damp and cold, and the skin moist. The boy shuns the society of others, creeps about alone joins with repugnance in the amusements of his schoolfellows.

Acton had lost his admirable objectivity. He was holding up a hollowed-out turnip as at Hallowe'en, and was urging all to keep the candle alight for the good of society. He set a tone for others to follow, and they did. The doctors of the middling order looked on Acton as a man who knew what he was talking about; like the ancient mariner, he held them with his glittering eye. Embarrassed, they looked in their looking glasses for the tell-tale acne and sallow complexion. Acton might not frighten happy masturbating boys, but he frightened them.

Like Paget, Acton thought that he knew best. He knew better than, for example, the primitive races, Moslems, Catholic theologians, or the great Greek physician Galen (130-201 AD), who thought that it did more good than harm. Diogones was praised by the philosopher Chrysippus (born *c.* 280 BC) for masturbating in the market-place, though by and large the Greeks were not so generous, thinking it unmanly, as did the Romans, though not a penal sin. Islam considered masturbation a Christian vice of not much consequence.

Historians of sex consider that the Moslems were correct, that before the coming of Christianity there were ample opportunities for those homosexual and heterosexual relationships that were later proscribed by the church. Masturbation was a way out of the impasse, though theologians disagreed about how significant it was, whether it was worth forty days' penance (seventh century) or merely a good talking-to by an understanding confessor (nineteenth century – as physicians were getting more and more worked up about it so the Catholic church was cooling it).

Under certain circumstances, Catholic theologians permitted a woman to masturbate, though naturally they put their reasons into Latin. A wife does not sin *quae se ipsam tactibus excitat ad seminationem statim post copulam in qua vir solus seminavit.* This promise rested on the erroneous assumption that women ejaculated like men; without ejaculation there could be no fertilisation; masturbation would help the ejaculation along.

Had those who waxed most on the subject bothered to consult history they would not have made the cardinal error of assuming that masturbation was something new, a vice of modern life. In their own recondite way, they were sentimentalists, looking back at a pure and healthy age and comparing it with the horrible nineteenth century. The romantic savage, it was roundly stated, did not do it, though the nearest the experts came to a savage was reading about Man Friday in *Robinson Crusoe.*

Typical of this point of view was Dr J. W. Howe, who in his *Excessive Venery, Masturbation, and Continence* (1883) wrote:

In savage lands it is of rare occurrence. Savages live in a state of Nature. No moral obligations exist which compel them to abstain from a natural gratification of their passions. There is no social law which prevents them from following the dictates of their lower nature. Hence, they have no reason for adopting onanism as an outlet for passions. The moral trammels of civilized society, and ignorance of physiological laws, give origin to the vice.

The belief that savages ran around with no clothes on, ate their enemies, and had it off when they wanted it, was cherished in Victorian myth and legend. It was one reason why the British Empire was such a good thing, to put an end to such naughtinesses. In many parts of the 'savage' world, people had a code of conduct that made nineteenth-century Britain seem barbaric. If this was known, it was kept to the pages of learned journals and sombre tomes on anthropology.

It was easy to define abstinence; it was less easy to define masturbation, or onanism as the learned term was (though Onan in the Bible practised *coitus interruptus*). The confusion of nomenclature shows confusion of definition. There was also auto-erotism (Havelock Ellis's invention, *not* auto-eroticism), *auto-erastia, geistige Onänie, onania psychica, autophilie*, and monosexual idiosyncrasy. How did one deal with accidental masturbation arising from day-dreaming, riding in railway carriage, cab, or omnibus, horse-riding, or even the rubbing of clothes? There were men and women who admitted that they felt that there was no sin provided that they did not use their hands. But if they used their hands accidentally?

This could be very dangerous, as E. B. Kirk declared in *Talk with Girls* (1905):

> There is one thing, however, which may most seriously hurt a girl's body, and that is touching the private parts in any way to make the sensitive nerves give a sensation of pleasure. Sometimes schoolgirls do this out of ignorance or curiosity, but they run the risk of hurting themselves for life through it. A tired dull feeling is often the result next day, and sometimes even nerve affections may be started which injure the brain.

Nothing, surely, could be more calculated to make a girl experiment. And experiment girls did. Bananas, cucumbers, candles, turnips, carrots, beetroot, pencils, sticks of sealing wax, cotton-reels, hair-pins, knitting-needles, compasses, glass stoppers, eggs, tooth-picks, and toothbrushes were all recorded. The banana was mentioned in the *Arabian Nights* and had a place in Polynesian mythology as a real impregnator, not a simulated one. The smaller instruments were used to tickle the urethra. This practice could be extremely dangerous, not for the reasons postulated by E. B. Kirk but because these small objects found their way into the bladder by accident. This was so common that in 1862 a German doctor invented a special device for extracting hair-pins from the female bladder. The English gynaecologist Lawson Tait declared that most cases of stone in the female bladder were due to the introduction of a foreign body, often a hair-pin.

These were the dangers of masturbation, not insanity, epilepsy, blindness, headache, skin tenderness, acne, asthma, heart disease, deafness, red nose, incontinence of urine, warts, smelliness, or hallucinations. There would have been many fewer thousands of anxious and hysterical men and women had propagandists been as concerned with telling the truth about masturbation as they were about spreading news about birth control. Many sensitive young men, accepting what they were told by their elders and betters, castrated themselves rather than submit to their passions; others used infibulation devices. Young women, told that their pelvises would be distorted and that they would not acquire breasts, were driven to hysteria and sometimes to suicide by their inability to drop the habit. In her diary of 15 March 1850, Florence Nightingale gave vent to her feelings on the subject. She had conquered masturbation. 'God has delivered me from the great offence and the constant murderer of all my thoughts.' But she relapsed. 'My enemy is too strong for me, everything has been tried.' For all her great talents and energy, Florence Nightingale suffered throughout her life from hypochondria and suppressed hysteria, one of many thinking people whose lives were made wretched by listening to those who did not know what they were talking about.

Once again, it was the middle orders of society who suffered. The poor 'wanked' and 'kept down the Census'. Guilt and shame only struck those who were capable of feeling them. The rich suffered less, having been broken into the habit at their public schools where masturbation was the rule rather than the exception and was accepted as part of life. As the rich and the poor were notorious for their lack of sexual inhibitions they enjoyed something of the freedom of the pre-Christian never-never-land of fun and frolic, and had less reason to pay tribute to, (the most unedifying and disapproving phrase of them all) self-abuse.

2

THE VERY ICE OF CHASTITY

CHASTITY is imposed from within, whereas abstinence is forced on the person concerned by external pressures, usually social. Often this is not realised by the abstainer. There is a good deal more kudos associated with chastity than abstinence, and those who were most chaste (or undeniably chaste, as in theory there cannot be degrees of chastity) often made certain that others knew it.

Its prestige was partly due to the support of the church, though chastity was a notion that fitted in with the romantic movement of the eighteenth century and after. It brought to mind the heroes and heroines of the age of knightly courtesy, the sexless creatures that inhabited the world of Sir Walter Scott at his most baronial Gothick, and the pure maidens of the ancient world (though they may have occasionally given in to the odd god in the guise of a bull, a swan, or a cloud).

There was a good deal of prejudice against chastity among those who only saw it as submission to an external law, or as a rule of morality imposed by one sex on another. William Morris saw chastity as exploitation; it was 'the most disgusting vice that afflicted human nature,' he alleged at a meeting of the Fellowship of the New Life.

The essence of chastity was that it could be triumphant amidst temptation. In its religious form, asceticism, temptation was deliberately encouraged so that the body could rise above it, so that from the first it was irrevocably tied in with sex. St Jerome in the desert was clad in a sack, was blackened by the sun, but thought of girls. 'My face,' he wrote, 'was pale with fasting and my mind within my frigid body was burning with desire; the fires of lust would still flare up in a body that already seemed to be dead.' St Magdalena de Pozzi rolled on thorny bushes to dispel sexual thoughts. St Anthony, whose array of temptations were pictorially graphic enough to make him a patron saint of artists who delighted in portraying acute discomfort, is perhaps the most typical of the ascetics.

The most adventurous of the religious ascetics were those who really challenged themselves, participating in brother and sister relationships, kissing one another, and indulging in nakedness at baptismal rites. Men and women shared the same room, and even the same bed, but they all remained *virgo intacta*. Men who really wanted to show off brought virgins into their houses, lavished kisses on them, and even caressed them voluptuously, but did not infringe such virginities. The glorification by the early church in these manifestations of self-control were a subtle counter to the open eroticism of the pagan world, but this kind of asceticism became absurd when nuns and monks shared the same bed and the same lascivious purpose.

The identification of chastity with physical virginity was inevitable. Admittedly, a chaste person would get a reward in heaven, but was that sufficient? Certainly for those who believed in the harsher Christian disciplines. As Milton wrote in *Comus*:

> So dear to Heaven is saintly chastity,
> That, when a soul is found sincerely so,
> A thousand liveried angels lacky her,
> Driving far off each thing of sin and guilt.

Virgins for Christ was a pretty idea, and many girls thought that it might be safer that way, for Nonconformism brought with it fear of eternal consequences for those who had strayed from the straight and narrow. During the eighteenth and nineteenth century chastity became more and more associated with women; Milton in the above four lines assumed that chastity governed women.

But men, and not merely the clergy, were looking at chastity in another light, as a target, the attaining of which would extend their personal consciousness. Nietzsche (1844-1900) clothed the idea in philosophical trappings. 'A fundamental and wise foresight in the face of erotic things, even in thought, is part of a fine reasonableness in life, even in richly endowed and complete natures.' Nietzsche was not a particularly impressive sample of this fine reasonableness; his cult of the superman has a lot to answer for in twentieth-century politics, and he became unhinged in 1889.

Enrichment of life was not a negligible ideal, but using chastity as a spiritual self-help had all the disadvantages of a smug formula. It could mean erecting artificial barriers to the consummation of a love affair, regarding chastity as a game of snakes and ladders. One was deflated, disappointed, sent down a snake by lewd thoughts, propelled up a ladder by some spectacular act of renunciation, but one knew that one would eventually get through if one tried long enough. This expansion of the sex impulse was called 'irradiation'.

One disadvantage of this was that it could be a fulltime job; the aesthetic equivalent of irradiation as set forth by Walter Pater was burning with a gem-like flame. But the more unfortunate could go up like a petrol can, and those who trod the primrose path of dalliance, working themselves up in chaste lubricity, could end up in pornotopia, where everything was seen and felt in sexual terms. 'Only the chaste can be really obscene,' wrote the novelist Joris Karl Huysmans, whose novel *À Rebours* (1884) fastened on sensation as the be-all and end-all.

À Rebours was not a novel for the chaste, but in the person of its hero (based on Robert de Montesquiou who took a gilt tortoise about with him everywhere he went) it demonstrated how sensation for the sake of sensation could be extraordinarily perverse. The hero orchestrated scents and perfumes, and no vice was too disgusting to investigate; external nature was of little interest compared with a bizarre inward life.

The professional male virgins found themselves detoured, and the pursuit of the ideal could end by their becoming crabbed hypocrites, with nothing gained but faded memories of long-lost sensations. In 1859, Prosper Mérimée wrote, 'I think that nowadays people attach far too much importance to chastity. Not that I deny that chastity is a virtue, but there are degrees in virtues just as there are in vices.' 'As chaste as unsunn'd snow,' says Shakespeare in *Cymbeline*. But chastity could be a searing red-hot brand as well.

There were the chaste who were storing their sexual impulses for the great day, and who were chaste because they wanted to be. There was Charles Darwin, who declared, 'My God, it is intolerable to think of spending one's whole life like a neuter bee

working, working, and nothing after all . . . marry, marry, marry.'
There were those who were playing a part, discussed cynically by
George Bernard Shaw:

> Formerly it may have been difficult to live in a modernised Jesus
> Christ style; but now it is easy, convenient, and cheap; and if a
> man makes a merit of it he is pretty sure to be a humbug.

Somewhat out of the normal run of the chaste was Beatrice
Potter, later to be Mrs Webb, pioneer Socialist and a strong formative influence on the creation of the Labour Party. She saw
chastity as somehow socially good, a contribution to the Utopia
she and her husband were working for. In her diary for 1887 she is
writing of her fiancé, whom she would marry in the 1890s:

> We are very fond of each other. A close intimate relationship
> between a man and a woman without sentiment (perhaps not
> without sentiment, but without passion or the dawning of pas-
> sion). We are fellow workers, both inspired by the same intellec-
> tual desire.

Chastity was very much a matter of class, the province of those
who thought before they acted. The respectable lower-middle
classes had their own idea of chastity – this meant not getting
married before they could afford it, and the corollary that the
womenfolk were to keep their virginity but not necessarily the
men. It was this class which was most devoted to the notion of
women as property; the men were obsessed with not getting
damaged goods. Some of the lower-middle class men were forced
by the nature of their jobs to be bachelors – clerks, bank cashiers,
the superior kind of shop assistants – and they were the ones who
helped to keep the middle range of the prostitutes in business.
Prostitutes were the guardians of middle-class virginity.

There were also upper-middle-class occupations that demanded
bachelordom. University dons were obliged to quit their jobs when
they married; they were regarded as clergymen until the early
1870s, though some of them never gave a sermon in their lives. The
High Church movement, variously called Ritualism or Puseyism,
now better known as Anglo-Catholicism, demanded celibacy from
its clergy. The Ritualists paraded their celibacy like medals for
good conduct, and with their hair plastered close to their heads and
their affected manners the Ritualists stood out from the ordinary

clergy like exotic birds. They sought to implant their ideas of celibacy in their flock, and brought back the confessional to the Church of England; the sceptics thought that the confessional was an excuse for secret vice, and sometimes they were right. The arch-priest of the movement, some said the anti-Christ, Dr Pusey, reproved his minions for preferring to hear the confessions of nubile young women rather than middle-aged frights worried lest divine retribution strike them for sacking their cooks.

The pornographers, both writers and artists, often used the High Church confessional as a subject. In his series *Pretty Little Games for Young Ladies and Gentlemen. With Pictures of Good Old English Sports and Pastimes*, Thomas Rowlandson includes an engraving called 'The Sanctified Sinner', described by Ashbee:

> A meanly furnished room, with a small window at the back, into which an ugly old man is peeping. On a low bed is seated a naked girl; and between her legs stands an old man, dressed in a hat and long cloak, with his breeches down. The girl with her left hand clasps the old fellow round the buttocks, and with her right handles his member, which is unnaturally large, and its shape quite *a la* Rowlandson; the girl is bald about her parts.

Although the argument of the engraving is not immediately apparent in the picture, there is a supplement in the form of a poem, either supplied by Rowlandson or more likely, the publisher Hotten when he reprinted the series in 1872:

> For all this canting fellow's teaching
> He loves a girl as well as preaching.
> With holy love he rolls his eyes
> Yet view his stout man Thomas rise!
> Tis sure enough to make it stand
> To have it stroked by such a hand.
> When flesh and spirit both combine
> His raptures sure must be divine.

The use of the confessional by High Church clergy to elicit erotic memoirs was frowned upon by their superiors, who were rarely of the same persuasion. The Rev. Alfred Poole was a curate of the parish of St Paul's, Knightsbridge, and was accused by several parishioners of 'habitually asking outrageous questions from persons who came to him in Confession'. The Bishop of London investigated, and thought that the matter was exaggerated. Poole declared that he had 'never put any questions of a nature, or in a manner, or in language calculated to bring scandal on the Church.' Nevertheless, Poole's licence was withdrawn.

There was also a scandal connected with St Saviour's, Leeds, and in 1850 the Bishop of Ripon wrote to the offender, the Rev. H. F. Beckett, accusing him of putting questions to a woman 'which she says made her feel very much ashamed, and greatly distressed her, and which were of such an indelicate nature that she would never tell her husband of them'.

A privately printed *Manual of Confession for Children* created consternation; it told the reader:

> A good Confession ought not only to be humble and sincere, but also *full*. You must tell your Confessor *all* the sins you can remember. For if you hide one sin on purpose, you lie to God; you would be guilty of a great crime; and you would not even receive the pardon of those sins which you have confessed.

That many High Church clergymen regarded the confessional as a perquisite is clear. In the anonymous *From Oxford to Rome* (1847) the author writes: 'Confession the young Anglican has been accustomed to regard as one of his *secret privileges. Scarcely ever spoken of, even in the most confidential intercourse*, it is yet practised very extensively, and, as we believe, most beneficially, in the English Church'. The Rev. Charles Jupp, of Houghton-le-Spring, enjoyed the secrecy. He heard confessions in his own house, and wrote to one young lady in 1872: 'Mrs —— has left, and we have the house to ourselves. Parishioners are so constantly coming on business of one kind or another that your visits would not be noticed'.

Women could find a session in the confessional with a well set-up young priest as exciting as an assignation. It must be remembered that to the Victorians sin meant sexual sin. The attitude of the Anglican priest guaranteed that no stone would be left unturned, and the High Church clergy were encouraged to dig deep. 'In the pulpit,' wrote the Rev. Augustus Worth in his *The Confessional* (1882), 'he can touch certain sins only with kid gloves, in the Confessional he probes the sores to the very bottom. In the pulpit he must be a lion, in the Confessional a fox.' It was a form of refined sexual pleasure quite in tune with those of the early

Christians, a voyeurism adapted for extraordinary social conditions. Without pleasure in telling all, there was no pleasure in the auditing and the necessary, if half-hearted, reproofs.

Some of the criticisms of Church of England confessionals were carried out by rabid anti-Catholics (Roman Catholicism was subject to considerable persecution when the High Church movement was at its height), but it is interesting that Roman Catholic priests were rarely suspected of the secret vices that were laid at the doors of the Ritualists, perhaps because it was thought that the Roman Catholics were blasé about confession, and that it was a meaningless ritual for both priests and lay folk.

Whatever women – and women were the predominant sex in the confessional – told their confessors, it was clear that outsiders thought it was pretty strong stuff. It was well understood that excess of spirituality was next door to sensuality, and the hell-fire-and-damnation preacher Spurgeon delivered a sermon on this theme. Ordinary decent girls did not need to go to tell their secret life to a hypocritical humbug who had 'fears and sorrows about the intense wickedness of the world ... a believer in the superior righteousness of celibacy' wrote Octavia Hill, pioneer in the provision of model dwellings for the working class, in 1857. She had cast a shrewd eye on what she described as a 'patent Puseyite'.

Because of the publicity given to his case, Alfred Poole was a chief target for criticism. He fulfilled all the requirements for a butt, and because he had been sacked by his bishop it was reasoned that the accusations made against him were true. The most literate exposé of Poole was made in the pornographic anthology of verse, *Cythera's Hymnal*:

> The Reverend Pimlico Poole was a saint
> Who averted from sinners their doom,
> By confessing the ladies until they felt faint,
> All alone in a little dark room.
> *Chorus*: But they never confessed, and it never was known
> What was done in that little dark room all alone.

The confessions did not shock the Rev. Alfred Poole

> But arranging his person, he sat in his chair,
> While his Tommy kept rising like yeast.

Eventually 'Mr Poole's constitution gave way/And his clock-weights [i.e. testicles] hung down to his knees'. The tone of disapproval in the attacks on Poole was often mixed with envy.

In retrospect the High Church confessional can be seen as a primitive form of psychoanalysis. The techniques are shared. In an article on the sexual element in sensibility published in *Psychological Review* in 1904 W. Thomas points out the means used to bring out confessional material – strong suggestion, an appeal 'not of the conflict type, but of an intimate, sympathetic, and pleading kind.' The women who made use of the confessional were incapable of holding out against a probing inquisition. The American psychologist Clara Barrus, writing in 1895, maintained that women who believe 'that they are the Virgin Mary, the bride of Christ, the Church, "God's wife", are sure, sooner or later, to disclose symptoms which show that they are in some way or other sexually depraved.' Many of the nineteenth century writers on sex argued that the strongest feelings of religious emotion were often unconsciously rooted in erotic emotion.

The close relation between sex and religion was explored extensively during the nineteenth century, and often obsessively. The findings could be extremely recondite. Coventry Patmore, the poet and glorifier of sexual love sanctified by marriage, pondered on the matter: 'The relationship of the soul to Christ *as his betrothed wife* is the key to the feeling [with] which prayer and love and honour should be offered to Him. In this relation is a mine of undiscovered joy and power'. The mystic Swedenborg enjoyed a vogue. He maintained that all knowledge is nuptial knowledge, and that sexual duality was the basis of all being.

The clergy, their feet on the earth, who were more interested in the contents of their collecting plates and getting every baby baptised, were not happy at the association. Dean Inge in his *Christian Mysticism* (1899) considered that the 'employment of erotic imagery to express the individual relation between Christ and the soul is always dangerous'. There was something of the decadent in Victorian High Church Christianity, just as there was something of the Ritualist in the decadent. There was an irritating perversity in Coventry Patmore's contention that 'between unequals sweet is equal love; and the fact is that there is no love and therefore no sweetness which is not thus conditioned; and the greater the inequality the greater the sweetness'.

One feels that Arthur Symons, expounder of decadence, could

have written that. His definition of decadence could equally have applied to the Christianity of incense, sleek young men, anguish, and a secret tryst with a fair penitent in a curtained alcove: 'an intense self-consciousness, a restless curiosity in research, an over-subtilising refinement upon refinement, a spiritual and moral perversity'.

There does not seem anything immoral in the behaviour of Ritualist clergymen, whether or not they were getting a kick out of sexual confessions; it is doubtful whether any of them ever raped a penitent. If so we would have heard about it; it would have made a stout volume on its own. Besides, no penitent was obliged to confess all. There was a free choice. A Church of England communicant who opted for High Church knew what the form was.

It is likely that most High Church clergymen thought that they were doing a good job, and that when they gave absolution for sins they thought it as efficacious as any Catholic absolution. Naturally there were hypocrites among them, but it was a hypocrisy that did little harm. Confession *was* good for the soul, whatever the motives of those who listened. What Patmore termed a 'greatly pangful penance' could uncork suppressed guilt and fear, and a muttered absolution by a red-faced young man in a state of tumescence was certainly no more heinous than the baying of a doctor promising madness, or early death, or probably both.

3

A QUEST FOR VIRGINS

RESPECTABLE men wanted unmarried women to be chaste largely for selfish reasons; when they or their sons married they wanted the package entire, without the seals broken. This sentiment could be easily rationalised as a reverence for innocence – provided that the female was young and comely. There was nothing particularly interesting about an innocent middle-aged woman, and *spinster* was, and is, one of the most loaded words in the English language, readily assumed to be applicable only to dry prune-mouthed women of a certain age (spinster: one who spins, young or old). This obloquy was often illustrated by malice and ill nature:

> There was a young man of Penzance
> Who rogered his three maiden aunts;
> Though them he defiled,
> He ne'er got them with child
> Through using the letters of France.

By a shift of emphasis, reverence for innocence became obsession with virginity, which could be suppressed into a consuming interest in young children. Lewis Carroll delighted in photographing young girls in the nude, and when they reached puberty he abruptly lost interest in them; John Ruskin found an outlet for repressed sexuality in a sentimental adoration of young girls. He never quite forgave the ancient Greeks for omitting to make sculptures of them.

Virginity was a loaded word, too. The urge to destroy virginity was part of the make-up of man as a sexual creature, the bridal night was the ravishing of a virgin bride. Logically a man could not expect to violate many virgins, marry he ever so often, and in the ordinary course of events there was a shortage of virgins for the respectable man who disdained the use of prostitutes. One of the factors that made virgins so appealing as love objects was the assumption that they would not know what was going to happen. Sexual ignorance ranged from complete unawareness that any bodily relationship occurred, to utter confusion. Some girls thought that the wife and husband lay side by side without doing anything, others that somehow the navel was the centre of sex life, while others were under the misapprehension, shared by writers of pornography, that the act occupied the whole night.

One woman of twenty-seven due soon to marry was lent a copy of Ellis Ethelmer's pamphlet *The Human Flower*. From this she learned that men desired the body of a woman, and this appalled her so much that it made her ill. When her fiancé tried to caress her she told him it was 'lust', and repelled him. Typical of the information books was *Talk with Girls* (1905) by E. B. Kirk. It was assumed that this book would be vetted by parents before the girl was permitted to read it, and half-way through the book there was a page 'to parents':

> You will see that here follow two pages, number 47a and 47b. The first of these gives explicit information, the second is less detailed . . . Before giving the book to her this page and one of the following are to be torn out. They are perforated so that this can easily be done.

The explicit information was succinct and to the point. 'Nature has made the man's sex organ to fit exactly into that of the woman in the most marvellous and beautiful way.' Good on you, Nature, but mystified brides-to-be would have preferred something more precise. For the unwary it was not marvellous and beautiful, but extremely painful. For the bridal night was the only time a man could indulge in socially approved rape (rape on a wife is not a criminal offence). This could result in what Alfred Adler termed permanent sexual anaesthesia. The unskilled, over-excited husband could become stricken with guilt on the morning after, but by then it was too late; the damage could have been done. A honeymoon could be as pleasurable an experience as a visit to a dentist for a bewildered wife, though this had to be concealed. Most wives got over it; the human organism is not so frail as that. But many did not.

Much of the distress could have been averted by sane instruction, but books which were down to earth and informed rather than prevaricated were reckoned as obscene, and suppressed. In 1894 the *New Review* did a symposium, asking many prominent men and women if girls should be informed about the facts of life. Most said that they should be. These included Thomas Hardy, Walter Besant, Hall Caine, and Max Nordau (the author of a sombre tome on degeneration, the others being novelists). The minority of two against included Mrs Lynn Linton, who, despite all the evidence, preferred virgins to be virginal minded.

Mrs Lynn Linton was typical of a kind of reactionary that flourished in the nineteenth century, waspish and prejudiced, with a life style of her own that made it presumptuous of her to pontificate on matters concerning sex. As one of twelve children of a country vicar, Miss Lynn was short-sighted, solitary, self-opinionated, and scruffy. She conceived an adoration for an artistic woman who lived nearby, referred to as Mrs X by her biographer, but, as she wrote herself, 'the strain grew too intense, and nature gave way. I had a sharp attack of brain fever, when I was for many days in danger'.

Totally self-educated, she went to London as a general purpose journalist on the *Morning Chronicle*, rubbed shoulders with the famous, and at the age of thirty-six married William Linton, a wood-engraver ten years older than herself. She was described as a 'tall, stately, handsome young woman', though at that time an unmarried woman of her age was preparing for the inevitable years of spinsterhood. She was Linton's second wife. Linton was impractical, woolly, untidy, debt-ridden, surrounded by children of the first marriage. 'How long will this last?' Mrs Lynn Linton asked after three months. Of course, she claimed, she had had offers, but she had 'gone through the wood and picked up the crooked stick'.

To judge by photographs of her taken at the time, Mrs Lynn Linton looked like a heavyweight boxer in drag. She started a salon in London, in which her smart acquaintances rubbed shoulders with her husband's rag-tail-and-bobtail friends, 'poor patriots and penniless propagandists'. Disenchantment set in, and the couple parted. In 1867 Linton emigrated to America.

Mrs Lynn Linton is not remembered because of her novels, including the curiously titled *Grasp your Nettle* (1865), but by her
crusade against modern young women in the columns of the *Saturday Review*. It was a time when Women's Rights were news; Mrs
Lynn Linton, argumentative as ever, took the opposite line. She
'found it paid better to attack women than to defend them'. There
speaks the true tabloid journalist. An illustration of lady footballers in the *Daily Graphic* drove her into a frenzy, and the Girl of
the Period (as she was called) was always good for half a column –
superbly dressed, with bust, arms, and shoulders bare, painted,
dyed, and powdered, her lips red with wine or moist with liqueur.
Not at all like the dear old queen, nor, for the matter of that, Mrs
Lynn Linton.

Envy, petulance, and the desire to deprive the young of the
pleasures that she had missed were characteristic not only of Mrs
Lynn Linton but of many of her contemporaries. It was hypocrisy
at its most blatant, but this could easily be sublimated into pretending that one was doing what was best for Womanhood. It was the
revenge of the old against the young. She half-realised it. In 1878
she wrote to a relative, 'Our youth has gone, and we have to face the
unpleasant fact of *decadence*'.

But women like this were listened to. Because she was taking the
part of the man against the woman, advocating keeping women in
submission, men lauded her. She had something of the prurience
of the High Church clergyman. Writing to a niece in 1880:

> Remember that you may trust me implicitly with all your
> thoughts and feelings, and even weaknesses and faults. I under-
> stand human nature and youth above all, and I can feel for even
> the sinfulness of men and women. And I am *safe*. . . .

Whatever information young girls received about the facts of
life, it would hardly include what Queen Victoria called the
'shadow-side' of marriage. In an editorial in the *British Medical
Journal* it was said that 'knowledge need not necessarily be nasty'
and it was clear that there was embarrassment on the part of even
the best-intentioned. Canon Lyttelton's comment in his *Mothers
and Sons* that children received information 'with native
reverence, truthfulness of understanding and guileless delicacy'
was simply not believed. Educationalists were too acquainted with
acres of giggling children to attempt to impart data, and those who

summoned up their courage usually restricted the information. Where children come from was their brief, and they stuck to it.

A correspondent of Havelock Ellis wrote about his wedding night problems. 'The first night she found the act very painful and was frightened and surprised at the size of my penis, and at my suddenly getting on her. We had never talked very openly about sex things before marriage, and it never occurred to me that she was ignorant of the details of the act. I imagined it would disgust her to talk about these things.'

Mrs B, another of Havelock Ellis's inimitable case histories, 'was somewhat shocked and sickened by the experiences of her wedding night. It seemed to her that her husband approached her with the violence of an animal, and there was some difficulty in effecting entrance. Coitus, though incomplete, took place some seven times on this first night. The bleeding from rupture of the hymen continued, so that for two days she had to wear a towel.'

Where there was affection between man and woman male pleasure at inflicting pain was tempered by the aftermath – regret, guilt and shame. The urge to deflower a virgin might be satisfied, but when the ex-virgin is still about the premises, as wife or lover, there were complications; it was impossible to visualise the woman as an object, to be used once, and discarded. An obsession with virginity necessitated the depersonalisation of the virgin.

A virgin adored from afar and a virgin raped have one thing in common. They are not real people; they serve to answer a need. We see this in pornography, where virgins cram the pages awaiting their traducers, the pallid reflections of readers' fantasies. Unfortunately virgin-taking was not restricted to dirty books; it was a minor industry in the Victorian underworld.

Of all the hypocrisy associated with Victorian sex matters, nothing was so blatant as the attitude towards the procuration of virgins, made less heinous by being included under the heading of child prostitution. The appalling thing was that it was not a crime; the common law of England made the age of consent twelve. It was reckoned that at that age a child was a woman capable of answering yea or nay to any proposition she received. A Royal Commission of 1871 thought that the age should be lifted to fourteen. It was open season for lechers. In Liverpool there were reckoned to be 500 prostitutes under the age of thirteen; they usually operated in pairs, one acting as look-out.

Naturally they were only virgins once, but they evolved elaborate means to simulate virginity *in perpetuo*, using broken glass in the vagina, blood-soaked sponges, and leeches. Sometimes they were sponsored by pimps, brothel-keepers and often by parents who provided their cover – selling matches or flowers. In March 1840 the salacious weekly *The Town* included a news item in the fashionable leering style pointing its editorial finger at one well-known frequenter of child prostitutes:

> It is a fact that the Reverend Mr Nickson is occasionally seen wandering about the parks; and rumour adds that he frequently discourses with ragged bipeds known to belong to the *small piece* family. The number of pincushions and pennyworths of lavender the reverend gent possesses is almost incredible.

The crusade of W. T. Stead against the procuration of child virgins in the columns of the *Pall Mall Gazette* led to a public outcry. Campaigners for women's rights and the Salvation Army joined in, 'wrestling with the powers of Hell'. A full account of the Stead case can be found in my *Worm in the Bud*, together with my assessment (which remains unchanged) that Stead himself was as bent as a corkscrew. The Criminal Law Amendment Act of 1885 raised the age of consent to sixteen. But not until the present century did virgin-taking ('the daughters of the people served up as dainty morsels to minister to the passions of the rich') lose its popularity.

The narrator of *My Secret Life* gives the flattest and most convincing account of why and how a flash man of the Victorian period picked up virgins:

> My friend L—— has often told me that he has picked up half a dozen virgins in the streets. That a sovereign, offered to lasses looking in at a linen drapers, will get them to a house and that the sight of the gold vanquishes them. He looks out for them quite young, for that turned sixteen they are scarcely ever virgins. He thinks that from a large acquaintance with these youthful strums, that their cousins and friends (all boys, merely street boys of their own age) get the virginities for nothing, and before the girls are fifteen years old.
>
> Few of the tens of thousands of whores in London gave their virginities either to gentlemen, or to young or old men at all.

Their own low class lads had them. The street boys' dirty pricks went up their little cunts first.—This is greatly to be regretted, for street boys cannot appreciate the treasures they destroy. A virginity taken by a street boy of sixteen is a pearl cast to a swine. Any cunt is good enough for such inexperience.—To such an animal, a matron of fifty or sixty would give him as much, if not more pleasure than a virgin.

On another occasion, the narrator violated a ten-year-old girl, and afterwards chatted with the woman who had provided the child. 'She was not the mother, nor the aunt, though the child called her so; the child was parentless; she had taken charge of her and prevented her going to the workhouse. She was in difficulties, she must live, the child would be sure to have it done to her some day, why not make a little money by her? Someone else would if she did not.'

Elsewhere he philosophises on the matter, and surprisingly comes up with the same answer as the psychologists and specialists on sex:

A [street] girl is not among nine-tenths of the population morally damaged by a little illicit fucking, as she is among those who look upon a hymen as a prize and guarantee in the woman they seek as a wife.

All said, the female who keeps her cunt hymenized and under seal among the well-to-do classes, only does so that she may get a higher price for it, either in money or position. She sometimes never attains either, and mostly has to wait long for it, wait for years, and frigs herself during her waiting, languishing for want of a prick and spermatic lubrication, which is health-giving to a female.

That the author of *My Secret Life* had to pay for his virgins would have marked him out among the connoisseurs as lacking *ton*. The debauchees with refined taste insisted not only on giving pain but on degrading the victim. Consequently in pornography, virgins are well-born, unpaid, raped, and flagellated. Pornography had the edge on reality in one respect. The virgin in pornography *was* a virgin, but on the streets there was no such assurance. When rich men bought a virgin (at about £20 or even cheaper) they made certain that she was medically examined to ascertain that she really was. There was also the menace of syphilis

in a pseudo-virgin; being new to the trade she was not likely to take
the precautions that were second nature to the trained prostitute.
Raping a virgin was said to cure syphilis, though no one knew
exactly how – the rakehells were as subject to folk myth as the
respectable.

Fact and fiction were also in conflict in the details of raping a
virgin. In fact the operation could be unsatisfactory, messy, and
inconclusive. The details of how the monomaniac in *My Secret
Life* ascertained that one of his pick-ups was a virgin must have
been distinctly clinical and unerotic to porno readers:

> Then the girl lay on the side of the bed, her thighs distended, one
> heel up so as to facilitate and keep the legs open, the little thin
> lips of her vulva gaping, and showing the pink lining. I took a
> candle and saw the orifice, inside it the membrane closing. The
> girl was unmistakably a virgin . . .

A run through Victorian pornography illustrates extreme dis-
association of sensibility. Virgins are objects. In *The Amatory
Experiences of a Surgeon* (1881) the narrator 'longed for an unripe
beauty, a young girl, a child even – I found a lovely little girl of
thirteen years of age who had been under my care for a spinal
affliction'. Consequently he debauches her, Hippocratic oath
forgotten. *Curiosities of Flagellation* (1875) deals at length with
virgins being flogged. These include Lady Flora Bumby, 'a
slightly-made, meek-looking, fair girl, of about fourteen' and Miss
Mason, 'a dark girl of about sixteen, with flashing eyes and burning cheeks'. Their humiliation is watched by the wicked Sir
Charles from a secret hiding-place. After the girls have been
flogged silly they retire upstairs for Lesbian games.

Sexual perversity at its most twisted occurs in the *Experimental
Lecture* by 'Colonel Spanker' on *The exciting and voluptuous
pleasures to be derived from crushing and humiliating the spirit of
a beautiful and modest young lady*, to wit, Miss Julia Ponsonby,
who has her bottom slapped, is subject to 'dreadful liberties', is
assisted at her toilette by the colonel 'which he aids by sundry cuts
with the birch', is forced to walk up a ladder holding upon her
drawers, is dressed in a ball costume and flogged on the shoulders,
shown to a masked company, made to undress ('slowly'), is pricked
with a pin, pinched, made to recount erotic experiences of her
schooldays, tortured with stinging nettles, flagellated upside down

tied to a ladder, and finally 'brutally ravished'. H. S. Ashbee, the erotologist dismissed it as the nightmare of a vicious, used-up old rake; but he admitted it was well written.

In *The Haunted House* (1880) another wicked nobleman intends to deflower Nelly, after going on the run. He had misguidedly 'got hold of a little girl of twelve or thirteen, and fucked and flogged her so unmercifully that the country was up in arms about it, and he had to cut.' Nelly is saved by the entrance of her affianced. 'Quite a denouncement!' says the nobleman, laughing, 'I will yield to the affianced husband so far as the first fuck of this sweet young lady is concerned . . .' *Love's Tell-Tale* (1865) has the heroine ravished by her foster-brother, after which she 'sank senseless, inanimate, exhausted, upon him'. *Scenes in the Seraglio*, probably written some time between 1855 and 1860, was a come-on. Adelaide does not get violated, though she is set up for it by a lustful Turk. *The Youthful Adventurer* has a surrealist plot that must have been diverting to those with undemanding tastes:

> On the wedding day his bride is surprised by her monthly ailment, and she induces him to satisfy himself, firstly with one of the bridesmaids in her own presence and in that of the other bridesmaids, then in the travelling carriage with her own lady's maid, and finally on arriving at their destination, allows him to sodomize her in a water-closet.

The most literate account of the voluptuous attractions of virgin-taking occurs in *The Battles of Venus*, published 1850-60:

> In the first place his fancy is heated with the prospect of enjoying a woman, after whom he has perhaps long sighed and had been in pursuit, who he thinks has never been in bed with a man, and in triumphing in the first sight of her virgin beauties, and first fruition of her virgin charms. This precious operation, then, of fancy, has been shown in the highest degree to prepare the body for enjoyment.
>
> Secondly, his body perceives, in that of a virgin, the cause of the greatest aggravation of delight. I mean not only in the coyness and resistance which she makes to his efforts, but when he is on the point of accomplishing them; when arrived, as the poet sings, 'on the brink of giddy rapture', when in pity to a tender virgin's sufferings, he is intreated not to break fiercely in,

but to spare 'fierce dilaceration and dire pangs'. The resistance which the small, and as yet unopened mouth of bliss makes to his eager endeavours, serves only, and that on a physical principle, to strengthen the instrument of his attack, and concurs with the instigation of his ardent fancy, to reinforce his efforts, to unite all the co-operative powers of enjoyment, and to produce an emission copious, rapid, and transporting.

Fancy has been repeatedly observed to heighten fruition. In this case, part of the delight arises from considering that the lewdest part of your body is fixed in the delicious centre of *her* body, that you may feel the convulsive wrigglings of the chaste nymph you have so long adored, and at last feel her diffuse her warm juice throughout her dewy sheath, and moisten the hot, ruby crest of your firm-fixed instrument.

The author then enthuses about the reward of rape:

I cannot conceive a higher banquet to a man of lustful humour, than to see a modest and beautiful woman forcibly stripped naked: to observe her struggling, and discording[sic] her hidden beauties by degrees, until she comes to her last shift, and then to lay her down and, notwithstanding her efforts, rifle all her charms, and penetrate even into her honeyed treasure!

Whoever the author was (allegedly posthumous Voltaire), he was not taking too many liberties with fact but narrating everyman wish-fulfilment, the bridal night without a blemish. Perhaps he was over-estimating the co-operation of the bride and the expertise of the groom, but he was writing for a reader who did not insist on truth to life.

It is conceivable that *The Battles of Venus* might well have been of more use to anxious brides and grooms than the laboured and inept explanations of bridal night etiquette propounded by the experts. Not that all of *The Battles of Venus* would be a suitable primer for a young married couple. The author also explains carefully how a woman may be enjoyed by two men at the same time. Even the most progressive of sex educationalists would have thought this inadmissible.

4

MODESTY AND DECENCY

ONE of the most important elements in sexual hypocrisy is the preoccupation with modesty. Modesty has a variety of meanings: humility; purity of thought and manners; chastity. The definition by Havelock Ellis was the most clinical: 'an almost instinctive fear prompting to concealment and usually centering around the sexual processes'. He maintained that although common to both sexes, in the woman it was important enough to be rated as the chief secondary sexual character 'on the psychical side'.

Modesty was not a peculiarly Victorian attribute, and in the ighteenth century the poet Edward Young (1683-1765) had appreciated what modesty really was:

> That modest grace subdued my soul,
> That chastity of look which seems to hang
> A veil of purest light o'er all her beauties,
> And by forbidding most inflames desire.

The last line defines the biological function of modesty. It was a device of Nature to make women more desirable. Stendhal went further. In his *Essai sur l'amour* (1822) he wrote:

As to the utility of modesty, it is the mother of love. As to the mechanism of the feeling, nothing is simpler. The mind is absorbed in feeling shame instead of being occupied with desire. Desires are forbidden, and desires lead to actions. It is evident that every tender and proud woman – and these two things, being cause and effect, naturally go together – must contract habits of coldness which the people whom she disconcerts calls prudery.

To men, modesty is a challenge. It was a no meaning yes, a token that the woman expressing it by blush or downward eye was a creature of sensibility and a worthy love object. Shame struggling with desire was sexually stimulating, and extremely flattering to the man, though it would have felt less flattering had the man known that the action took place on an instinctive level, and that reactions associated with modesty occurred in all savage races (though they were often being modest about something other than sex, such as eating in public).

The isolation of modesty as a desirable attribute in itself was an antique practice promulgated mostly by men who were projecting their own feelings. The women themselves were largely bemused by the praise they were being awarded for having acted instinctively. As Celine Renooz, a woman psychologist of the nineteenth century wrote: 'They have, in appearance at least, accepted the rule of shame imposed on them by men, but only custom inspires the modesty for which they are praised; it is really an outrage to their sex.'

Self-congratulation on the part of man, succeeding in creating consternation in the fair sex, could have its disquieting sequel. After modesty had played its part, the male had been won, and sexual gratification had been obtained on the part of the woman, the wiles, the coyness that seemed part of modesty, were abruptly discarded. Many men who had married a delicate shrinking violet found that they had instead a voracious Venus fly trap whose abandonment was as provoking, though not so pretty, as the one-time reticence. Many men were disillusioned by what was in fact a commonplace process, and considered that they had been selected by a malignant God for special treatment. To preserve the proprieties the transformation was usually kept quiet and the concept of modesty remained unsullied, and if anything, was raised to an even higher pedestal.

The corollary was obvious. If modesty was laudable, then immodesty was not. Modesty represented a sequence of actions carried out for a biological purpose, and it was an error to suppose that it was something else, such as virginity. If modesty disappeared with marriage, then marriage itself must be to blame, especially the rites of marriage. The husband himself must take on the guilt.

This guilt varied from person to person. Some were ashamed because they had brought out a hitherto undiscovered animal nature in their wives, others felt that they had forced their own animal natures on their wives and by doing this had destroyed their inherent delicacy. Guilt was mostly unwarranted. The man was merely following a predestined course, predatory because he was the pursuer but because he was under social and religious pressures he was obliged to rationalise. It was best, in the sense that it was the most rational, to accept matters as they were, as did the psychologist Hans Menjago:

> I cannot imagine anything that is more sexually exciting than to observe a person of the opposite sex, who by some external or internal force, is compelled to fight against her physical modesty. The more modest she is the more sexually exciting is the picture she presents.

It was a rite played out between men and women, and could be extremely complex on both sides. The man was torn between his idolisation of woman and his desire to despoil innocence, even to pay back the loved one for her coquetry. The woman was torn between the innate feeling that she ought to play by the rules, be cool, withdrawn, and respectable, and her own ill-understood but peremptory desires. The involved called it love, the sceptics chemical attraction. Love, declared C. E. M. Joad, was the trick of Nature that guaranteed the perpetuation of the species.

One of the few things that seemed clear was that there was, apparently, a pursuer and a pursued, and this realisation brought in several conventions. One of these was that the woman had to pretend that she was not being pursued, and was therefore obliged to repel or ignore the male on certain occasions. Though were he selected as a possible mate, there had to be a certain amount of encouragement, which should come as a surprise to the man and often came as a surprise to the woman. The favour should be gained by sudden surprise, not by mutual agreement. A bared shoulder, a glimpse of cleavage, a hint of nipple that may have been genuine or the illusion of a bust improver, these were the enticements offered.

These were the equivalents of what is today known as a 'flash', a glimpse of bare thigh between knickers and the tops of stockings, and produced a weird variety of erotogenic zones. Any part of a woman's anatomy could rouse a man, provided that it was seen *en passant*. As one foot fetishist told Havelock Ellis: 'It is the *stolen* glimpse of a pretty foot or ankle which produces the greatest effect on me'. By extension, activities that were associated with the sexual parts were of great interest to connoisseurs, especially those concerned with urination and defecation.

Even the most shakily modest of Victorian maidens hesitated over allowing their admirers to 'accidentally' see them on chamber pot or in the lavatory, though a surprisingly large number of married women overcame their scruples and let their husbands watch them, sometimes taking a keen delight themselves especially when urinating from a standing position. Some devotees of undinism, as it was called, advocated the setting up of *pissoirs* similar to those supplied on the continent for men, thinking it ridiculous for women to shut themselves in a box for such a natural and rewarding natural function. Failing that, to urinate against a wall.

In his *Studies in the Psychology of Sex*, Havelock Ellis, himself an enthusiast for this harmless aberration, paid great attention to the case history of Miss E, quoting her letters to a man she had never met, suggesting a tryst at the seaside. 'If you sat on the shingle and I stood in front of you, I could make water so that you might watch me . . . If I were with you I should like to stand with my lower part bare and I should like you to kneel in front of me with your face against my part there and I should like to make water then . . . And I should like you to stand about a yard in front of me and to make water from that distance, steadily, against my part.' In the event this never happened, for though Miss E could transgress modesty by letter she considered that she was too 'craven-hearted and nervous' and too old to follow it through. Miss E was temperamentally bisexual, and wrote to a woman friend saying that she would like to see her stand and make water. Her favourite fantasy was to see a man dressed in woman's clothes. 'I should like to turn up his petticoats in front as he stood, and pull his drawers, and get his chemise out of the way; and directly his thing could be seen I should like him to begin making water instantly, as if he had been in a great hurry to do it.'

The realisation that men much preferred to see modest girls behaving in an immodest way communicated itself to prostitutes, who were forced to act out an innocent role, at the most extreme pretending to be virgins violated. Many of them became very accomplished in these charades, and the wide use made of prostitutes by apparently happily married men is explained by their skills in catering for men's innermost desires. Many women, once they had married, did not feel inclined to carry on their coquetry now that it had served its purpose, and accepted their menfolk as their duty, phlegmatically and with no great enthusiasm.

Modesty used as enticement is one major aspect of the subject, but another element is social modesty, which often acted against sexual modesty, thereby causing even more confusion. Thus the sexual organs were both alluring and disgusting, and the urge to reveal all was countered by the desire to conceal everything. This was not necessarily the prerogative of civilised races, though the emphasis on what was significant shifted. In some parts of the world where the natives ran about naked the face was considered that part to be hidden. Eccentric as this might be thought, it was not nearly so odd as the *reminders* of sexual and quasi-sexual organs that were proscribed in the west, such as table legs, which were though to arouse lascivious thoughts because they obliged viewers to think of human legs, that most forbidden of Victorian erotogenic objects.

Why were sexual organs thought to be disgusting? Perhaps because they were near the anus and were associated with defacation. It has been suggested that if the woman's vagina was placed between the shoulder blades many of the problems associated with sex would have disappeared. The church played a major part in deciding that sexual organs were disgusting. St Augustine in his *De Divitae Dei* (413-26) maintained that erections of the penis did not occur until Adam and Eve had been ejected from the garden of Eden, and throughout the history of the Christian church sexual matters have been treated with contempt and disgust. Significantly enough, it has not been the celibates who have been in the van, and the Roman Catholic church has frequently adopted a sane and refreshingly realistic attitude towards sex. Non-abstinent Church of England clergymen have often been the chief castigators of what they have usually equated with Original Sin. Shame in their own shortcomings has obliged them to over-compensate.

Shame was one of the key factors in social modesty. Shame was defined by the psychologist Hohenemser as 'a certain psychic lameness or inhibition' sometimes accompanied by the sinking of the head and inability to meet the eye. And of course blushing. These characteristics were precisely the same as those met in modesty as a womanly come-on. Sexual ideas tended (and tend) to evoke shame, because they are apt to pass into sexual feelings. Only when they do not develop in this way, as in scientific discussion, do they fail to produce the physical and psychological phenomena associated with shame.

The evocation of shame depended not only on the projection of sexual ideas or the awareness of one's own or others' sexual organs, but on the environment. There were certain environments that were shame-proof, that were psychically without charge. The marital bed had some of this magic, and had, as it were, a certificate of exemption. Another was the public bath, where, throughout history, mixed bathing in the nude was the rule rather than the exception, and this phenomenon persisted into the Victorian age with the seaside replacing the public bath.

At the public baths in Sofia in 1717 Lady Mary Wortley Montagu commented on the grand ladies and their slaves 'without any distinction of rank in their dress, all being in a state of Nature; that is, in plain English, stark naked, without any beauty or defect concealed. Yet there was not the least wanton smile or immodest gesture among them.' In St Petersburg in 1774 Sir Nicholas Wraxall noted 'the promiscuous bathing of not less than two hundred persons, of both sexes . . . There are, indeed, separate spaces for the men and women, but they seem quite regardless of this distinction, and sit or bathe in a state of absolute nudity among each other.' In Victorian Britain, men would bathe quite naked in the sea, emerging clutching their penis with one hand to give an aura of respectability to the operation, sanctified by tradition. In the anonymous *Letters of a Gentleman from Scarborough* (1734) the author mentions the practice: 'The gentlemen go out a little way to sea in boats and jump in naked directly.' The ladies 'have the use of gowns and guides', and later bathing-machines catered for the fair sex, though there is every evidence that they were prepared to display their charms in the sexually antiseptic atmosphere of the seaside. In *Punch* of the 1840s, the humorous writer Albert Smith dealt with Brighton in the series *Guide to the Watering Places*:

The ladies seem to take great delight in the sea-bath, and that they may enjoy the luxury in the most secluded privacy, the machines are placed as near the pier as possible. This is always crowded with men who, by the aid of opera-glasses, find it a pleasing pastime to watch the movements of the delicate Naiads who crowd the waters.

For their edification the various seaside corporations erected telescopes, ostensibly to view passing ships etc.

In Rowlandson's cartoon *Summer Amusements at Margate* a group of Regency bucks are seen focussing their spy-glasses on to nude bathing women, and a painting by Benjamin West (1738-1820) of Ramsgate shows that naked women in the sea were not the fantasy of wits and cartoonists. The machine invented by the Quaker Benjamin Beale in 1753 that resembled a large pram hood under which, in almost pitch darkness, a lady could bathe 'in a manner consistent with the most refined delicacy' was not to the liking of the voyeurs on the promenade nor, one imagines, to all the gambolling Naiads.

The freedom from censure of unquestionably modest girls bathing naked in the sea was noteworthy in an age that prided itself on its modesty and decorum, and to a slight extent social permission extended to other select areas of water, such as the ponds on Hampstead Heath, though during the nineteenth century the sexes were kept strictly segregated. The ability to feel free to bathe naked was restricted to women of the superior classes, and in the day to day business of life the working and lower-middle class women were the most concerned with shame, especially when they were in contact with men and women of a higher caste.

One reason for this was their ignorance about sex, and their taking on trust the view that sex was dirty. In particular they accepted that menstruation was disgusting, that it was indeed a curse. Not until late in the nineteenth century was it discovered that menstruation served a purpose. The less instructed women thought that the vagina and the womb were associated intimately with the bowels and evacuation, and that they passed water through their vaginas and not through a separate urethral passage. The absence of any form of sex education for the lower classes meant that they picked up information haphazardly. Sex was something to snigger at, and even when, as was usual amongst the poor, a girl ceased to be a virgin at the age of twelve or thirteen, she was still overcome with shame when she had to discuss sexual matters with someone of a higher class, such as a doctor.

Eccentric and arbitrary modesty may be, but it is also rigid, having its effect on even those supposed to be without it, such as prostitutes. In European countries where prostitutes were licensed during the nineteenth century (including naval and military towns in Britain for a period, after the passing of the Contagious Diseases Acts of 1864-9, repealed in 1886) it was found that prostitutes looked askance at being examined by the authorities during menstruation, protesting with a vehemence that was considered most inappropriate.

Modesty, especially when concerned with the process of capturing a man, is understandable and a perfectly respectable phenomenon. Considering lack of knowledge about sexual matters and the willingness to accept the opinion of those who, presumably, knew better, shame about sex is also understandable. There was nothing hypocritical about a woman who preferred to suffer cancer of the womb rather than permit a doctor to examine her private parts, only something sad and unnecessary. The hypocrisy lies with those phantom people who were acknowledged as knowing better.

But modesty could be transformed into decency, defined by Havelock Ellis as 'modesty fossilized into social customs'. Decency was genteel, and became a prerogative of civilised races. People thought before a consideration was made of what was decent and what was not. It became more important than modesty – consider the difference in emphasis between immodest (a girl showing an ankle in a breeze) and indecent (a strip-tease, the publication of pornography, a man buggering an animal). Decency was a concept that lent itself to hypocrisy.

The fossilisation of modesty into decency was not accomplished in one fell swoop. The word was first recorded in 1567, meaning appropriateness to the circumstances of the case, fitness, seemliness, propriety, due regard to what is becoming, and, in 1751, respectability. Decency infiltrated, creating problems where none had existed before. It permeated life, literature, and art. Observing the decencies became important, and permitted those with the power to decide what was decent and what was not irrespective of whether their considerations served any useful purpose except as a weapon of class. Inferiors did not decide what was decent or not.

The concept of decency did not necessarily mean that men and women behaved differently, only that they had to pretend to. Animal instincts in courtship proved more pressing than recommendations to adopt a set pattern of behaviour. The only difference on the woman's part was that she knew now why she was being modest, or at least thought she did. Blushing was a pretty convention, not as G. Stanley Hall wrote in 1897, 'a vicarious genital flushing of blood, diverted from the genital sphere by an inhibition of fear'.

Due regard to what is becoming, one of the subsidiary definitions of decency, could be counter-productive. In his *De l'Amour* (1834), Senacour declared that a useless and false reserve is due to stupidity rather than to modesty.

By the eighteenth century far too many people were giving advice. Sex is a one-to-one relationship, by and large, and in most cases men and women can get along very well without gratuitous advice. Information is another matter, but information was notably lacking. Many writers, from whom indications of becoming behaviour were never in short supply, found that the new periodical press offered them a fine platform. In *The Spectator* of 1711, Richard Steele, most refined and primmest of essayists, declared that he was against short engagements:

> The passion should strike root and gather strength before marriage be grafted on to it. A long course of hopes and expectations fixes the idea in our minds and habituates us to a fondness for the person beloved. Before marriage we cannot be too inquisitive and discerning in the faults of the person beloved, nor after it too dim-sighted and superficial.

Nevertheless, Steele has some wise things to say about the modish cult of correct behaviour. As soon as a girl leaves her nurse she is handed to a dancing master:

> The pretty wild thing is taught a fantastical gravity of behaviour, and forced to a particular way of holding her head, heaving her breast and moving with her whole body; and all this under pain of never having an husband, if she steps, looks or moves awry.

Typical of the manuals catering for the new age of decency was Adam Petrie's *Rules of Good Deportment and of Good Breeding*

(1720), in which readers were cautioned not to spit into the fire, break wind ('even among inferiors'), or fail to give ladies a chance to ease their bladders ('If you pass by one easing Nature you should turn your face another way'). Unless, of course, you were sexually excited by undinism.

Ladies who did not behave by the rules, who 'tigged' or indulged in horseplay with men, could expect paleness of the face, heaviness of the eyes, squeamishness of the stomach and a tumour in the belly. In the following century such warnings became commonplace, but we can see from Adam Petrie that what is commonly regarded as Victorian behaviour had its roots more than a hundred years earlier. The habit of extending decency to cover almost anything was also promoted in the eighteenth century. To us, the reading of banns has no naughty connotations, but to the opponents of Lord Hardwick's Marriage Bill of 1753 there was something incredibly salacious about the operation. The MP Robert Nugent declared that 'it shocks the modesty of a young girl to have it proclaimed through the parish that she is going to be married'.

The pursuit of decency meant that girls were to be prevented from encountering anything that would shock their sensibilities, and with the coming in the late eighteenth century of the romantics who believed in love but not necessarily marriage this took on the nature of a crusade. This could be difficult, for young ladies had the quaint habit of not reading what was prescribed for them but what excited them, and could hardly be prevented from seeing life as it was, the bucks and the dandies with an eye and a groping hand for a pretty girl, and their amorosie with their dress, according to William Hazlitt, disclosing 'each full swell, each coy recess, obtruding on the eye each opening charm, the play of muscles, the working of the thighs . . . moving pictures of lust and nakedness'.

Efforts to prevent girls from coming across the indecent in word, thought, or deed reached an apotheosis in the Victorian period. The coming of the chaperone indicated that the girl was not fit to look after herself, and could not be trusted. The care and attention of a chaperone seemed to self-satisfied parents an indication that they had their daughters' interests at heart, though another factor had entered into it. A daughter, in a capitalist age, was property, and damaged goods were not negotiable.

The employers of chaperones were largely middle class. Upper-class girls had their governesses, but when these girls had reached an age when they could not absorb more education the governesses were despatched into the outer darkness where, presumably, aged governesses lived. Upper-class girls were trusted further than their middle-class contemporaries, and if something unfortunate did happen and an inconvenient little bundle was on the way there would be found means to circumvent the difficulties.

Middle-class parents were leaders in the propagation of the double standard. In an age that had seen the emergence of a true social mobility, many of them had risen from the ranks, bringing with them their mores, their half-baked ideas, and their hypocrisy. Decency was not seemliness or propriety, but a fetish. They did not look behind the rules to see if they had any sense, but regarded them as if engraved on Moses' tablets, the orders of the day to disregard which was to invite retribution. The middle classes conceived it their duty to codify decency, first of all for their families, then for all those multitude of inferiors left far behind.

Decency in public life meant that all sexual feelings were to be kept hidden so far as possible, and that courtship was to be a polite ritual with every spark of the spontaneous eliminated so that it would not offend. Secret and clandestine meetings between prospective lovers should be frowned on, since these were frequently injurious throughout life. Visits to the loved ones' parents should be strictly limited, as familiarity breeds contempt. A written proposal of marriage was infinitely preferable to an oral one (as the parents had time to assess the situation and a letter was an economic weapon – if only as an exhibit in a breach of promise case). Courtship in public was vulgar, selfish, indelicate and offensive (as it might lead to actions that were even more vulgar and indelicate), and flirting with others was indescribably selfish. Jilting, the young were earnestly advised, often led to insanity.

Taking the fun out of sex, that widespread Victorian pastime, was pursued for a variety of reasons, not the least of which was the awareness of those who laid down the law that they were too old to indulge in young love, and they did not see why the new generation should have pleasures from which they themselves were debarred. The general tenor of advice was pompous and windy, but often a practicality crept in that was difficult to reconcile with muttered pronouncements upon sexual behaviour. Naturally this practicality dealt with property. A young married man should insure himself if he had no property, and as, until the Married Women's

Property Act was passed, a wife's property went to the husband on marriage, a settlement should be drawn up by experienced lawyers to make certain that any property she had did pass automatically to him. By law, the wife's earnings belonged to the husband (many successful lady authors were aggrieved by this), and there was no way to circumvent this. The married woman had only one prequisite – any bills she ran up were the responsibility of the husband.

Naturally enough, many spirited unmarried ladies resented being placed by their elders in an emotional straitjacket for the sake of decency, and patronised by men and women authors who always seemed to take the trouble to remain anonymous. *Courtship As It Is and As It Ought To Be* (1877) was typical of the genre. The author complained that most courtship was riddled with hypocrisy, dishonesty and cupidity, and that a woman's heart ('a golden fort') should be stormed by ardour, intellect, integrity and truth, not beleaguered by pretending pride. Chicanery, foppishness, or 'nature smothered in the glare of art' (whatever that might be) were also reprehensible, if not actually criminal.

Statistics, beloved by the Victorians though they were not very good at them, do not state how many spirited Victorian maidens there were compared with the docile and the compliant who did what they were told, and what was expected from them. Such women lived in a closed world. A seraglio or a harem would have seemed impossible freedom to them. There was a conspiracy to keep them from finding out what life was really like, and until they were given away in ritual marriage they lived as if drugged, passing the time in needlework, drawing, piano playing, and in reading 'nice' novels from Mr Mudie's circulating library (and all the novels from Mr Mudie's establishment were nice – that was why he was successful).

Is conspiracy too strong a word? In the first place the word conspiracy presupposes a number of conspirators, and if a doting father, anxious to protect a daughter from the world, is one, who are the others? The parents supplied the environment and nourishment, hirelings such as governesses suitable instruction, while mental nutriment came from a variety of sources that had one thing in common – the furthering of Victorian decency. These were the more insidious conspirators, distinct from the pornographers only in that they were peddling cleanliness for money, not filth.

This conspiracy, as with new ideas about modesty, was in full swing by the time Queen Victoria came to the throne. A key word among the conspirators was delicacy. In Congreve's *The Way of the World* (1700) delicacy was subtlety, well illustrated in the dialogue between Fainall and Mirabel:

> FAINALL: I'd no more play with a man that slighted his ill fortune than I'd make love to a woman who undervalued the loss of her reputation.
>
> MIRABEL: You have a taste extremely delicate, and are for refining your pleasures.

In 1712 Addison, Richard Steele's co-essayist on *The Spectator*, attempted to draw a distinction between true and false delicacy; the first was a love of virtue, the second squeamishness, but within half a century delicacy had taken on other meanings, denoting sensibility and feeling. It was considered a good thing to be shrinking, easily wounded by coarse behaviour. Delicate people broke into tears at the slightest provocation. It need hardly be mentioned that they were intensely modest and decent, so intense that these qualities were overpowering. They blushed so often that they resembled human traffic signals.

Delicacy had its propagandists, some of whom had learned from the cult of feeling in France. One of the most influential was Samuel Richardson (1689-1761), described as a stout, rosy, vain, prosy little man, whose novel *Pamela* (1740) was the first middle-class fiction of sensibility. In the 1770s Lady Louisa Stuart was worried when she read *Pamela* for fear that she 'should not cry enough to gain the credit of proper sensibility'. It was only a short step to being an accomplished hypocrite, when the reader would emerge tear-stained from her labours – provided that there was an audience to register the fact that she (it was more often she) had been properly overcome by her feelings. The awareness that delicacy did not operate in a vacuum but usually in a social setting exasperated the level-headed, such as Vicemus Knox, author of an essay *Delicacy of Sentiment* (1778):

> The appearance of a toad, or the jolting of a carriage will cause a paroxysm of fear, but it is remarkable that this delicacy and

tenderness often disappear in solitude, and the pretender to uncommon sensibility is frequently found, in the absence of
witnesses, to be uncommonly unfeeling.

However, there was money (and kudos) in being an advocate of
sensibility and delicacy, and if it could be extended, so much the
better. As John Bennett wrote in *Letters to a Young Lady* (1789):

> Delicacy is a very general and *comprehensive* quality. It extends
> to everything where woman is concerned. Conversation, books,
> pictures, attitude, gesture, pronunciation should all come under
> its salutary restraints.
> [The girl of sensibility] vibrates to the most distant touch of
> what is proper and becoming, and would tremble like the sen-
> sitive plant, where any thing that could stain the delicacy of her
> *mind* was conveyed in the most *distant* allusion.

In the eighteenth century it was extremely difficult to protect a
young girl from indelicacy, near or 'distant'. It was the age not only
of *Pamela* but Henry Fielding's *Tom Jones* (1749) (that 'exquisite
picture of human manners', as Gibbon declared), not only of the
poetess Hannah More ('Sweet Sensibility! thou keen delight!')
but of Hogarth and public hanging, filth and squalor. A girl *could*
avert her eyes from the more unseemly aspects of eighteenth-
century life and pretend that they did not exist. This was a good
training for hypocrisy.

The systematic protection of delicacy can be seen as arising from
three major phenomena. The first was the ascendancy of
evangelical religion, the second was the industrial revolution
which produced a new kind of middle class, and the third was the
provision of intellectual nourishment guaranteed not to infringe
the sensibilities of the consumer.

Evangelicalism was both a religion of enthusiasm and a religion
of modesty. It tried to make Christianity wholesome and chaste, to
fit it up for the new age. Evangelicalism in essence can be well
illustrated by John Wesley's sermon on dress:

> Let it be observed that slovenliness is no part of religion; that
> neither this, nor any text of Scripture, condemns neatness of
> apparel. Certainly this is a duty, not a sin. 'Cleanliness is, in-
> deed, next to godliness.'

   The evolution from a rural economy to an urban economy had, as one of its features, the breadwinner working away from home. On a farm, the wives and especially the daughters were too near the centre of things to completely avoid the indelicate and that which offended their sensibilities. Spouses and fathers could be seen to behave in a manner that was not in goody-goody novels, and which could be downright brutal and nasty. They were angry, swore, were obliged to engage in indelicate tasks. Furthermore, farm workers were not the epitome of delicacy; if anything they swore more than husbands and fathers, and were not averse to copulating with the female help and indulging in dirty talk when the farmer was not about.

   The urban middle classes usually worked away from home, and what they did to their employees was no business of anyone except themselves. Middle-class shopkeepers no longer lived over their shops, and could behave as they wished to their assistants without the inhibitions of a family within earshot. Industrialism and city life was fierce and harsh, and few writers failed to comment on the chasm between the *laissez faire* of factory and the sanctuary of home life. Man had to go out and fight corruption or get corrupted, but it was his prerogative, as Ruskin says, to guard the woman from all this. 'Within his house, as ruled by her, unless she herself has sought it, need enter no danger, no cause of error or offence.'

   The sealing of the house from moral and intellectual infection became easier as the nineteenth century progressed. If the ladies of the house wanted to read there was literature suited to them, the bland productions of the decency machine or the expurgations of those anxious to promote delicacy, modesty, and decency. The Bowdlerisers moved in force. Their aim was to eliminate everything that savoured of the salacious, that encouraged impure thoughts, or that fractured the fragile hymen of innocence.

5

A SWEET DISORDER IN THE DRESS

THERE are certain things,' wrote Montaigne in his essays, 'which are hidden in order to be shown', and nowhere is this truer than in the dress of woman. In his master work *History of Human Marriage*, Edward Westermarck, professor of sociology at London University from 1907, contended that ornament and clothing, often in combination or intermingled, were at first not intended to conceal or protect the body, but to make it sexually attractive.

At first this seems to contravert common sense, though the theory gradually became accepted as it would account for otherwise incomprehensible phenomena. If woman's dress is seen as the counterpart of the plumage of the bird there is one drawback; it is the male bird which attracts attention by the colouring, whereas the Victorian male was beginning to attire himself in a sort of uniform that was the reverse of sexually stimulating. The brightly coloured waistcoat could still be seen though, and the young men of the day were addicted to loud checks (described as 'uncommon nobby' by the loutish swells in Leech's cartoons in *Punch*).

Certainly in the past men's clothes had been contrived to flatter the wearers and draw the attention of women to their good points. That clothes were designed to pretend to hide what in fact they exploited is most evident in the case of the cod-piece, introduced 1450-70, 'whereby the attributes of manhood were accentuated in the most shameless manner'. It was, in fact, the avowed aim at that period to attract attention to these parts. The cod-piece was sometimes coloured differently from the rest of the garments, often stuffed out to enlarge it artificially, and decorated with ribbons. Female fashions of the nineteenth century did not produce anything quite so explicit as the cod-piece, though there are several close analogies.

Victorian women often did not know why they dressed as they did. They were numbed by confusion. Even the most strait-laced of matrons would in the evening adopt a garb that displayed most of the breasts except the nipples, and cleavage was the rule rather than the exception. Devices to accentuate the breasts were used quite unconsciously, the most obvious of which was tight-lacing. In theory this was to provide a tiny waist, but this has never been of much interest to men as an erotic stimulant. Tight-lacing pushed the breasts up into melon-like objects, which was what the men liked. They would have liked to have seen legs even more, but the cult of the bosom meant that alternative portions of the anatomy were *verboten*. The legs were hidden not in order to be shown, but to be inferred. It is prosaically recorded that children believed their mothers to be tree-shaped, with the torso ending in a single substantial limb.

The confusion was compounded by fashion magazines. In 1886 the *Queen* decreed that 'the upper part of a ball dress should be both modest and picturesque'. It was often difficult to combine both, even with the aid of patent palpitators and bust improvers, in which air, feathers, and wire springs helped to do what Nature had forgotten.

The fact that the nineteenth century was breast-orientated was resented by many, who could not reconcile proclamations of modesty and its manifest absence in those who made the most noise. In the anonymous *Handbook of the Toilet* (1841) the writer asserted that 'bare shoulders in evening dress is largely instrumental in starting consumption'. Disgust at the spectacle of protruding breasts was hidden under the guise of attacking tight-lacing, which produced 'injurious pressure upon those forms which Nature has given women as fountains of nourishment for their offspring' and, from 'a moral point of view, is opposed to all laws of religion'.

In 1867 and 1868 the *Saturday Review* ran a sustained campaign against over-exposure. The woman of fashion is described as wearing

. . . a white or spotted veil thrown over the visage in order that the adjuncts which belong properly to the theatre may not be immediately detected in the glare of daylight; and thus, with diaphanous tinted face, large painted eyes, and stereotyped smile, the lady goes forth, looking much more as if she stepped out of the green-room or from a Haymarket saloon, than from an English home. But it is in evening costume that our women have reached the minimum of dress and the maximum of brass. The female bosom is less the subject of a revelation than the feature of an exposition. A costume that has been described as consisting of a smock, a waist band and a frill, seems to exceed the bounds of honest liberality. At the Opera two gentlemen were heard remarking on such a costume. 'Did you ever see such a thing?'— 'Not since I was weaned.'

The *Saturday Review* considered that the low-necked dress and 'bold look of the wearer' were indications of the 'fast, frivolous and indecorous age'. In 1869 it returned to the battle – 'they are really wicked, those ball-dresses, wicked for cost and indecent for cut; with only a little gold strap across the shoulders, that look as if a good shake would shake them off altogether.'

The pursuit of the tiny waist could become a full-time occupation. In 1861 a girl under the pseudonym of 'Seraphine' wrote to the *Englishwoman's Domestic Magazine* boasting of her 15¾ inch waist, and asking what the record was. The magazine cut her down with rare common sense, pointing out that the Venus de Milo had a waist of 23½ inches, and she was considered by the best judges to have the perfect figure. Seraphine further claimed that this was her natural waist measurement, acquired without tight-lacing.

The magazine did not believe her. 'If we had not Seraphine's word for it, that she did not tighten, we should say that she must have endured many hours of misery and wretchedness in consequence of trying to alter her natural figure by squeezing it into so very small a compass. . . . If Seraphine wishes to enjoy good health, and preserve the beauty of her complexion, let her avoid tight lacing.' The magazine was later to be involved deeply with tight lacing, and the correspondence columns echoed with the pros and the cons.

A letter in 1866 came from a schoolgirl who described her boarding-school as 'Whalebone House Establishment'. Corsets were compulsory, and were sealed up every Monday morning. One

hour off was allowed on Saturdays for the 'purposes of ablution'.
By this stern regimen it was possible to reduce a waist of 23 inches
at the age of thirteen to 13 inches at seventeen.

All was not as plain as it seemed. Included in the correspondence
was a most curious letter, the writer of which stated: 'Everyone
must admit that a slender waist is a great acquisition; the so-called
evils of tight lacing are so much cant. To me the sensation is superb
and I am never prouder than when I survey the fascinating undulations that Art affords to Nature.' Others were less circumspect,
speaking of the delicious sensations, half pleasure, half pain,
echoed in History X of the Appendix to 'The Development of the
Sexual Instinct' in Havelock Ellis's *Studies in the Psychology of
Sex*. The subject found the effects of sexual excitement increased by
keeping the bladder full, 'but the chief method which she had
devised for heightening and prolonging the preliminary excitement consisted in wearing tight stays (as a rule she wears loose
stays) and in painting her face ... Self-excitement is completed by
friction, or sometimes by the introduction of a piece of wood into
the vagina.'

The 1870s were no less dominated by the spectre of the small
waist than the 1860s. A woman's magazine of 1873 stated:

> Of late years fashions have greatly improved in elegance and
> taste. The tight-fitting jacket shows the dainty little waist; the
> looped up skirt displays the feet in pretty high-heeled boots; and
> a fullness in the skirt behind and at the hips gives grace to the
> figure and makes the waist look smaller, and is a development of
> that contour which is universally considered a great beauty in
> the female form.

Universally considered? Not by sensible doctors faced with a
succession of ailments rising from tight lacing, which could have
the effect of nearly slicing the liver in two. Modern technology had
made lacing more efficient with the evolution of elasticated
material and the commonsensical hook and eye. Even as insides
were being compressed, there were elder women who looked back
at the old days, 'the days of wooden and steel busks, of short waists,
of scanty skirts, of overwhelming sleeves, of general suffering and
barbarous torture'. Did the older woman, reflected the
Englishwoman's Domestic Magazine of 1861, 'forget the consequences of a too-rapid dance, the fainting-fit likely to ensue, the

rapid retirement, the ultimate fainting, the sal volatile, unconsciousness, a sudden report sounding in the ears like a pistolshot, a glorious sense of expansion, of recovered breath, of life, and then the awful discovery that the lace had been cut?' And the subsequent agony all over again, 'the staylaces tight to bedposts for better purchase'.

The preoccupation with the small waist was seen as conquering nature, as the first step to the good figure, pronounced in 1873 as 'a well-developed bust, a tapering waist, and large hips'. By obtaining all these, parity with other women was accomplished, no matter at what cost.

From the number of prescriptions for improving breasts it is clear that it was a major industry. Among these was bathing in sage-tea, and the application of 'virginal milk', a concoction that included rose or orange flower water. To reduce the size of breasts it was recommended that ten grammes of sulphate of iron, ten grammes of alum, sixty grammes of vinegar, and a hundred grammes of water should be mixed with breadcrumbs into a creamy paste, spread over the bosom, and left all night. Flabby breasts were refurbished by using white wax softened by alcohol. Sage was a panacea for all ills. As Mme Bayard wrote in her *Toilet Hints*, 'Cover yourself with sage. Sit on it, walk on it, sleep on it.'

To acquire a full bust the method was to eat plenty of black grapes, drink Serkys Tea – a preparation sold at 2 New Bond Street at 12s. 6d. and 24s. – and gently rub the bosom with a mixture composed of tincture of myrrh, pimpernel and elder-flower waters, musk, and spirits of wine. Fruit baths were also recommended. The ingredients consisted of twenty pounds of fresh strawberries and three pounds of ripe strawberries. Bust improvement was not a pursuit for the poor.

Attention on the breasts was permitted, provided that they were not called that. Globes were allowed, and so was titty (and had been since about 1740), but they were not the primary sex organs, as might be believed from the evidence of mild porn. They served to draw interest from more fundamental parts; a partly exposed breast was allowable, even respectable, a partly exposed leg, never.

It is interesting to see pornographic writers react to the breast as they were meant to, as if taken in by the current emphasis. In *The Disembodied Spirit*, published in the pornographic magazine *The Boudoir* of 1860, the hero 'could inhale the sweets of her delicious breath, and here I could also catch glimpses of part of her lovely breasts, as they rose and fell in the calm undulations of innocent sleep'. In the *Adventures and Amours of a Barmaid*, published in the same magazine, 'Her lovely blue eyes languishing with desire, and her snowy bosom half exposed to view, could not, she thought, fail of captivating any beholder'. *The Pearl* was racier than *The Boudoir*, but in *Sub-Umbra, or Sport Amongst the She-Noodles* the writer was similarly preoccupied with the permitted zones. 'Annie, a finely developed blonde, with deep blue eyes, pouting red lips, and a full heaving bosom, which to me looked like a perfect volcano of smothered desires.'

In *Voluptuous Confessions of a French Lady of Fashion*, purported to be by a female narrator, the 'lady' claimed 'I had an admirable bust, the breasts apart firm and well placed; my figure was neat and supple with voluminous buttocks that were perfectly handsome.' In *Miss Coote's Confessions* in *The Pearl* the heroine has 'pretty white rounded globes, with dark brown nipples that looked impudently above her chemisette, which only reached a little way down her thighs.' However, concentration on the breasts could produce behaviour that was *not* approved. From *Sub-Umbra* part two, where the hero is done with ogling: 'I could feel the nipples of her virgin bosom stick out as stiff as little cocks, and whispered to her to allow me to kiss them'.

The pornographic magazines often resorted to asterisks and hyphens to give added emphasis to the breast, as if conscious that it was being oversold and that making it mysterious would give it more potency to the male fantasy-mongers who bought such magazines. In *The Exquisite* is a poem that is ostensibly coy, and can only be evaluated by realising that the writer is trying to be subtle:

> While her b———s and t——s
> Sink and rise,
> Like stormy waves on a milky main.

Elsewhere in the magazine the naughty words, plus others even more reprehensible, were printed in all their provoking glory.

Towards the end of the nineteenth century, a curious fashion arose that nullified the effect of tight-lacing – the high-necked dress that concealed the breasts, though they were pushed up above the corset in the traditional manner. This may have been an instinctive reaction against the over-exposure of the breasts, and came at a time when the legs were beginning to have a part of the action.

The cult of the breasts gave an opportunity for unconcealed hypocrisy. Women pretended that they dressed in a provocative manner to conform to fashion, knowing that they did it to attract men. Fashion was a convenient excuse, and anything that savoured of immodesty could be laid at its door. And, as a writer of a previous age, Colley Cibber, had said, 'as good be out of the World as out of Fashion'.

Women *did* know that they were dressing to please men, even when they pretended that it was not so; they were also dressing to please themselves, which could be narcissism or a subtle form of sex warfare, using dress as a snub to a husband. But there was also a new factor in fashion; middle- and upper-class women dressed in a manner that would show that they were not expected to work – a manner in which they could not work. The simplest example of this was the crinoline, which made woman a ridiculous hooped creature.

The crinoline evolved from a hooped skeleton, through a wired petticoat, to the Watch Spring Crinoline. As the years went by the skirt expanded until it became less of a dome and more of a pyramid; in 1859 the Sheffield factories were producing wire for half-a-million crinolines a week. The crinoline vogue was one of the few fashions to have a permanent result on architecture; the wide staircases of mid-Victorian houses derive directly from the demands of the crinoline.

There was no hypocrisy involved in the fashion for the crinoline; hypocrisy implies that the victim is aware that he or she is acting out a role, whereas women wore the crinoline without knowing why, except that everyone else was. *Punch* attacked the crinoline with forced joviality (but only when it was going out of fashion); so did the *Englishwoman's Domestic Magazine* with a delicate irony that would have been lost in the most famous humorous magazine of all time. Speaking of the evils of tight-lacing, the magazine concluded that victims 'died slowly, perhaps, but died. Fashion demands a more rapid supply of victims now-a-days . . . Death *a la mode* is effected at present by the combustion of crinoline skirts. The abolition of some portions of the crippling machinery for the manufacture of a perfect figure may have given greater impunity to the staylace, but the skirts make speedy end of their votaries, who are offered up upon a funeral pyre of silk and muslin, stretched upon a ghastly skeleton altar devoted to their insatiable deity.'

This was no exaggeration. The newspapers were rarely without an account of some poor girl who was burned to death. The *Englishwoman's Domestic Magazine* looked back to the ancestors of the crinoline:

> [It] seems to me to have been handed down by tradition from some savage belle, and I can remember having seen a picture of her somewhere – I think in 'Captain Cook's Voyages' – where the elaboration of skirt and its enormous amplitude of extension are, if possible, more perfect than they have yet become amongst ourselves. I take it to be a proof of the close connexion between the two states of society in the matter of dress that the expansive petticoats of the 'belle sauvage' are not accompanied by any remarkable fulness of material in the body of the dress, the neck and shoulders being left, if I remember rightly, to the full amount of exposure.

Far from being appealing to men, crinolined women were annoying. Three or four women filled a drawing room, keeping the men penned up against the door or the wall, and an omnibus designed to take 'eight inside' would have its work cut out to accommodate four of these pyramidic structures. As if to point the uselessness of the crinoline, there arose a fashion for longer dresses, so that women not only had to cope with the crinoline but a dragging skirt. A means had to be found of holding up the skirt when walking. 'This is generally managed by the aid of *porte-jupes*, and ladies are seen in the streets with their skirts looped up over their petticoats, quite in the Pompadour style.'

The existence of the crinoline demonstrated a delight in conspicuous consumption, and illustrated confidence in one's role in society. Men, it was assumed, would give way to women, even when irked and forced to move into the gutter off the pavement when outside. They would, hopefully, take care not to crumple her skirts when they sat down with a woman. In the main, they did; it was a quiet triumph for women, and so it was recognised at the time.

Above the skirts were oceans of white material, frothy lace, delicate pastel colours, and needlework that had perhaps cost the eyesight of some poor drab in a sweat-shop. Through it all bulged the bosom. It was spectacular, expensive, and proved that the wearer did not work. However, the servants and the working classes who came into contact with their betters – the shop assistants, the laundresses – caught the infection, and these too wanted crinolines. When the crinoline craze died and its successors came on the scene, the lower orders wanted to wear these too. The most curious of these refinements was the bustle, which gave woman the appearance of a letter S, the behind sticking out, sometimes at such an angle that a tea-tray could be balanced on it. The more aggressive bustle lasted from 1881 to 1888. The crinoline, if worn by a pretty young woman, could be alluring, but the bustle, never. It has been suggested that it came at a time when women were becoming actively hostile to men, realising that they could do very well without them and that they could take up careers in which they need not preen themselves.

The most percipient historian of women's fashions, Dr C. Willett Cunnington, argues that the bustle was 'an unconscious expression of a maternal craving, and the fashion was accompanied by a significant arrangement of the front of the skirt, which was draped as though a further addition to the family might presently be anticipated.' In Mrs C. S. Peel's *A Hundred Wonderful Years* (1920), one of her correspondents looked back in nostalgia:

> My coming-out dress had a bustle. Not, I think, the 'cushion' bustle, but one with wires tied together with tapes to make a half-hoop which waggled as one walked. Sometimes a steel poked through, which was most embarrassing. One of my cousins as a boy staying with a large family of cousins hid all their bustles on a Sunday morning (these were the horse-hair cushion bustles), and none of them would go to church because they 'felt so flat and indecent'.

The involved technique that was needed to cope with the bustle was described in *Cassell's Family Magazine* in 1885:

> Skirts now require a vast deal of adjustment because in order to look fashionable, they should be full and much puffed out at the back, but straight and narrow at the front and sides. In order that they may fall well in any position, the steel springs must be placed very high at the back, and every skirt must be mounted on

a foundation; four breadths of silk form the best, though inferior materials are often used – and these are furnished inside with either elastic bands or sets of strings. The first set are five inches below the waist; the two next are elastic bands with ribbon or tape or tie them ...

As with all fashions demanding a lot of time, the novelty eventually became a bore, the bustle was reduced to a mere pad, called the half-bustle, and at length sanity was restored for a while. The Victorians did not have any monopoly on absurdities; at least the wearer could walk in a bustle, or proceed in somewhat the same way as a camel, but with the Edwardian hobble-skirt even walking was difficult.

Monolithic woman below the waist, provoking siren above it – except during the day, when the high neck carried all before it. Transparent and semi-transparent materials began to be utilised, and even, the perverse cut indeed, a flesh-coloured velvet that imitated the body. The wearers of such clothes were obliged to pretend that they did not know that they were showing sufficient details of their anatomies as to be embarrassing. This game of pretend extended to prostitutes, who knew perfectly well what they were doing. In *My Secret Life*, that much discussed copulation epic written about 1890, the narrator visits a prostitute: 'It was a night of summer. The woman stood with a very fine chemise on, made of such exceedingly slight, thin, gauzy material that I could plainly see through it her entire form, and the dark hair of her motte'.

The chemise, introduced about 1849 to replace the shift, was a necessary ingredient in pornographic tales. In decent society, no one mentioned the word underclothes, though there is no doubt that married men were excited by them and unmarried men had fantasies about them. There was a fiction that no person but the wearer ever saw underclothes, even when they came in a rash of bright colours in the 1860s, with magenta, 'the queen of colours', the favourite.

A possible exception was the petticoat, of which four to six were often worn, for when the crinoline became popular in the 1850s-60s – it began to decline in 1866 – it was hardly possible for a viewer to avoid seeing the occasional flash of petticoat, flounced, embroidered, crocheted or decked out with lace.

The evolution of the blouse in the 1860s gave a great opportunity for the modest use of immodest materials. There was some doubt about the respectability of the blouse, to judge by the names it went under – bodice, chemisette, canezon, and Garibaldi shirt. New materials were constantly being invented or imported. India provided a variety of exotic semi-transparent materials, and towards the end of the century clinging materials were used that accentuated the body form and, if selected carefully, left little to the imagination. 'Veiled, trimmed with chiffon, jewelled with flimsiest of gauzes' comes not from a pornographic magazine but from the *Lady's Realm* 1898-9.

One of the great disadvantages of the nineteenth century fashion scene is that almost total exposure combined with decency had to wait for the invention of the brassiere in 1912. There was no way to display an expanse of semi-transparent flesh from the bust to the waist without problems of technique. Another was that the clothes industry could not really capitalise on stockings, though, strangely, considering that in theory they were never seen by anyone but the wearers, they evolved from plain white through bright colours matching petticoats in the 1860s to black in the 1890s.

The ostensible purpose of stockings was to show off ankles. As a fashion writer of the 1890s put it, 'nothing is so becoming to the ankle, so ladylike or so smart, as an openworked black stocking, or one quite plain with the ever-pretty clockings'. For the man in the street (literally) the glimpse of an ankle was considered the greatest of favours a woman could bestow, though if he kept his wits about him he could see a good deal more, for during much of the Victorian period women did not wear drawers or knickers, a word that was introduced into the English language in 1881.

This seems rather amiss for an age that prided itself on its delicacy, and the paradox was that initially drawers were only worn by prostitutes. When the King of Sardinia saw a lady-in-waiting trip over her crinoline at the court of Queen Victoria he observed that the gates of Paradise were always open. Drawers are an Oriental garment and probably reached Europe through Venice. In Britain they were considered masculine, and as they were associated with prostitutes and ballet girls, who were obliged to wear them after an unfortunate experience that was widely seen and reported, respectable women scorned them.

There is some controversy about the date drawers became

proper, and from what the gynaecologist Tilt wrote in is *Elements of Health* (1852) it is evident that they were not widely worn then. He advocated drawers made from fine calico, not to extend below the knee. 'Thus understood, the adoption of drawers will doubtless become more general in this country, as, being worn without the knowledge of the general observer, they will be robbed of the prejudice usually attached to an appendage deemed masculine.' By 1868 drawers were being sold made of silk, flannel, lace, and plush, so between 1852 and 1868 they had passed from reprehensible to acceptable, to the fashionable. Combinations, introduced in 1877, a 'new style of combining chemise and drawers' did not catch on.

There were two kinds of drawers, split legs anchored at the waist, and closed drawers. According to Pepys' *Diary*, 1663, his wife, born of French parents, wore drawers of the closed kind, something of a novelty in the London of the day. The open drawers were sensible considering the cumbersome dresses worn by women, often involving more than forty yards of material, the petticoats, frequently starched, and the crinoline frames, which were in engineering terms a series of connected hoops of diminishing size. Graphic details of the various kinds of drawers in use were supplied by the author of *The Mysteries of Verbena House* (1882):

> There were little minxes whose breeches only reached to the knee, and others whose trowsers only came mid-leg, and a few who wore the old-fashioned drawers, which came down to the ankle, and well nigh covered the boot . . . Some of the elder girls wore drawers almost as tight as nun's pantaloons, and whole seated – that is to say not slit up the back. These buttoned at the sides, and necessitated the letting down of a hinder flap when the wearer went to the watercloset . . . Others, again, patronized knickerbocker drawers of crimson or purple flannel – Zouave breeches in fact, secured by 'elastic' at the knee – but the majority of the elder girls wore the ordinary undergarments of English ladies, young and old, linen or longcloth tongs, slit up the front and the back, tying round the waist with a string, the drawers themselves reaching to the middle of the calf of the leg, and decorated at the extremities with several tucks, or with embroidery or insertion.

The author of *The Mysteries of Verbena House*, who called himself

Etonensis, was activated by drawers sufficiently to attack them violently, hypocrisy at its most archetypal:

> Peasant women, who are chaste enough as times go, don't wear drawers; and when they stoop you may see the bare flesh of their thighs above their ungartered stockings. But the bigger the whore – professional or otherwise – the nicer will be the drawers she wears, while the prude, or the cantankerous old maid will either wear the most hideous breeches imaginable, or none at all.

That it was not considered immodest not to wear drawers or knickers might be something of a surprise to those who tend to see Victorian life as all of a piece. The phenomenon shows that nothing is modest or immodest unless it is discussed. There is nothing in general literature to indicate that drawers were not worn; Dickens's women do not go to the lavatory, and Thackeray's do not know what a lavatory is.

It would seem that drawers were forced on women for hygienic reasons and as an aid to good health by doctors. For those dealing with hypochondriacs or those afflicted with the vapours it was a good sales line. But another factor might well enter into it – the realisation by man that woman was a property, and that drawers would help to safeguard this property. It was reasoned that a daughter wearing drawers would be more secure from sexual violation than one without. The same went for a wife. To judge by a passage in *Rosa Fielding, or a Victim of Lust* (1876) this was not so.

Two of the characters in this novel, reckoned to be one of the more literate offerings on the pornographic market, are discussing the matter: 'Woman's pants are made, to speak plainly, with openings at the front and rear, corresponding to her natural openings'. Consequently, the garments 'are no obstruction whatever to a man who is determined to violate a woman'. And that, so far as pornographers were concerned, put paid to that, but to millions of women up to the last decades of the nineteenth century (and well into the present century in Europe) there must have been some uneasiness in their freedom from drawers whereas other parts of the body were tight-laced so energetically that it was customary for them to faint, and when three inches of ankle was a cause for scandal.

6

THE GREAT SOCIAL EVIL

THE Great Social Evil might be thought by cynics to refer to matrimony instead of prostitution. It was a euphemism that was widely used, even by those who did not regard prostitution as an evil but as a useful social safeguard. The whole subject was surrounded by myth, and it was a field in which hypocrisy ran riot. There was no need for myth, for oddly enough there was no shortage of writers on prostitution, writers not of pornography but of sociology. Prostitution forms a large chunk of Mayhew's *London Labour and the London Poor*, endlessly plumbed by twentieth-century writers since it was reissued in a cheap format edited by Peter Quennell.

There was no real need for hypocrisy either. Nobody in their right minds could pretend that prostitution did not exist, though well-bred ladies taking their promenade through the West End were obliged, by tradition, to ignore the serried ranks of street-walkers. Often the street-walkers were better and more expensively dressed than they were; only when they opened their mouths was it apparent that they were not all sisters under the skin.

No one will ever know how many prostitutes there were in London, whether there were 8,000 – as the police maintained, or 80,000 – the estimate of the Bishop of Exeter. All we do know is that there were a lot of them, catering for the entire spectrum of society from sailors and Irish navvies to noble lords. Some would have suppressed them entirely, some would have let them alone, and others would have had them organised, medically inspected and forced to live in approved brothels. Most of the prostitutes were let alone. The British people, to their credit, were tenacious of their rights and privileges, and liberty was more important than clearing London of its gay ladies. Consequently the police, who considered the presence of prostitutes on the streets a personal affront, were unable to enter brothels and houses of ill-repute unless to suppress disturbances. Individual policemen, poorly paid (30s. a week in 1878), were not too displeased by the inhibitions; they received a pay-off from prostitutes on the beat, and a constable would turn his back while the prostitutes solicited for custom.

Hypocrisy had a powerful opponent in some sections of the public, especially among the men. They liked the colour and gaiety of the West End whores, and they brought a sense of excitement into their observers' lives, even though a good percentage would not have dreamed of using them. Prostitutes were picturesque at a time when life could be dull and grey.

Not all prostitutes were picturesque; some did not need to be because they were cheap, though the sixpence a time earned by the drabs in the slums of Drury Lane would have been high pay for workers in the sweat-shops who had to work several hours for as much. In the East End, by the docks, and south of the river the whores were often ugly, filthy, and diseased. Mayhew looked at one in the prison cells, charged with nearly murdering a man with a poker. 'Her face was bad, heavy, and repulsive; her forehead, as well as I could distinguish by the scanty light thrown into the place by the bull's-eye of the policeman, was low; her nose was short and what is called podgy, having the nostrils dilated . . .'

Another low prostitute had a grimy and unwashed face, 'and her hands [were] so black and filthy that mustard-and-cress might have been sown successfully upon them'. A black woman was also in circulation, sometimes venturing into the Haymarket, 'a shameless hag, with her thick lips, sable black skin, leering countenance and obscene disgusting tongue, resembling a lewd spirit of darkness from the nether world'. The other prostitutes paid her to go away. The ugliest and most diseased prostitutes operated at night in the parks; Mayhew was told 'that an old woman, whose front teeth were absolutely wanting, was known to obtain a precarious livelihood by haunting the by-walks of Hyde Park, near Park Lane'.

When there was any kind of disturbance, such as a visit from the police or a fight between whores, 'the noise caused the adjacent lanes to be emptied of their occupants . . . it was like a human sewer suddenly discharging its contents'. So wrote Hippolyte Taine, whose *Notes on England* (1861) show great observation not un-mixed with wonder at the way they managed things away from his native Paris. 'Every hundred steps,' he went on, 'one jostles twenty harlots; some of them ask for a glass of gin; others say, "Sir, it is to pay my lodging." This is not debauchery which flaunts itself, but destitution – and such destitution!' They managed things much better in the West End, too.

Why did women become prostitutes? There were almost as many reasons as there were prostitutes, but the three main ones were poverty, inclination, and seduction. It was often asserted that economic conditions lay at the root of prostitution, and that morals fluctuated with trade. A girl had a much better life on the streets, in terms of variety, and money, than in a factory, a sweat-shop, as an outworker, or in service. A Royal Commission found that as many as sixty per cent of prostitutes had been servants; laundresses, dressmakers, and milliners were also well represented in the profession. It was popularly supposed that the girls soon regretted leaving their respectable occupations, but Charles Booth in his monumental *Life and Labour of the People* found out differently. Unless they had caught syphilis they were glad they had made the change. One prostitute summed up the sentiments of thousands: 'I am taken out to dinner and to some place of amuse-ment every night; why should I give it up?'

Middle-class employers did much to contribute their servants to the cause. In *The Dens of London* (1854) Vanderkiste declared that 'domestic service is a complete slavery', and that mistresses exer-cised a misplaced ingenuity in 'obtaining the largest possible amount of labour out of the domestic machine'. A domestic servant was also a 'kind of lightning conductor' for the ill-temper and morbid feelings of her mistress and any members of the family who happened to be about. Another feature of domestic life was the traditional habit of young men of the family trying out their sex appeal on the servants, and the equally time-honoured ceremony of servants seducing sons. Either could persuade a girl that what she did for pleasure could be done for money. Prostitutes not only enjoyed the perquisites of the trade, the free meals and entertain-ment, but prostitution itself.

Continentals noticed with amazement that British prostitutes obtained gratification from them, often leading to orgasm, and this apparently was little known among European prostitutes who provided their services without great enthusiasm. The tendency of prostitutes to masturbate (and not mind admitting it) encouraged writers on the subject to consider prostitutes criminals. A London magistrate named Lane decided that prostitution was 'at once a symptom and outcome of the same deteriorated physique and decadent moral fibre which determine the manufacture of male tramps, petty thieves, and professional beggars, of whom the prostitute is in general the female analogue'. This was merely the waffling of the establishment which saw what it wanted to see; it was simply not true. There is every kind of evidence to suggest that prostitutes were in far better health and in better physical shape than their contemporaries of the same class. The French sexologist Féré made a most curious judgment: 'Prostitutes and criminals have as a common character their unproductiveness, and consequently they are both anti-social'.

Unquestionably there was resentment that prostitutes were prettier, in better health, and more contented than they should have been. The wages of sin were apparent in the parks, in the slums, and around the docks, but not in the West End or anywhere where there was a middle-class clientele. It was also claimed that prostitutes were uneducated, but this does not fit in with facts. One of the diseased park women had been a skilful painter in water-colours. William Gladstone, who attempted to rescue fallen women and who took an impish delight in frequenting the streets on the look-out for candidates, treated the prostitutes whom he brought back home as equals; and Gladstone did not treat numbskulls lightly. It is also clear from the involvement of statesmen and intellectuals in the plight of the prostitute that all whores did not come from the ranks of washerwomen and tweenies, barmaids and shop assistants; nor were they brought up in the back streets of Shadwell or Whitechapel.

Interesting statistics were supplied by an investigation into the backgrounds of 14,000 prostitutes who passed through Millbank Prison (where the Tate Gallery now stands). No more than half were London born. Many came from military and naval towns such as Colchester and Devonport, nice girls seduced by sailors and soldiers and forced to leave home, or hardened prostitutes who specialised in the naval and the military. Many came from the country, healthy girls who found no work for them in the agricultural depression that began in 1875, when farmers were forced to sell out to speculators. As R. C. K. Ensor wrote in his *England 1870-1914* (1936), 'for twenty years the only chance for any young or enterprising person in the countryside was to get out of it', and this applied to the young women as well as the young men.

Prostitutes filled a demand. But from whom came the demand? Popularly, from the debauched and the dissipated, the perverts and the drunks, the diseased and the riff-raff of the streets. This happy assumption comforted Victorian wives. Nor did the prostitute exist solely for the benefit of licentious young unmarried men with more money than sense, though these did provide a cadre of customers. Men of a respectable rank in society married later than they do today; it was considered irresponsible to marry before they could afford it, and many young men considered that the moderate use of a prostitute was better than sticking it out with all the associated tension.

It was accepted by wives that married men, even happily married men, had recourse to prostitutes simply because wives were obedient but cold, were unwilling when they were willing, were pregnant, or were averse to indulging in prohibited sexual pursuits, such as oral sex, probably no less in demand then than now. People do not change much in a hundred years. There was also a craving for variety, the celebrated seven-year itch, a desire to show that they were virile after x-years of marriage. There was guilt and repentance, but there could be a driving force that brooked no repression.

The author of *My Secret Life* related his struggles with his conscience:

> I have wept over this weakness, I have punished myself by self-imposed fines, giving heavily to charities, thus disposing of the money which I would have paid for other women. More than that – I have masturbated to avoid having a woman whose beauty has tempted my lust. I have, when about to accost a lovely frail one, jumped into a cab and relieved my passions by myself, though unavoidably thinking of the charms I had not seen. I have avoided Argyll and Cremorne, and any other places to which whores resort, for fear of being tempted.

There were plenty of goodies on the stalls:

> Luckily one finds among courtesans every type of physical

beauty to gratify the taste, together with a libidinousness which seems to be becoming more and more important to me. Fortunately, too, there are also to be found among them those who are willing enough to gratify every taste of mine . . . But even in those aberrations I am sure some gay ladies would be willing to indulge with me, providing I am able to pay for their services.

A husband could venture into this attractive world without any strong convictions, not desirous of breaking up his marriage, not wishing to cause distress to his wife, but drifting in a trance, instinctively trying to find something that he could not find at home, but also insuring himself against a permanent liaison. Paying for services was a guarantee; a prostitute, it was reasoned, would not laugh at a customer on account of an innocent fetishistic whim. Brothels were well equipped with black dresses and nuns' outfits to answer obscure and harmless demands, not to mention riding boots and frilly knickers.

Some of the fetishism was odd. One prostitute whose beat ran along the Strand had a customer who always brought with him a pair of live pigeons. The prostitute and the girl with whom she lived had to undress and wring the pigeons' necks, during which the customer had his orgasm. Another man's 'letch' was to lick the boots of a prostitute; another's was to have the prostitute urinate in his mouth. Although such customers were undemanding in a physical sense, the better class of prostitutes avoided them unless they knew beforehand what exactly was expected of them. A pervert could be harmless, or he could be a sadist of the school of Jack the Ripper. During the time when he was in circulation (1888-9) many prostitutes went under cover, only giving service to old and favoured customers.

A successful prostitute, especially if she was a loner (or seclusive) had to be a shrewd judge of character, able to ascertain if the prospect was a pervert and how much she could take him for. There was the question of approach. 'Are you good natured, dear?' was an ambiguous form of address that could serve any purpose and was often heard in the dance rooms and introduction houses, as well as in the shops in the Burlington Arcade, a favourite pick-up spot. The prostitutes had 'arrangements' with the shop managers. A successful prostitute making her way to the top of the tree (to be a rich man's mistress) also had to gauge whether to be sympathetic or brassy.

The sovereigns could be enticed from a man's purse by mere companionship and understanding. Havelock Ellis wrote, 'In every great city, it has been said, there are thousands of men who have no right to call any woman but a barmaid by her Christian name.' In such cases a prostitute was as efficacious as a telephone call to a Samaritan. It was a failure of society to shut out the lonely; it is a failing that still exists. It was also society's loss that the therapeutic value of the street-walker was not appreciated. It was a typically Victorian generalisation to group all prostitutes under one heading, as low life no better than they should be.

The well-dressed and presentable street walker also represented glamour; she was abreast with the latest fashions, and her equivocal social position made contact with such a creature tantalising, especially to country people. There were directories of better-class prostitutes containing names, addresses, specialities, and prices, plus hints by 'a sporting surgeon' on how to prevent infection. A countryman or, as he was invariably termed, a yokel, knew what to expect.

Many men preferred their prostitutes to be genteel, and as the nineteenth century progressed there were more prostitues about whose appearances did not shriek their trade. Brothels tended to disappear, and the prostitutes were more inclined to work in ones or twos. There were more high-class girls coming on to the market, whether they were discarded mistresses of the rich who changed their women as they changed their shirts, or respectable girls enticed from their homes under the pretence of being employed as governesses (an overstocked profession and a certain lure), or emancipated girls. These did not see why they should not batten on men as men had exploited them for hundreds of years. They were also in a van in calling for an end to traditional marriage, and would have agreed with Ellen Kay in her *Essays on Love and Marriage* when she declared that 'the development of erotic personal consciousness is as much hindered by socially regulated "morality" as by socially regulated "immorality" '.

The claims of the emancipationists show the trend. Kathleen Cuffe in *The Nineteenth Century* (1894) declared, 'Our desires to develop our Personality (with a very big P), satisfy the cravings of our souls for something beyond the commonplace (the com-

monplace of home duties and making the best of our natural sur-
roundings), are inseparable from an equally intense longing to
frequent music-halls and possess latchkeys.' Alys Pearsall-Smith
in the same periodical penned in the life of the suppressed emancipationists:

> They must arrange the flowers, help with the housekeeping, pay
> the family calls, entertain the family visitors, always be at hand,
> well-dressed, cheerful, and smiling, like household angels, as
> they are often called, without any personal preferences or pur-
> suits, ready to meet every call, and to contribute to everyone's
> pleasure but their own.

It was a short step to contributing to a man's pleasure and getting
paid for it. Miss Pearsall-Smith married the Fabian Socialist B. F.
Costelloe, so there was an out for her, but others were not so
equitably accommodated.

Mrs Lynn Linton, on behalf of the anti-emancipationists, did
not point out the logical end of the keenest emancipationists, only
hinted. 'Their idea of freedom is their own preponderance, so that
they shall do all they wish to do without let or hindrance from
outside regulations, or the restraints of self-discipline.'

That emancipationists were joining the ranks of the prostitutes
as a gesture was not recognised by respectable middle-class opinion
unless it was labelled free love, which was prostitution on the truck
system with goods given in exchange for services instead of money.
Free love was widely practised among the Fabian set which included H. G. Wells and George Bernard Shaw, and by changing
the terminology they changed the image.

The idealistic free lovers were often disappointed, for life outside
the home brought in its own chain of problems. The prostitute
with a real talent for the game was a pragmatist, and this the free
lovers, be they mischievous, libidinous, even lecherous, never were.
They were as much entangled in the web of convention as their
reactionary parents. Hypocritical parents were, but so were their
daughters. As for their sons, they were hypocritical in a different
way.

Escape from the family thus provided prostitutes and clients.
'Subduing and subdued, the petty strife, Which clouds the colour
of domestic life' wrote Hannah More in her poem 'Sensibility'.
Petty strife was one of the elements of Victorian family life, which

had been systematically upgraded in a conscious attempt to preserve the status quo. 'Many an enlighted intellect, many a sensitive spirit,' declared Eliza Cook in the pages of her weekly journal, established 1849, circulation 50,000-60,000, 'is bitterly restricted in sympathies and hopes, yet wearing the mien and manner of elevated content'. She thought that it was a strong lesson to see 'a mind and soul of Nature's finest workmanship take the scanty pittance doled out to them by Fortune, and bravely, honourably, and cheerfully "make the best of it" '. Miss Cook, and many others, could see the mind-bending effect of family life.

It was, of course, respectable. Queen Victoria, breeding with exemplary energy, made a fetish of family life. The middle classes considered the family the centre of their universe – especially the women. They modelled their life on what they imagined was the life of their betters. The merchants moved from above the shop to a square, preferably not unlike Berkeley Square, the well-to-do farmers moved from their muddy farmhouses into something in red brick, and the professional men moved into the suburbs. It was like the present-day move of Cockneys from the back streets of Bethnal Green into high-rise flats – it was an upgrading of their environment, but the result was stifling and boring.

Women thought they ought to behave in a manner to suit their station, and preoccupation with etiquette took spontaneity out of behaviour, and consequently life itself. There was more interest in what was 'proper' than in following one's inclinations, whether in entertaining, eating, visiting – or in bed. Men found themselves in an irritating position. Nominally in a commanding position, they were obliged to kowtow to a matriarchy, unable to smoke except outside, in the stables, or somewhere where 'the weed' would not inconvenience the ladies, and constrained in a social strait-jacket.

In 1844, *Punch* came out with one of its excellent waspish little articles, 'More Hints to Make Home Happy – to Wives'. It advised wives, 'be at no pains to look well of a morning. A long toilet is tiresome . . . Indulge your taste in dress to the utmost. Be always buying something new; never mind the expense of it. Payments belong to husbands . . . If your husband is astonished at the bill, pout; if he remonstrates, cry. But do not spoil your finery by domestic wear. Reserve it for promenades and parties. It is the admiration of society that you should seek for, not your husband's . . .' Wives were also instructed to take every opportunity of making a cheap purchase, and when asked of what use it was, to reply that it was 'a bargain'.

> Enjoy ill health. Be very nervous: and, in particular, subject to fits; which you are to fly into as often as your husband is unkind, that is, whenever he reasons with you. . . . Put yourself under no restraint in your husband's presence. Sit, loll, or lie, in just what way you like, looking only to the ease of the posture, not to its grace. Leave niceties of conversation and sentiment to the single; never mind how you express yourself; why should wives be particular? When your husband wishes to read or be quiet, keep chattering to him; the more frivolous and uninteresting the subject, the better. If he is disposed for conversation, be dull and silent: and whenever you see that he is interested in what he is talking about, especially if he wishes you to attend to him, keep yawning . . .

There seems no reason to think that this is exaggeration. To many of the readers of *Punch*, precisely that class to go off the rails, it would all have seemed too near the bone to be funny. If the reader had been a subscriber to *Punch* for some time he would have become familiar with the campaign. In 1841 *Punch* ran 'A Dictionary for the Ladies', with the following definitions:

> *Husband*—a person who writes cheques, and dresses as the wife directs.
> *Marriage*—the only habit to which women are constant.
> *Brute*—A domestic endearment for a husband.
> *Honeymoon*—a wife's opportunity.
> *Nice; Dear*—expressions of delight at anything, from a baby to a barrel organ.

It was the boredom and exasperation of family life that most encouraged a husband to take time off, not inordinate sexual appetite. 'The nymphs of the pavement' were made to seem irresistibly fascinating when compared with a complacent nag of a wife, and the Great Social Evil can only be seen in perspective when it is understood that those who were most aghast at the presence of prostitutes in their midst, the middle-class women, were partly responsible for their numbers and their success. Often they had only themselves to blame; after marriage far too many of them dropped into a smug middle-age, as if they had reached their goal and that was sufficient. They were not interesting, and they let their looks go. As Oscar Wilde put it, 'A man who moralises is usually a hypocrite, and a woman who moralises is invariably plain'.

The venom with which middle-class women attacked prostitution arose from the recognition that it was a threat to the stability of the home. A lapse on the part of even the most brow-beaten of husbands was always possible; he was almost by definition a fool who could be infatuated with any painted hussy of the streets. And the most infuriating thing was that a wife had no defence; the double standard operated on behalf of the husband in all matters concerning marital infidelity. He could divorce her if she committed adultery, but for the wife to get a divorce adultery had to be combined with something else, such as physical cruelty.

There was no hypocrisy on the part of women who hated prostitution, but they confused their motives. They did not hate prostitution for what it was but for what it could do to them personally – damage their position in society, deprive them of housekeeping money, or perhaps infect them through their husbands with venereal disease. And whatever happened they had to grin and bear it. If they left their husbands the husbands would keep what property they had, and customarily retain custody of the children. Even if the husband was cruel and a divorce was legally possible it was usually too expensive (at least £700).

A wife may have been a shrew, a nag, a dominating termagant, but in the eyes of the law she was property, a second-class citizen. A man need never fear that an escapade now and then would injure him financially, except in the sense of paying the prostitute her fee. A wife, half-fearing that her husband was not being faithful, always had the dread that a perambulating prostitute would be replaced by a living-in mistress – in the same house as the wife. That would have been an even greater social evil, and in nine cases out of ten a wife would still have had to suffer it. The law of the land was not on her side at all.

One of the most pressing of wives' fears was contracting venereal disease from a husband who had been with prostitutes. The long-term effect of syphilis had begun to be realised, that it could lie dormant for years and appear at any time in the future, perhaps in the form of that most fearful disease, general paralysis of the insane. Furthermore, syphilis, wrote Dr Spencer Thomson in 1856, could 'be transmitted to circulate in the young blood of innocent offspring'.

There was no certain cure for syphilis. The mercury treatment could be as bad as the disease, rotting the jaws and causing the teeth to drop out. Morbid fear of syphilis was so widespread that the term syphilophobia was coined. It was no consolation that many clergymen and some doctors thought that syphilis was the just reward of sin, 'a Divine Judgment against moral transgression' reported *The Times* in 1869.

As with other offences against wives, the transmission of syphilis was not illegal. 'A husband knowingly and wilfully infecting his wife with the venereal disease cannot be convicted criminally either under a charge of assault or of inflicting grievious bodily harm', stated Sir W. Nevill Geary in *Law of Marriage* (1892). The injured wife had lost again.

7

THE WAGES OF SIN

THERE was an evangelist in a London street engaged in the task of rescuing young females from themselves. He saw a likely candidate, and approached her bearing a tract for her to take home to her squalid lodgings and read. She looked at him in bewilderment, and then explained, 'Lor bless you, sir, I ain't a social evil, I'm waiting for the bus.' Another diligent soul pounced on a young lady walking along the street, and had her put in charge for soliciting. She was merely walking home, and there were some red faces in the police station when the 'victim' of her soliciting had to sign his name with an X. Illiteracy was no bar to evangelical fervour.

There could be a lot of confusion on the London streets, and no less ambiguity about prostitutes. There is something oddly significant about the synonyms that were coined for them; they were not merely circumlocutions to avoid calling a spade a spade, but terms that were almost tender. In 1862 the *Saturday Review* looked askance at this practice. Speaking of the 'highly-tinted Venuses who form so favourite a study of the connoisseurs of the Haymarket' the writer went on to analyse this phenomenon, coming to the conclusion that 'on the whole, the nicest, the softest, the most poetical designation we have heard is that which the Penitentiaries have invented – "soiled doves" '.

The *Saturday Review* had been complaining about this kind of thing for some years.

The very fact that we have lost sight of the old-fashioned language is significant. We purposely use the term 'street-walker' just now; but nobody else uses the phrase, nor that of prostitute, to say nothing of more homely language. The term 'Social Evil' by a queer translation of the abstract into the concrete has become a personality. 'Unfortunates' and 'fallen sisters' are the language of the sentimental.

That was the crux of it. Prostitutes, like the poor, were of sentimental interest especially at a distance. They were ogled from fifty yards away, the mysterious girls who were 'fond of a kiss and fond of a guinea', as was the subject of Rossetti's poem 'Jenny', written in 1858.

The attitude of Rossetti towards prostitutes was typical of that of the Bohemians, who even if they did not take advantage of their services used them as 'copy'. Artists and writers found that there was a lot of mileage in prostitutes; they thought they were interesting, even quaint, and acted as public relations men. The prettier and more fashionable prostitutes received the kind of coverage, not to mention adulation, enjoyed by pop stars today.

The analogy may seem extravagant; but both species operate on the fringes of the establishment, and both have a reputation for speaking their minds.

All this was provided that the prostitutes were pretty and fashionable – in other words, successes. In an odd sort of way, they were illustrations of the advantages of self-help, that most moral of all qualities. The drabs in the back streets were failures; they were the scum, the worthless riff-raff, the repugnant. One or two of the most lauded prostitutes had started off that way, yet this did not stop them being taken up by the media when they became established in the West End and had a well-born clientele. This was crucial. The dominant Victorian class, the middle, loved a lord, and a prostitute who had lords as her clients partook of some of the charisma. It was snobbery at its most curious.

The aristocracy gave their whores protection, as well as money and gifts that enabled them to live far better than middle-class women. Lord Yarmouth selected Louisa Turner as his love-object, gave her a horse worth £200, and although he set her up, taking her from a brothel in Titchfield Street, near Oxford Street, to which she had graduated from the opera house, she continued to ply her trade as before. She was in competition with Ellen Clarke for the Duke of

Brunswick, who was one time a possible suitor of the young Victoria.

The most prestigious of the superior prostitutes was Catherine (Skittles) Walters (1839-1920), whose conquests included Lord Hartington, who almost became prime minister, Aubrey de Vere Beauclerk, and Achille Fould, the finance minister to Napoleon III. She was admired by the Prince of Wales and Lord Kitchener, not to mentioned the society poets who dribbled over her as if she were Venus come to town. Beauclerk had, wrote Sir William Hardman, lawyer and gossip, 'four thousand pounds a year, which will be even as fourpence halfpenny to such a woman'.

As for her appearance

> She was a little woman dressed in black
>> Who stood on tiptoe with a childish air.
> Her face and figure hidden in a sacque,
>> All but her eyes and forehead and dark hair.
> Her brow was pale, but it was lit with light,
>> And mirth flashed out of it, seemed in rays,
> A childish face, but wise with woman's wit,
>> And something, too, pathetic in its gaze.

So wrote one of her tame bards, William Scawen Blunt. The matrons would have dearly loved to have seen Miss Walters, as Blunt wrote, 'hidden in a sacque', but they were helpless. In the days of the ancient Greeks, a courtesan had been a religious figure demanding awe, and such was true in the 1860s when Skittles was in fashion. She rode at the fashionable hours in Hyde Park:

> Though scowling matrons champing steeds restrain,
> She flaunts Propriety with flapping mane.
> *(Alfred Austin, later Poet Laureate)*

She rode with the Quorn, she was the subject of a Royal Academy picture of 1859 – 'The Taming of the Shrew' by Sir Edwin Landseer – she was taken into Society by Lord Hartington and presented at the Derby in 1862, and earned the gratitude of milliners for popularising the pork-pie hat. Gladstone presented her with twelve pounds of Russian tea and took her on a conducted tour of St Paul's Cathedral.

She had the reputation of being 'the greatest horsewoman of her age' (having jumped over railings in Hyde Park for a £100 bet), and, according to Edith Finch, biographer of Blunt, was 'interested in modern art, knew something about music, liked serious reading, even on religious subjects'. She and her sister had a house in South Street, Mayfair, and an apartment in Brown's Hotel, Dover Street. If she had not been a whore, she may have been Britain's first lady prime minister, such is the impression one gets.

Incidents in the life of Skittles Walters reveal the uneasiness of the establishment when an outsider is deposited in its midst. She did not see why she should not ride with the Quorn, and neither did its Master of Fox Hounds, the Earl of Stamford, nor her escorts to the Shires, Lord Hopetoun and Jem Mason, a well-known jockey who had been taken up by the sporting set. The Earl of Stamford's wife had other views, and insisted that her husband 'should not permit that improper woman to go out with the Quorn'. Those who were neutral in the matter veered towards Skittles, as Lady Stamford was the daughter of a local gamekeeper and her airs and graces were resented. The Earl of Stamford said, 'My decision is she can hunt with this pack whenever she wants to, and damn all jealous and interfering females!' In the end he lost and the objectors won.

Miss Walters also wanted to hunt with the Fitzwilliam, and Lady Cardigan made a formal complaint. Miss Walters retorted, 'As you are the head of the profession to which we both belong, I shall have to meet your wishes.' It was a delicate situation; to call a titled lady a whore was decidedly indiscreet, whatever the truth of it. Lady Cardigan, well-born, presented at Court in 1842, created a scandal by consorting with the lecherous hero of the Crimean War, Lord Cardigan, and their subsequent marriage did not prevent her exclusion from county society.

Skittles Walters and her *contretemps* with the various hunts received a good deal of press coverage. It was a test case. How high could a prostitute climb? Being accepted by a prestigious hunt was not quite so epoch-making as being presented to Queen Victoria, but it was a near run thing. Under the heading 'Attempted Extinction of the Social Evil in Leicestershire' one sporting paper led off with:

A certain fair equestrienne has just been warned off the Quorn Hunt, and driven to those packs whose Masters are not so straitlaced, and whose lives have been distinguished by a proper appreciation of those cardinal virtues, modesty and chastity . . .

3

That she should have flourished is not remarkable; that she should have been adulated, almost revered, is. To be a worldly success was more important than the means through which it was accomplished ('selling their miserable bodies for the purposes of debauchery' declared the *Daily Telegraph*). If one had money and aristocratic protection, one had position. The appearance was more important than the reality. Skittles Walters did the right things and did them well. She did not copulate in the Royal Enclosure at a race meeting, she did not flash a gartered thigh at the pantomime to which she was taken by a rabid rescuer of fallen women, Baroness Burdett-Coutts, and she did not try to seduce Gladstone, or at least not in front of Mrs Gladstone. More important still, she did not make a spectacular repentance, and so draw attention to the chasm between her public and private life.

Others of her kind did. Laura Bell was ten years older than Miss Walters, and had also climbed into respectability. She rode in the park in her open phaeton, the idol of the fast men of the time, but made the cardinal error of marrying in 1852, compounding it by turning to religion, proclaiming herself 'a sinner saved by grace through faith in the Lamb of God'. It tarnished the image. A sinner did not live in great luxury in Grosvenor Square.

Many of the fashionable prostitutes of the mid-Victorian period had books written about them, and Miss Walters was not the only one to be painted by a society artist. Laura Bell sat for a picture called 'The Nun'. But the basic requirements were to spend money like water, wear diamonds worth a king's ransom, be seen consorting with the great, and not act like a common whore. They did not have to be particularly pretty; Cora Pearl, nee Emma Crouch, was downright ugly. The favourite of Lord Pembroke, Miss Schaeffer, was as 'flat as a pancake and had hands and feet like a stable boy', redeemed by 'rather nice shoulders'.

The narrowest of dividing lines separates the fashionable prostitute from the mistress. The mistress came in all shapes and sizes. Henry Mayhew thought that a mistress was still a prostitute, for 'prostitution does not consist solely in promiscuous intercourse, for she who confines her favours to one may still be a prostitute'. The police thought differently. They divided prostitutes into three classes, girls in brothels, street-walkers, and the lowest of the low in rough neighbourhoods; if they wanted to pull in a few in response to an outburst of public opinion they concentrated on the last category.

A mistress could be as respectable as a wife, the consort of a man who did not believe in the institution of marriage or who could not marry for one reason or another. A mistress was defined in *The Town* in 1837 as a 'sucking pump, which stops working only when the source from which it is supplied happens to dry up'. But a mistress could be as formidable a proposition as George Eliot the novelist, who lived openly with G. H. Lewes from 1854 to 1878, when Lewes died. Lewes was a highly respected literary man. 'As a populariser of philosophy he was inferior to none,' declared *Chambers's Biographical Dictionary*, 'as a populariser of science inferior to few.' His *Physiology of Common Life* (1859-60) had nothing to do with the circumstances of the Lewes-Eliot home life; whatever could be said of their *menage*, it was not common.

There were many who were perplexed that those who were most prejudiced against irregular unions not only passed over George Eliot's transgressions but praised her freedom from convention. Mrs Lynn Linton dealt with this sensibly in a letter to the philosopher Herbert Spencer in 1885:

Mr Lewes and Miss Evans [George Eliot's real name] were perfectly justified in their union – perfectly – but they were not justified in their assumption of special sacredness, nor was the world, in its attitude of special reverence, which was more than condonation. It is the sense of favouritism and consequent unfairness that has animated me in all I have said . . . [Mr Lewes's] union with Miss Evans was no other, no more, than any other of the same kind, and that the holiness and solemnity ascribed to it came solely from her success. Had she been exactly the woman she was, and not the authoress she was, she would have been left in the shade by all those who sought her in the sunlight.

Admirers of George Eliot the authoress were willing to gloss over the many odd features of the union. In early life Lewes had been involved in a *menage à trois* (his wife had two children by the journalist Thornton Hunt), and he showed a lively interest in his wife's women admirers. One of them, Edith Simcox, thought this 'innocently boyish' but others were not so sanguine, especially those who built up a Lesbian attachment with George Eliot.

Literary liaisons seemed to avoid censure. After his death it was found that the historian Henry Thomas Buckle (1821-62) had kept a Mrs Faunch as his mistress, the novelist Samuel Butler had a mistress in Islington whom he visited every Wednesday afternoon at half-past two, and Wilkie Collins lived with Mrs Caroline Greaves whom he picked up one summer evening. When Mrs Greaves inconsiderately married again Collins took up with Martha Rudd, though eventually Mrs Greaves returned to him. Martha Rudd, otherwise known as Mrs Dawson, was not forgotten, however, for she presented Collins with a child four years after Mrs Graves' return. John Chapman, editor of the *Westminster Review*, kept his mistress, Elizabeth Tilley, in the same house as his wife.

Some of these liaisons were known, some were not. Collins did not take any particular care to keep his amorous exploits quiet, and was probably proud of them. The author of *The Woman in White* and *The Moonstone*, Collins has the happy reputation of inventing the detective novel, but in private life he was a spindly legged, scruffy individual, noted for his dirty gloves. In later life he grew a beard to hide behind. It was said that it was he who drew Charles Dickens from the straight and narrow.

Perhaps Charles Dickens was the most devious of them all. When he died in 1870 he was lauded as the greatest name in English literature since Shakespeare, the foremost moral reformer and benefactor of his time, as holy as a surpliced priest (an American view). The first two were reasonably based on fact, but the last, never, though the full story was not known until 1939. Dickens left his wife and ten children to take up with Ellen Ternan, whom he met as an amateur actress, set her up in Windsor Lodge, Peckham, renting the property in the name of Charles Tringham, writer of mystery stories. 'My father was like a madman,' recollected his daughter, Kate Perugini. 'He did not seem to care a damn what happened to any of us.'

When Dickens visited America he was in a quandary whether or not to take Miss Ternan with him, and arranged a telegraphic code with his friend and sub-editor W. H. Wills, a talented journalist who followed Dickens around from paper to paper, a code which would tell Wills whether it was safe for Ellen Ternan to join him in the United States. Dickens decided that it was too risky. Whether it was to recompense Wills for having acted as go-between or as a token of appreciation for his work as journalist is difficult to say, but Dickens had Wills proposed as a member of the Garrick Club.

Wills was blackballed, and Dickens resigned from the club in a huff.

The laison between Dickens and Miss Ternan lasted for something like twelve years without the knowledge getting through to his wide adoring public. Although, as Thackeray said, the English people might be 'grateful for the innocent laughter, and the sweet and unsullied pages which the author of *David Copperfield* gives to [its] children', they might well have withdrawn some of their adulation if it had been known that their hero had feet of clay and was no less a hypocrite than those he had lambasted in his novels.

Irregular liaisons flourished amongst the upper classes. Lady Arundel lived with the painter Basil Hodges, and maintained that among her set she did not think 'there are half a dozen certificates to be had among the lot, and no one that I can see is a penny the worse'. The affair between Lady Aylesford and Lord Blandford, brother of Randolph Churchill (and therefore uncle of Sir Winston) involved the Prince of Wales, who had written compromising letters to Lady Aylesford. Churchill claimed that he had the Crown of England in his pocket. Most liaisons were conducted with more decorum, though without much secrecy. Nevertheless Lord Ernest Hamilton declared in his *Old Days and New* that 'with a few lurid exceptions, the Mid-Victorian aristocracy of Great Britain stood out as bright and sunny examples of connubial constancy'.

Secrecy was impossible, even if required, because it demanded too much of the participants in matrimonial musical chairs. Diligent as men were in pursuit of fox and slaughter of grouse, their practical skills left something to be desired and keeping things secret was not in them. They had estate managers, lawyers, and hordes of servants to do the mundane things of life. It was far too much trouble to run an illicit love affair on the quiet, if only on account of the impossibility of pulling the wool over the eyes of servants. Obsequious and diligent as they might seem, servants were tuned in to a below-stairs network of gossip. If Lord Torrington was sleeping with Lady Molesworth (and he was), the servants knew, and it would be a fresh titbit to swap in butler's pantry, housekeeper's room, or in draughty attic filled with giggling maids.

The low standard of morality of the Top Ten Thousand was

partly due to boredom. Baccarat, charades, piano playing, needlework, curio collecting, dancing, whist, and the whole range of manly sports, left a lot of time for amorous dalliance. A hostess who at house parties did not allocate the bedrooms according to preference rather than respectability was considered an arrant spoil-sport.

Obviously Hippolyte Taine in his *Thoughts on England* was not thinking of the aristocracy when he reported that 'an Englishman in a state of adultery is miserable: even at the supreme moment his conscience torments him'. It was perhaps true of politicians, who had to seem to be above reproach, who were not worried about the pricking of conscience, only being thrown out of parliament. Whether this was done depended on how powerful their friends were, and what was expedient. Expedience guided Gladstone when Charles Parnell was involved with Mrs O'Shea; in her book on Parnell, Mrs O'Shea claimed that Gladstone had of their relationship for ten years, but preferred to keep quiet about it for the benefit of his political career.

Scandal also wrecked the career of Charles Dilke, who was cited as co-respondent by Donald Crawford on the eve of his marriage to Mrs Pattison, widow of the celebrated Oxford don. Mrs Crawford said that she had been forced to go to bed with Dilke and a maidservant. The newspapers waxed merry on the 'Three in a Bed' case. Furthermore, it was alleged that many years before Dilke had committed misconduct with Mrs Crawford's mother. Again the papers had a field day.

Dilke did not survive, but others who had indulged in rather more than group sex were more fortunate. Gladstone sent Henry Labouchere to sweeten Mr Crawford – Crawford wanted to be a judge but Gladstone said no – but Labouchere himself, MP and journalist, wit and one-time circus clown, was no less vulnerable than Parnell and Dilke at the bar of public morality. If anybody had been interested. Sir William Harcourt, at one time or another home secretary, chancellor of the exchequer, and leader of the Liberals, was extremely careful about his image, but the gossip Julian Osgood Field let his posthumous memory down in 1924.

Harcourt 'was not averse from carefully considering pretty young female human documents bound in diamonds and illustrated by smiles', and two were named, Caroline Letessier and Caroline Hasse. Lord Palmerston, known as Cupid, was a co-respondent in a divorce case in his eightieth year, and had once tried to seduce one of Queen Victoria's ladies under her very nose at Windsor Castle. Gladstone himself was not above suspicion, believed to be eminently vulnerable to the young prostitutes he rescued and took home to tea, and at one time he was widely thought to have been one of Lily Langtry's lovers, along with the Prince of Wales. At another time there was a rumour afoot that he had been seduced by a woman agent of the Tsar, but, as Lily Langtry said herself of her relationship with Gladstone, 'What does it matter what people say as long as they don't actually know?'

Agreements not to tell were exchanged in the corridors of power like order papers. Divorce cases brought out the pressures put on injured parties to keep quiet, but for every divorce there were a dozen convenient arrangements between the principals. 'Domestic treachery, systematic and long continued deception', sounded off *The Times* in November 1890. The topic under discussion was the Parnell case, but it had a wider application, especially among the Top People who even then took *The Times*.

The penalty of being found out could be total wreckage of a career. Dilke did return to public life after his enforced retirement after the trial; the odds are that he was not guilty and was the victim of a smear campaign so his partial rehabilitation shows that there could be natural justice. Sir Travers Twiss, QC, was less fortunate, and his misadventures stemmed from an announcement in the *London Gazette* of one morning in April, 1872: 'The presentation of Lady Twiss at the Drawing-room attended by her in 1869 is cancelled.' This curious message meant that the approval of the queen had been withdrawn.

Little was known of Lady Twiss; there was an element of mystery in her background. As for her husband, he was born in 1908, the son of a Welsh clergyman, a scholarship winner at university, then the bar, where he specialised in international and ecclesiastical law. Professor of international law at King's College, London, Regius professor of civil law at Oxford, he was knighted in 1867, a diligent lawyer who had merited his advancement. While staying in Germany in 1862 he had renewed acquaintance with Marie Van Lynseele, only daughter of a high-ranking Polish officer, whom he had met in Brussels and in London, and married her.

Mrs Twiss made her entry into society, presented at the wedding of the Prince and Princess of Wales in 1863, and six years later curtseyed to the queen. Soon after her appearance at Court the Lord Chamberlain received a message from a fly-by-night solicitor that prior to her marriage Lady Twiss had misconducted herself in London and elsewhere. The Lord Chamberlain investigated, and found that there was no substance in the charges. The solicitor, Alexander Chaffers, had done some work for Lady Twiss before her marriage; he had met her casually soon afterwards and congratulated her, and then began blackmailing her, demanding payment in connection with drawing up a will, £46 that rose to £150 when the demand was unanswered. Lady Twiss told her husband, and as there was some money due to Chaffers he paid him off with £50. When no more cash was forthcoming, Chaffers made a statutory declaration before a magistrate that Lady Twiss was not the daughter of a Polish officer, but a Marie Gelas, who had been a prostitute in London. One of her clients had been Chaffers himself. Not surprisingly, Sir Travers and Lady Twiss instituted proceedings against Chaffers.

Acquitting herself well in the witness box, Lady Twiss strenuously denied anything savouring of misconduct with anyone. As for the name of Marie Gelas, that had been the governess she had had in Poland. They had shared a house in London, during which time Miss Gelas had been ill. It was on her account that Chaffers had drawn up the will. Lady Twiss declared that she had never called herself Marie Gelas, that her father was not Pierre Deny, carpenter. A Belgian piano manufacturer was called; his cousin had been Count Van Lynseele, and Lady Twiss was as she purported to be, the count's daughter.

The case was moved from a small police court to the Sessions House at Newington, and it was beginning to attract the crowds. On the eighth day it seemed as though the odious blackmailer was going to get his just deserts for impugning the honour of a lady. But Lady Twiss did not turn up; she had fled the country, and she never returned. A week later Sir Travers Twiss resigned all his posts, living for another twenty-five years on his memories, good or bad depending on whether his wife was a Polish officer's wife or a common prostitute.

8

THE EXPURGATORS

A S with modesty, decency, and delicacy, the mania for expurgation was in full flow by the time Victoria ascended the throne. The Victorian censors were busier as there were far more books published to cater for what Coleridge called in 1816 the Reading Public. He gave it capital letters, though he did not think much of it (though his *The Ancient Mariner* might well be thought beautifully tailored for it). By 1844 the *Edinburgh Review* reckoned that this new Reading Public numbered 300,000. The reading elite amounted to 30,000.

This elite did not need protecting, but the 300,000 did. They were protected by individuals and by bodies, one of the earliest and most powerful of which was the Society for the Promotion of Christian Knowledge, founded in 1698, which moved away from strictly religious books and pamphlets into the secular field in 1817, sponsoring but not publishing the innocuous. Publishers were eager to support the SPCK, which guaranteed a big turnover, and there was no problem about issuing an expurgated version of *Robinson Crusoe* in 1826.

The Religious Tract Society was later on this profitable scene, formed in 1799, interdenominational and international, taking the good book to the far-flung corners of the world, a pioneer in the provision of 'sound' and cheap literature. It began to provide tracts for China as early as 1813, but it was mainly known to the general public for its magazines and periodicals, such as *Sunday at Home*, the *Leisure Hour*, the *Boy's Own Paper* and the *Girl's Own Paper*. These had immense circulations and were triumphant money-spinners. The *Leisure Hour* was one of the few periodicals allowed into prisons. It was as respectable as the Bible; some would have thought that it was a good deal more so.

Both the Society for the Promotion of Christian Knowledge and the Religious Tract Society ran profitable business organisations, but unlike commercial publishers they also had a considerable income from donations and legacies. What was more commendable than taking pure literature to the potentially impure? With the surplus the SPCK maintained bishoprics, helped schools and churches, and distributed largesse to deserving Christian causes amounting to an average of £50,000 a year, a considerable sum of money in nineteenth-century England.

These societies were not primarily expurgators, and only promoted and encouraged them. There were a good many worthy men in their ranks, as well as those who realised that they were on to a good thing and marketed Bibles and religious tracts as if they were packets of tea. The periodicals run by the Religious Tract Society provided an opening for journalistic hacks, though it is fair to say that the *Leisure Hour* contained informative general articles as lively as those that appeared in less didactic periodicals.

Such societies were only promoting what they would be expected to promote, but commercial publishers, including those of the highest probity, entered the profitable sphere of the expurgated book. The same publisher who authorised

> A little still she strove, and much repented,
> And whispering 'I will ne'er consent' – consented.

was only too willing to jump on the bandwagon. John Murray the second (1778-1843), the publisher of Byron at his sauciest and most unambiguous, found himself able and willing to undertake the Family Library in 1829, with classics 'adapted for Family Reading and the Use of Young Persons, by the Omission of Objectionable Passages'. That it was a profitable venture is clear from the run extending to forty-seven stout volumes.

One would expect emasculation from some, but not from a publisher with such a reverence for literature as John Murray. One would expect John Wesley to be a fervent expurgator, as indeed he was. When the Countess of Huntingdon (an early convert to evangelicalism who started her own church, the Countess of Huntingdon's Connection with sixty-four chapels) wanted an anthology of pure poetry Wesley was only too eager to oblige. Of the 250 poems in his *Collection of Moral and Sacred Poems* (1744) no less than a hundred had lines missing and words changed. Oliver Goldsmith did much the same thing with his *Beauties of English Poesy* and *Poems for Young Ladies*, though he did leave passages such as 'Pissing Alley' from Dryden to be the despair of the genteel who actually bought the books. Goldsmith would have written anything for money, and frequently did.

The poems selected by Goldsmith 'were not only such pieces as innocence may read without a blush, but such as will even tend to strengthen that innocence.' Goldsmith in his own work could be as trenchant as the next man. No self-respecting expurgator would have said, as Goldsmith did in *The Vicar of Wakefield*, 'By the living jingo, she was all of a muck of sweat'. However, Goldsmith made no pretence to be anything more than a collector of poetical snippets in his two anthologies. He had been contracted to do them, and had done them, not very well. The actions of Bishop Hurd (1720-1808), known as the 'Beauty of Holiness' on account of his comeliness and piety, were different. He published a 'definitive' edition of the poet Cowley in a scholarly format, and trusted that this was all of Cowley that would go down to posterity.

Fortunately reverence for text was more important to eighteenth century lovers of literature than the demands of delicacy, and reviewers took issue with Hurd. The 1773 *Monthly Review* declared that the less perfect productions should abide under the protection of better and happier works. Samuel Johnson, an advocate of the unexpurgated, was himself not free from the temptation to carve away with scissors, though the work that he did, as he put it, 'castrate' was perhaps the smuttiest of all, the *Poems* of the Earl of Rochester. 'Extremely gross', evaluates the Everyman *Dictionary of Literary Biography* (current edition) and that is an underestimate. Rochester's works are still under lock and key in the Private Cases of the British Museum, and are likely to remain there for some considerable time.

The expurgators considered that they, like the old advert for Waverley pen-nibs, were a boon and a blessing to men; the anti-expurgators thought that they were squeamish prudes, and that there was something ludicrous about omitting dubious passages, forcing the reader to think that they were worse than they were and make feverish guesses. But imperceptibly, the expurgators were winning. The new book-buying public was not so intent on verisimilitude as the old reading elite. The classics were to be made respectable, not revered; it was more important to have literature that could be read aloud after dinner than everything in its awful and shame-making completeness. When Dr Joseph Warton (1722-1800), poet and critic and a staunch supporter of the romantic movement in English literature, was attacked by Thomas Mathias, librarian at Buckingham Palace, he was sufficiently alarmed to become an expurgator instead of a resolute non-expurgator. Mathias had written: 'I solemnly impeach him of a high crime and misdemeanor before his country'. Mathias was a true hypocrite; the lines from Warton's edition of Alexander Pope which he refused to quote because they were so naughty were certainly no worse than his own poetry.

Expurgation being all the rage, Sir Walter Scott was approached to castrate Dryden. He refused. 'What would you say,' he retorted indignantly, 'to any man who would castrate Shakespere, or Massinger, or Beaumont and Fletcher?' Alas, they were soon to be done, Massinger by the croneys of John Murray, Shakespeare by the arch-expurgators themselves, the Bowdler family. The *Family Shakespeare* appeared in 1807. Sixteen of the thirty-six plays in the canon were cut out in their entirety.

In an introduction to a later edition Dr Bowdler wrote that he had been prompted to create his *magnum opus* by recollections of his father reading Shakespeare, and his father's good taste, delicacy, and prompt discretion, in omitting anything that savoured of the salacious. *Hamlet* was not entirely without the Prince of Denmark, but it might just as well have been. Dr Bowdler's mother had also been at work, taking her knitting scissors to the Bible; she would have preferred the bed in the *Song of Solomon* to be a bridal chariot, and where there is a will there is a way.

There was a distinction between the original Bowdleriser and his later disciples. The successors to Dr Bowdler and family, most of whom were involved in the expurgation trade, were mainly concerned with getting sex out the books they were involved with. Irreverence and blasphemy were the chief Bowdler targets. That the *Family Shakespeare*, later the *Family Shakspeare* when a new Bowdler got to work on it, was not received with a blaze of trumpets was not Bowdler's fault, though he could take comfort from the *Christian Observer* which thought that Bowdler had not gone far enough. Furthermore, it was not a good idea to do Shakespeare as it might provoke people to read him; the implication was that if he was encountered in an unexpurgated edition the heavens would fall.

The snag about expurgators is that they can always be accused of being prurient. If they could pick out smut at a hundred paces, how did they learn to do this? Surely they must have spent an apprenticeship wallowing in mire finding out what all the dirty words meant? Dr Bowdler was vulnerable. Why did he let everyone assume that he was a bachelor, when he married at fifty-two the widow of a naval officer? Why was no mention of this made by his nephew in a long obituary? Why did Bowdler live apart from his wife after a few years? Perhaps this is not fair to Dr Bowdler, assumed to be turned on by early exposure to Shakespeare at his most unbuttoned, for the odd fact is that it was not he who was the key figure in the *Family Shakespeare*, but his sister Harriet, the archetypal spinster, censor-in-chief to the clan. Her mission was to purify Shakespeare, but she made certain that this glorious role was not known to anybody outside her immediate circle.

Of course, there was not only the mission. There was the money. In 1817 Dr Bowdler, as front man, was involved in negotiations with Longmans, and money was forthcoming – a lot of it, £400 after Longmans had sold 750 copies. A working man could support a family for ten years on £400. Few Shakespeare editors received as much, and the Bowdlers did not have to indulge in scholarship but merely chip and chop and provide a preface. The *Family Shakespeare* remained in print for more than eighty years; it sold in all 15,250 copies. It had been a good buy for Longmans.

Condemned by *Blackwood's Magazine* as 'prudery in pasteboard', applauded by the *Edinburgh Review* as 'very meritorious', the *Family Shakespeare* was a monument to what could be done in the cause of delicacy. As late as 1894, when the edition was at last beginning to run out of steam, Swinburne declared that 'no man ever did better service to Shakespeare'. He did not mention the other expurgations of Shakespeare of his own time: the novelist Charlotte Yonge's; Valpy's 'Cabinet Pictorial' edition of 1832-4; Charles Knight's 'Pictorial' edition of 1838-43; Barry Cornwall's 1839-43 edition with illustrations by the early *Punch* cartoonist Kenny Meadows in which the incompetence of the illustrations is matched by the editor's lack of scholarship; the

Reverend Dyce's edition of 1857 (his first work had been *Specimens of British Poetesses* of 1825); Rolfe's American 'Friendly' edition of 1884; or Lewis Carroll's abortive the *Girl's Own Shakespeare*. If nothing else, this roll call shows that the bard, especially if illustrated and tidied up, had something to offer to the Victorians.

If Shakespeare's humour offended, though left in by Bowdler, then take it out. 'Humour is the quality least appreciable by the class of readers for whom I have laboured' said Miss Rosa Baughan introducing her *Plays, Abridged and Revised for Girls* of 1871. If sore feet were not considered worthy extremities for the bard, then Miss Baughan lopped them off in the interests of good taste. She was almost, but not quite, at one with John Styles who in 1806 doomed Shakespeare to a wretched oblivion:

> Barefaced obscenities, low vulgarities and nauseous vice so frequently figure and pollute his pages that we cannot but regret the luckless hour he became a writer for the stage.

Nor did she take the high moral tone of the Rev. Thomas Best, preaching in November 1864. He lamented the

> almost idolatrous honour to the memory of a man who wrote so much that would not be tolerated in any decent domestic or social circle and whose works, taken as a whole, whatever amount of genius and talent may be manifest in them – whatever literary beauties they may exhibit – notwithstanding the moral sentiments interspersed in them – and however esteemed among men, yet are, I doubt not, an abomination in the sight of God.

There was, to Miss Baughan and her contemporaries, a place for Shakespeare, if treated properly, just as there was a place for his Victorian commentators. He was a Classic, even though extremists regretted that he was ever published at all. Some of the expurgators knew, and some knew and did not care, that the presence of asterisks and blank lines would arouse the curiosity of the young reader. Fortunately for youthful pruriency there were still editions of Shakespeare about that kept in the rude words (though they were not so rude as the asterisks implied). It was far more satisfactory to substitute a suitable word than omit it altogether. In a reconditioned *Macbeth* 'Out, crimson spot' would not send a youngster mad. 'Out ... spot' might lead a boy to believe that Shakespeare had used that forbidden, but widely known, word beginning with f.

A simpler way to find out what Shakespeare had really written was not to search around for an unexpurgated edition (there was no sure way to find out what was an unexpurgated edition – editors of complete Shakespeares rarely mentioned it) but to consult a concordance. Public opinion might be diligent and severe, but it was rarely consistent; many concordances to Shakespeare were published in the nineteenth century, and some were very good, indexing the prohibited words without repugnance. It was said that the best was Bartlett's of 1894.

The complete concordance was also the answer to those thwarted by a truncated Bible, an early example of which was the *Sacred History*, a favourite of Dr Johnson, by Sarah Trimmer (1741-1810), mother of twelve children, who at the age of forty produced the first of her works for children, an *Easy Introduction to the Knowledge of Nature*. The *Sacred History* in six volumes cut the Bible by half, and although intended for the young she discovered that adults were using it. A revised version eliminated the baby talk, but Bible indelicacies remained out also. Mrs Trimmer hedged her bets; Biblical scholars were thick on the ground, and would have soundly trounced her had she maintained that she was compiling an expurgated Bible, but at no time did Mrs Trimmer claim this, though this was what it was and was recognised as such. Usually it was a happy recognition. The authorised version was published in a coarse age, 'translated in terms not now generally made use of in polished society'. Mrs Trimmer filled a long-felt want.

There was nothing very subtle about *Sacred History*, but there was about Bishop Porteus's version. Beilby Porteus (1731-1808) was made Bishop of Chester in 1776 and Bishop of London in 1787. Porteus did not meddle with the Bible itself, but provided an index, in which he points out those parts that are worthy of special consideration, which are uplifting, which can be read to sick friends, and which are dully historical and replete with begats. Some parts are not worthy of special attention, and these are not marked; these contain the saucy bits and Jacobean smut.

Human nature would insure that the unmarked sections would be dog-eared far sooner than those dealing with historical matters, but Porteus used double bluff, advising readers to turn to the un-

marked sections in language cleverly calculated to promise them
extreme boredom if they made the effort. This masterly exposition
deserves to be quoted in full:

> Although a considerable number of the chapters, *not* dis-
> tinguished as above [ie marked], relate to the Jewish laws,
> genealogies, and other subjects not so generally interesting to
> the youthful reader, yet it is manifest, there is among them an
> extensive distribution of important portions of Holy Writ:
> which are earnestly recommended to the attention of the advan-
> cing reader, and indeed which cannot fail inviting and rewar-
> ding his more general and thorough research.

In the event the Porteusian Bible Society had a considerable success
for a time, though eventually his reputation waned and his Bible
joined his *Lectures on St Matthew's Gospel* on the shelves devoted
to theology in second-hand bookshops. The *Holy Bible, Newly
Translated* by John Bellamy (1818) was written to counter the
notion that Old Testament characters were not prim English
gentlemen of the first quarter of the nineteenth century. Noah had
been drunk because the translators of the authorised version of the
Bible did not know Hebrew and had mistranslated. Bellamy
learned Hebrew, but he did not learn it very well, and the Biblical
scholars, who had left Mrs Trimmer alone, came at him in hordes.
So far as one knows, no one quoted Job xxxv. 16 at him: 'He
multiplieth words without knowledge'.

Dr Benjamin Boothroyd with his *New Family Bible and Improved Version* (1824) was an apologist rather than a full-blooded
expurgator; in the form of a commentary he made excuses for the
'offensive and indelicate', though often his commentary was so
muddled and singular as to tantalise a reader who would have
passed the passage by without a second thought. Boothroyd
seemed to indicate that Lot had incest with his daughters because
he did not want them to marry outside the family. William Alexander's *Holy Bible, Principally Designed to Facilitate the Audible
or Social Reading of the Sacred Scriptures* (1828) was a divine
muddle in which familiar narrative was split up in the manner of
the television version of a classic (episodes that were missed could
be seen later in the repeats).

As with Boothroyd, Alexander was sexually motivated, sub-
stituting the word harlots for whores, while he who had crushed

testicles or broken stones had instead a rupture, which was not quite the same thing. Calling a spade a digging implement often led into semantic difficulties. 'The outcasts and pariahs of our female population' of de Quincey's *Confessions of an English Opium-Eater* of 1856 had been 'prostitutes' in the first edition of 1821.

Oddly enough, except in America with Noah Webster's version, the Bible ceased to be a target for expurgation after Boothroyd and Alexander. It *was* a sacred book; more than that, it was a sacred object. In strongly evangelical households no book was permitted to be placed on top of the Bible. The Victorians took to heart the warnings given to the learned men who created the authorised version of 1611, that the Bible used in church known as the Bishop's Bible was the authority to be followed, and that it should be followed as near as possible.

The case of the Bible, and its freedom from meddlers, is significant. It shows that expurgation cannot be carried out if a formidable body is opposed to such an action, and irreligious as the masses were becoming there is no question that the power of the established church during the Victorian period was very great. There were men and women, especially of the middle classes, who had when young perused the pages to see what temptation lay in the story of Onan (Onan gave his name to onanism, the customary synonym for masturbation), who would have preferred something more delicate for their offspring. But for once in a way the middle classes were powerless, even though they thought that the young were obtaining from the Bible a sustenance that was the reverse of religious.

The middle classes were right. An anonymous 'literary man' confirmed it:

So many men and women gain sexual ideas in childhood from reading the Old Testament, that the Bible may be called an erotic text-book. Most persons of either sex with whom I have conversed on the subject, say that the Books of Moses, and the stories of Amnon and Tamar, Lot and his daughters, Potiphar's wife and Joseph, etc., caused speculation and curiosity, and gave them information of the sexual relationship. A boy and girl of fifteen, both friends of the writer, and now over thirty years of age, used to find out erotic passages in the Bible on Sunday mornings, while in a Dissenting chapel, and pass their Bibles to one another, with their fingers on the portions that interested them.

By those who were disgusted by the prudery of the age it was considered that the Bible performed a salutary service, and was a tonic corrective in its realism and absence of coy suggestiveness. Something of the earthy vigour of the authorised version of 1611 was lost when the revised version was mooted by a convocation of bishops in 1870, but the revised version still held a high place as a source of information about sex and as much misinformation. The Bible escaped the attentions of the smut-hunters; it and its anonymous authors were too prestigious to bring down.

Even the ubiquitous James Plumptre could not get his hands on the Bible, though it was his declared aim to purge the whole of English literature and change its course. If he had had his way, all the drama of the past would exist only in Plumptre's versions. Plumptre was almost unique in that he wanted to clean up something that was already clean, such as Steele's play *The Conscious Lovers*, the purpose of which, in Steele's own words, was 'to chasten wit, and moralize the stage'. Shakespeare was 'doubly likely to mislead'.

Plumptre did not succeed in obtaining a theatre to show off his versions of great plays of the past, nor did he evoke much interest among those concerned with the purity of their daughters. Well-bred daughters did not go to the theatre to be confronted by scantily dressed actresses and provocatively clothed actors. There was far more danger in material that was insidiously introduced.

Although an atheist with lurid sexual tastes, Shelley was regarded by Victorian mums as a nature poet. No one could take exception to 'Hail to thee, blithe Spirit' or his statement that 'Poetry is the record of the best and happiest moments of the happiest and best minds'. It was a sentiment wholly in accord with Victorian thinking. But with the publication of *The Cenci*, a chamber drama not for performance, Shelley entered forbidden areas – incest. The *Literary Gazette* referred to 'pollution, impiousness and infamy', and the Victorian parents tightened their lips and determined to be more careful next time.

The Victorians read a lot of poetry, and this could cause problems to the expurgators, as the more enthusiastic could read more into poems than their authors intended. The 'outrageous grossness' of Herrick could not be ignored, least of all by Francis Palgrave (1824-97), whose *Golden Treasury* (1861) was perhaps the most popular of all anthologies. Palgrave was perhaps the Victorian expurgator *par excellence*; he did it, but did not talk about it. A failed poet, he occupied the Chair of Poetry at Oxford for ten years, and was a close friend of Lord Tennyson.

There was no question that, unlike many expurgators, Palgrave was a hypocrite. In his 1877 edition of Herrick's poems he declared that 'much that was admissible centuries since, or at least sought admission, has now, by a law against which protest is idle, lapsed into the indecorous'. In his private life he had no such reservations. He appreciated the bawdy of Tennyson, enjoyed the incisive wit of the least buttoned of Victorian ladies, Jane Welsh Carlyle, and was not shocked when Tennyson read his favourite morsels that included the decidedly indecorous *Dunciad* of Alexander Pope (unexpurgated).

Palgrave had two faces, the public face and the private face. He was known as an obsessive chatterer, and was unnaturally nervous. Although he was well into his thirties, Palgrave was so upset by the absence of his father at a spa on one occasion that Tennyson felt obliged to stay with him. There were those who thought that Palgrave nourished a sense of inferiority because of his racial background (his father changed his name from Cohen when he became anglicised).

W. M. Rossetti (1829-1919) was another quiet expurgator. Always in the shadow of his rumbustious poet/painter brother Dante Gabriel and his talented but weird sister Christina, he spent fifty years of his life at the Inland Revenue Department but regarded himself principally as an art critic and wrote criticism for many periodicals. Home life among the Rossettis was Bohemian, and during his long life William Michael became acquainted with the oddest and most exuberant of Victorians.

He had in common with Palgrave and other expurgators a sense of grievance. Palgrave could not compare as a writer with his historian father, as a poet with his friend Tennyson, nor as a critic and man of letters with his university friend Matthew Arnold. William Michael Rossetti could not be a painter like his brother, though as a founder-member of the Pre-Raphaelite Brotherhood he tried, a poet like his sister, nor an art critic as influential as the one-time Rossetti family friend, John Ruskin. To compound matters, he married the daughter of one of the greatest of Victorian painters, Ford Madox Brown, yet another person possessed of remarkable talents.

Peevishness as well as prudery helped William Michael play the hypocrite when he expurgated Walt Whitman's *Leaves of Grass* for the first English edition. This was more heinous than dealing with Shakespeare, as there was always an unexpurgated Shakespeare within reach for the assiduous. Whitman (1819-92) was at war with the conventions of polite society, and proclaimed at great length his determination to be different. He was a great favourite among homosexuals, who thought that Whitman was one of them on account of his passionate friendship with a tram conductor. Somewhat disturbed, Whitman boasted about the illegitimate children he had sired across the United States of America.

Leaves of Grass came to Rossetti by accident. A cork-cutter of Sunderland, Thomas Dixon, one of the improved working-class who escaped from the industrial hell-hole of Tyneside into the never-never world of the Pre-Raphaelites, found the book in the stock of a book-pedlar who had been in the American Civil War at the same time as the poet. Dixon sent it to the painter William Bell Scott (who believed that he had committed the original sin without quite knowing what it was), who sent it in turn to William Rossetti. Brother Dante Gabriel dismissed the book as 'sublimated Tupper' but William decided that this was something on which he could work his wiles. To do William justice, Whitman agreed to the expurgation, though later he regretted it.

Rossetti said in his preface that he did not aspire to 'Bowdlerian honours' but was omitting half the poems because he and Whitman lived in a 'peculiarly nervous age'. He assured readers that he would not excise parts of poems; he said nothing about Whitman's prose, and as Whitman's prose was poetry and his poetry was prose it was a meaningless assurance. There was nothing particularly dirty in Whitman, only ambiguous, though Rossetti felt obliged to act as though he was confronted with the choicest works of the Earl of Rochester. 'Prostitute' was a word that he felt could not be faced by a delicate reader, and that had to come out, to be followed by others that either offended him personally or might conceivably offend someone else.

His brother was aware that William was becoming decidedly

odd and prudish, and thought that marriage would help, 'a great boon to his somewhat fossilized habit of life for years past'. William did not appreciate his brother's attentions. When a doctor told him that he was giving up the care of Dante Gabriel, an addict of the Victorian drug chloral, William said that he understood why, and that the doctor must have endured much 'unpleasant and capricious demeanour'. William Rossetti was exercising the Victorian privilege of being snide.

Another expurgator of other people's poetry was Frederick Locker-Lampson, a talented writer of light verse. His anthology *Lyra Elegantiarum* (1867) started off in a promising way, despite the unbearable title. Locker-Lampson (the Lampson was added for snob appeal when he married for the second time in 1874) had included forty poems by Walter Savage Landor, permission for which had not been obtained from the executor. This executor, John Forster, tore up a copy of the offending anthology when he saw it on a table in the Athenaeum. Sweet reason did not work with him. This event was

> not overlooked by the wily race of second-hand booksellers, the best servants of literature this country possesses, who, when they manage to get hold of one of these early copies, never fail to mark it high, and to advertise it in their catalogues as containing *the suppressed verses*, words which, when printed in italics, seem to possess in the trade a certain, but in this instance, a misleading, significance.

Locker-Lampson prided himself on his delicacy, and although his own library included first editions, and therefore unexpurgated, of Burns, Herrick, Donne and a host of others, he was not averse to wielding the blue pencil. His anthology was not intended for children or those who could be corrupted, but for adults with a taste for light perky verse. Why should he be an adjudicator, when he himself admitted a taste for the naughty?

Locker-Lampson was a sycophant, neurotically anxious not to offend anybody. He was a clerk in the City, in Somerset House, and then occupied a minor position in the Admiralty. Marriage with a daughter of the Earl of Elgin took him out of clerking and into a precious world where he could ruminate on his dyspepsia, send copies of his *London Lyrics* to all the literary people he could think of, and meditate on where he went wrong. In his autobiographical *My Confidences*, published posthumously in 1896, he wrote: 'I would not care to live my wasted life over again, and so prolong my span. Strange to say, I have but little wish to be younger. I submit with a chill at my heart.'

An exponent of the (one) small slim volume (*London Lyrics*), Locker-Lampson is especially interesting as probably a typical unconscious hypocrite. He expurgated because it seemed the proper thing to do. It is doubtful whether he had any strong feelings about exposing readers to the miasma of indecency. He joins the ranks of those who behaved prudishly because it did not occur to them to behave otherwise. The indelicacies he took out were wholly concerned with the passable erotic, though by the 1860s the erotic could encompass almost anything.

It might seem that nothing would pass the eagle eye of a Victorian publisher of poetry if it savoured of the salacious, but editors nodded. Alfred Tennyson could be trusted, but how about Robert Browning? Browning was acknowledged to be difficult, his actions in eloping with Elizabeth Barrett irregular, but it was felt that there was more of the reprehensible in the verse of Elizabeth Barrett Browning than in Robert.

By and large Browning was left alone, simply because of his inherent difficulties. His poem *Sordello* (1840) gave him a reputation for obscurity which he never completely threw off even in the days of 'The Pied Piper of Hamelin'. It was considered, logically, that something that was not understood even by those who knew about poetry could not corrupt the Reading Public. He was taken to task principally by those who looked askance at his technique. The Cambridge parodist C. S. Calverley disapproved of Browning rhyming 'silence' and 'a mile hence' and drew attention to a phrase that in someone more accessible, and preferably dead, would demand the blue pencil treatment:

> The more I read Browning, I regret to say, the more I dislike him – so much for my taste. Having in one place to describe a who paints, he says she is 'a masterplaster from scalp to udder'.

But there was worse in Browning, unknown to Calverley, and also to expurgators, not especially noted for their knowledge of slang. It occurs in *Pippa Passes* (1841), now known for the phrase 'God's in His heaven/All's right with the world'. Towards the end is the verse:

> Then, owls and bats,
> Cowls and twats,
> Monks and nuns, in a cloister's moods,
> Adjourn to the oak-stump pantry!

Twat defined by Eric Partridge in his marvellous *Dictionary of Historical Slang* as 'the female pudend', came into use in the mid-seventeenth century and can still be heard among the ill-informed (though twat-rug, pubic hair, is less common). Partridge refers to its use by Browning as 'a hair-raising misapprehension – the literary world's worst "brick" '. Long after Pippa had passed, the editors of the *Oxford English Dictionary* wrote to Browning asking in what sense he was using it. Browning, still innocence personified, said that he used it to mean a piece of headgear for nuns, comparable to the monk's cowl in the same line. Presumably they did not believe him, decreeing him a disgusting old reprobate, for it is not in the *Shorter* OED. Not surprisingly, they permitted cowl. Even the most prurient could not find anything improper in this.

Like many of his contemporaries, Browning could have been suspected of inserting hidden indecencies unconsciously into his work. His manly no-nonsense facade hid a streak of prudery, as is clear from a letter he wrote to Isabella Bladgen in July, 1862:

> I was at a House four days ago, where an English young bride of a year's standing began the dinner by getting hold of her husband's hands, with other significancies before us all – me an entire stranger; by the evening she was resting her head on his shoulder, and *I* did not stay for the little more that could well happen, and which probably *did*, for the edification of boys and girls.

One is entitled to wonder what sort of houses Browning was invited to when modest tokens of marital affection were expected to lead to, presumably, orgies.

Henry James, who observed the English with a detached and unique irony, was not taken in by Browning:

> Robert Browning, I am sorry to say, does not make on me a purely agreeable impression. His transparent eagerness to hold the *di de la conversation* and a sort of shrill interruptingness which distinguishes him have in them a kind of vulgarity. Besides which, strange to say, his talk doesn't strike me as very

good. It is altogether gossip and personality and is not very beautifully worded.

Not many Victorian poets did falter in the manner of Browning, even those of the Decadence, who knew if they were indecent. One other did – Arthur Hugh Clough, an Oxford friend of Palgrave, if in a more scholarly way. In 1848 his *The Bothie of Toper-Na-Fuosich* was published; bothie was a hut, but the rest was to Clough a meaningless jumble of words taken from a map. Although Scots maps are no more pornographic than English, 'toper-na-fuosich' meant the same as twat. Someone knew, for Clough altered the title to the equally arcane *The Bothie of Tober-Na-Vuolich*; so did the more erudite reviewers. But they kept quiet about it. They had their jobs to consider.

TO DEPRAVE AND CORRUPT

P ROVIDING anthologies of expurgated verse for the young did not carry any guilt, and anthologies for mature readers did not carry much more; definitive editions of poets and dramatists could create problems among those with a respect for the written word, but there were few who stood up for their principles when the task of expurgation was urged on them. It was gently pointed out to them that it was their duty. The writers of the past, great as they may have been, lived in coarse, unmannered ages, and had they been writing in the nineteenth century they would have suited their matter to the times.

It was rarely necessary to tell editors what exactly needed to be omitted. Brutality and savagery could safely be left in, and so, if it was not too strong, could blasphemy and irreligion. The indecent and the obscene meant, to the Victorians, sex. Sex could mean anything, and from the 1860s the smut-hunters, or, as one writer calls them, the censor-perverts, were seeing sex in everything, from the shape of grand pianos to the Elgin marbles.

It took a considerable act of will to ride against the current, and needed an even greater degree of perception to recognise that there was something decidedly odd in the situation, that there was something bizarre in hiding the legs of pianos under skirts and referring to the bosom of a chicken. For some, at the top and the bottom of the social scale, there were no problems; sex was a pleasurable activity for the former, together with its art and its literature; for the latter, it relieved the monotony of a life, and with drink was the only compensation for living.

Those who thought about sex found it all incredibly confusing,

not to say frightening. As every person that has ever been born has
come into the world by the process that could not be referred to, it
was not a minority interest. Those with a taste for speculation did
wonder what harm it would do if the subject was openly aired, but
such speculation was not only fruitless but dangerous. It was
tacitly agreed that there was a body of people, mainly men, who
were able to face up to the stern facts. It did not seem fair that they
were deprived of material that they needed for their livelihood.

The men who were assumed to be able to stand up to raw sex
were scholars, and the formula was to print unexpurgated books in
small editions at a high price for this specific market. This
procedure would seem to be sensible enough, but the editors involved in this laudable enterprise felt guilt, doing what they knew
was right but uneasy about their presumption. Typical of these
editors was Alexander Grosart (1827-99), the son of a Scots builder,
and a minister of the English Presbyterian Church. Although little
known today, Grosart did sterling service to literature with his
Fuller's Worthies Library, thirty-nine volumes (1868-76) *Occasional Issues of Unique and Very Rare Books*, thirty-eight
volumes (1875-81), and the *Huth Library*, thirty-three volumes
(1886).

In 1872-3 he tackled one of the suspect poets of the day, John
Donne, and his qualms were aired in the preface to his limited
edition of 156 copies, 'printed for private circulation'.

> I do not hide from myself that it needs courage to edit and print
> the poetry of Dr. John Donne in our day. Nor would I call it
> literary prudery that shrinks from giving publicity to such sen-
> suous things.

That Grosart did provide a considerable corpus of unexpurgated
texts for a specialised public does indicate that there were some
who, despite inner uncertainty, were willing to take the risk, or at
least share the risk of publishers and printers. The publishers and
printers were far more vulnerable than the editors, open to police
raids and the persecutions of the Society for the Suppression of
Vice, formed in 1802. In its early years the Society was not noted for
its crusading policies or efficiency, and the celebrated wit Sydney
Smith called it the society for suppressing the vices of persons
whose incomes do not exceed £500 a year. Later the Society became
more formidable.

There were a number of laws that could be invoked to trim adventurous publishers – the Vagrancy Act of 1824, an amending act to it of 1838, the Metropolitan Police Act of 1839, the Town Police Clauses Act of 1847, and, most important of all, the Obscene Publications Act of 1857 which could make it open season for publishers. It provided that a search warrant could be issued on sworn information that obscene publications were kept at the premises concerned for sale or distribution, and that a sale of such a publication had actually been made.

The last provision was met by using plain-clothes police, who went into publishers and printers, or bookshops, and asked for a copy of the book about which there had been a complaint. The least that could happen would be the confiscation of all copies of that book, but the police were rarely content with that; they usually went through the stock and ordered the destruction of all books that could be interpreted as obscene, just going by the titles. Theological books as well as unoffending novels came under this heading. That was bad enough for business, but town magistrates, unlike country JPs who had a well-deserved reputation for commonsense, were relentless smut-hunters by proxy, and for the mildest of offences it was considered that nothing less than prison would do.

Not surprisingly the ordinary commercial publisher wished to steer clear of the law, and only published books that were above suspicion. This applied equally to contemporary books and literature of the past. Among the older non-fiction expurgated was St Augustine's *City of God*, Sir Thomas Browne's *Religio Medici* (1642), Robert Burton's *Anatomy of Melancholy* (1621), Charles Lamb's letters, and Pepys' diary. Contemporary fiction translated into English or imported from America was also expurgated. Herman Melville's *Moby Dick* was suspect because there was a reference to the captain's underclothes (it is fair to add that the Americans were equally suspicious of *Tom Brown's Schooldays* because of an ill-advised reference to beer).

The nervousness of publishers was therefore a key factor in the sexlessness of much Victorian fiction. Some were irked by the self-censorship they were forced to carry out. In his preface to *Pendennis* (1850), Thackeray declared:

Even the gentlemen of our age – this is an attempt to describe one of them, no better nor worse than most educated men – even these we cannot show as they are, with the notorious foibles and selfishness of their lives and education. Since the author of *Tom Jones* was buried, no writer of fiction among us has been permitted to depict to his utmost power A MAN. We must drape him, and give him a certain conventional simper. Society will not tolerate the Natural in our Art . . . You will not hear – it is best to know it – what moves in the real world, what passes in society, in the clubs, colleges, mess-rooms – what is the life and talk of your sons.

Thackeray avoided the censor by subtle innuendo, but this drove Walter Bagehot to wrath:

> He never violates a single conventional rule but at the same time the shadow of immorality that is not seen is scarcely ever wanting from his delineation of the society that is seen. Everyone may perceive what is passing in his fancy.

It would be easy to see Thackeray as a blatant hypocrite, but whatever he was in private life (he was sexually excited by flagellation and public hanging, but concealed this by pretending to crusade against the latter, necessitating attendance at any public hangings that were going), he was being deliberately coy in his novels through necessity.

Charles Reade, whose novels are sterner stuff than those of Thackeray, was equally exasperated. In a open letter he wrote, 'There is a kind of hypocrite that has never been effectually exposed, for want of an expressive name. I beg to supply that defect in our language and introduce to mankind the PRURIENT PRUDE'. The prurient prude attracts attention 'by a parade of modesty (which is a mild form of disease) or even by rashly accusing others of immodesty (and this is the noxious form)'. Lady novelists were vulnerable to accusations of immodesty, with the exception of Jane Austen in whom even the most rabid could only see sweetness and light. When sexual indecency was hard to find, the prurient took another tack, as Lady Eastlake did in her criticism of Charlotte Brontë's *Jane Eyre*. Miss Brontë had committed 'the highest moral offence a writer can commit . . . that of making an unworthy character interesting in the eyes of the reader'.

The review by Lady Eastlake, then Miss Rigby, appeared in the influential *Quarterly Review* in December 1848. The novel appeared under a pseudonym, though Lady Eastlake thought it was by a woman. Others were not sure. The critic of the *Economist* praised the book if written by a man, odious if the work of a woman. The critic of the *North British Review* said 'if *Jane Eyre* be the production of a woman, she must be a woman unsexed'.

No Victorian novel is today more appreciated or freer from opprobrium than *Jane Eyre*, but the chorus of distaste with which it was greeted established a precedent. Charlotte Brontë was upset by the reviews. As she wrote to W. S. Williams, reader to the publishers Smith and Elder, 'I now feel vulnerable: I should grieve to see my father's peace of mind perturbed on my account'.

Charlotte Brontë defended herself. 'To critics I would say, "To you I am neither man nor woman – I come before you as an author only. It is the sole standard by which you have a right to judge me – the sole ground on which I accept your judgment" '. However, such a defence was irrelevant. Miss Brontë had explored female psychology with a precision that was considered improper, as though she had publicly exposed herself and by association womankind itself. It was better to slate the author as desexed instead of accurate.

The conspiracy of silence concerning sexual matters, or, as in the case of *Jane Eyre*, womanly matters, did not apply to what we see as far more shocking topics. The dark underbelly of industrial life was explored in Mrs Gaskell's *Mary Barton*, private asylums in Charles Reade's *Hard Cash* were relentlessly investigated, while the work of Dickens in uncovering abuses ranged from workhouse to the legal system. But Dickens obeyed the rules. In 1837 he was engaged in writing operettas under his journalistic name of 'Boz', and two Miss Smiths complained of the immodesty of one of his verses:

> A winter's night has its delight,
> Well-warmed to bed they go:
> A winter's day we're blithe and gay
> Snipe-shooting in the snow.

In a letter to the song-writer and pioneer of Sol-fa singing, John Hullah, Dickens wrote:

If the young ladies are specially horrified at the bare notion of anyone going to bed, I have no objection to substitute for the objectionable line, 'Well-warmed to bed they go', 'Around old stories go'. But you may respectfully signify to Cramers [music sellers and music publishers] that I will see them damned before I make any further alterations . . . you will see that we ought not to emasculate the very spirit of the song to suit boarding schools.

However Dickens did not have any objection to doing the same sort of thing in his novels, and in the preface to *Pickwick Papers* he makes it clear that there was nothing in its contents to bring the faintest blush to delicate maidenhood. Although he could create turmoil in the human breast, reducing the most awesome of literary celebrities to tears, Dickens never stepped out of line. Harrowing but unsalacious, his novels could be read by papas to their brood in their entirety, which was precisely Dickens's intention. His novels were written in monthly parts, each one eagerly awaited (*Pickwick Papers* appeared in twenty instalments of thirty-six pages each).

There was nothing to mark the transition of Dora from child to child-wife that any reader could take exception to; although Nancy in *Oliver Twist* was a prostitute, Dickens never mentioned it. Although Dickens's comic characters are vulgar, they are never given to obscenities in word or deed. Impressionable readers took Dickens at his word. The heroes always behave with perfect decorum to the heroines, and the heroines always wait in perfect contentment for the heroes when they have inconsiderately gone off or married someone else (who would die in due course). Heroes rarely had pre-marital sex, and did not importune their beloved ones to anticipate the marriage ceremony, as was frequently the case in real life (more than half working-class married women were pregnant on their wedding day).

Dickens gave a false picture of life, and because he was universally read he might be accused of helping to form mass attitudes, but he was writing for a specific market, not especially individuals but households. He provided the perfect product for the household, lively, colourful, incident-packed, eminently suited to be read aloud. A writer who obliged the household reader to stumble over suspected indecencies or to surreptitiously skip doubtful sections was a writer who would soon be out of a job.

The duty of novelists to provide material for reading aloud cannot be overemphasised; today, it would need an extremely permissive father to read out a modern novel to a child of tender years. Some novels were cunningly structured so that reading aloud would be a pleasurable process. Wilkie Collins's *The Woman in White* (1860) used the trick of assigning different parts of the narrative to different people in the expectation that one part of the tale would be read by one person of the family and another by someone else.

Stretching the novel over twenty instalments would enable the pleasure to be long drawn-out, and this was true of novels that were serialised in the magazines of the time. Magazine editors did not want anything in the least damaging to their reputation. A book once bought was money in the bank for the publishers, but a magazine depended on the future; if each serialised episode of a novel could end on a question mark . . . that was what the magazine editors wanted.

Many of the best-known Victorian novels were published in magazines. *Bentley's Miscellany* was the original home of *Oliver Twist*, Mrs Gaskell's *Lizzie Leigh* was first read in Dickens's weekly *Household Words*, and Dickens gave Wilkie Collins's novels their first airing in his subsequent weekly, *All the Year Round*. Magazine proprietors *could* get away with far more than book publishers, and what is known as the 'Salisbury Square School of Fiction' showed that it was possible to serialise the lurid and even the sexually stimulating in such papers as *The Weekly Penny Miscellany* and the *Penny Atlas and Weekly Register of Novel Entertainment*, both started in 1843.

The sensationalist weeklies were known as 'Saturday trash' and they were the despair of those anxious to improve the taste of the lower orders, a Reading Public that did not want to have merely what was foisted on them by their betters. The Noncomformist lecturer and preacher, George Dawson of Birmingham, was assured of a hearty reception among the worried middle classes when he speculated upon the great popularity of 'Saturday trash'.

We give the people an appetite to read, and supply them with nothing. For the last many years, in England, everybody has been educating the people, but they have forgotten to find them any books. In plain language, you have made them hungry, but you have given them nothing to eat.

Dawson pointed out that the penny tax on newspapers of the time made them expensive. For that penny a working man could buy his weekly periodical. Not that there was very much obscene in it. The writers, as skilled in their own way as the tabloid journalists of today, their logical successors, tantalised and prevaricated. These periodicals were suggestive, as Thackeray was suggestive in *Vanity Fair*, but they were attacked not for what was in them, for the attacker rarely demeaned themselves to reading them, but for the effect they would have on their lower-class readers, inflaming them with sexual urges that were destined to lead to rape.

Of course, some of those who reviled the 'Saturday trash' *did* read it, and were probably disappointed that it was not more potent. It was the respectable man's surrogate for pornography, obtaining which could be something of an adventure. But even secret readers not finding quite what they expected found the material refreshingly spicy after the respectability of the standard magazines and periodicals. In what he called the 'conductorship' of his own periodicals, Charles Dickens was as watchful and fearful of offending as the most prudent publisher. A story by Mrs Lynn Linton was thought by him to be in the style of the awful French blackguard Balzac, and a tale about an unhappy marriage by the now forgotten Holm Lee was returned for 'fear of waking too painful emotions'. Perhaps Holm Lee is forgotten because the material was true to life; in the best run of magazines this could not happen, except with topics that were not concerned with sex. Then the periodicals run by Charles Dickens provided some of the best factual reportage of the century.

Self-censor or censor-in-chief of his staff, Dickens knew what he was doing, though he lapsed when he proclaimed the break-up of his marriage in the columns of his own periodicals. He was more knowledgeable and more perceptive than most of his contemporaries; his instinct told him what was acceptable and what was not. Lesser mortals needed a guide line, and a guide line was not available, least of all to respectable publishers operating from the 1860s onwards.

Their only compensation was that the deterrent for publishing the obscene was not nearly so great as had been the case when blasphemy was in vogue. But the blasphemous was fairly easy to spot; not so the obscene. It could lurk for years (as it did for Browning and Clough), a literary time-bomb.

The classic publisher-victim was J. B. Payne, of the highly reputable firm of Moxon, founded in 1830. Edward Moxon had been dead eight years when disaster struck J. B. Payne through *Poems and Ballads* by Swinburne. Payne had had trouble with Swinburne before. Swinburne's first book for Moxon, *The Queen Mother*, had sold seven copies in two years. It had had one review. The *Athenaeum* had said: 'We should have conceived it hardly possible to make the crimes of Catharine de Medici dull, however they were presented. Mr Swinburne, however, has done so.'

Between *The Queen Mother* and *Poems and Ballads* Swinburne had become famous, 'shot like a rocket into celebrity' said Edmund Gosse. His *Atlanta* had been rapturously received, though there had been raised eyebrows concerning *Chastelard*, which was so perverse that the critics could not recognise it. Sado-masochism in verse had befuddled them. But as the word spread, as the brighter reviewers gave the dimmer ones an inkling of what *Chastelard* was really about, so was the net spread. 'I have heard low mutterings already from the lion of British prudery,' reported Swinburne's friend George Meredith, himself to suffer at the hands of the smut-hunters in due course.

Swinburne's friends and relations gave him gentle warnings. 'Do let it be a book that can be on every one's table,' urged Lady Trevelyan. Lord Houghton, who had one of the finest collections of pornography in the country, released hints of the contents of *Poems and Ballads*. It was not a book one could leave on a table. On 4 August 1866 John Morley reviewed it in the *Saturday Review* in terms that left no doubt about his opinion of it – 'mixed vileness and childishness of depicting the spurious passion of a putrescent imagination, the unnamed lusts of sated wantons . . . tuning his lyre in a stye . . . nameless, shameless abomination . . . pieces which many a professional vendor of filthy prints might blush to sell . . .'

On 5 August, Payne told Swinburne that the book had been withdrawn from circulation. Swinburne's friends Rossetti (Dante Gabriel, not the sanctimonious William Michael) and the Pre-Raphaelite painter Sandys went to Payne to intercede on behalf of Swinburne. They found him, wrote Edmund Gosse, 'distracted with terror of the Public Prosecutor and desired nothing so much as to be rid of the poet and his friends'. Thirty years before Moxon & Co had been prosecuted for publishing Shelley; he thought the same was to happen again. Payne had also heard that *The Times* was preparing a crushing review of *Poems and Ballads*.

Swinburne turned on Payne. 'That pellet of decomposed dung technically known as Payne,' he wrote to W. M. Rossetti at the end of September. 'That bottomless and drainless cesspool of lies and counterlies, the mouth of Mr J. B. Payne,' he wrote a week later. In the end, Swinburne found another publisher, John Camden Hotten, a man of dubious repute now best known for his history of signboards and his considerable catalogue of curiosa. Hotten took the precaution of having it vetted by a police magistrate, who assured him that it was neither 'seizable nor indictable'. J. B. Payne, pellet of decomposed dung or a worried publisher doing what he thought was best depending on viewpoint, was not sent to prison.

Other publishers were, for issuing material not nearly so hot as *Poems and Ballads*. Few read Swinburne today for his indelicacy. 'The beauty of her bosom a good deed', is neither here nor there, though typical. It was the theme of sexual cruelty that disturbed the reviewers:

> I would find grievous ways to have thee slain,
> Intense device and superflux of pain;
> Vex thee with amorous agonies, and shake
> Life at thy lips, and leave it there to ache.

or

> Ah that my lips were tuneless lips, but pressed
> To the bruised blossom of thy scourged white breast!
> Ah that my mouth for Muses' milk were fed
> On the sweet blood thy sweet small wounds had bled!

The glorification of sexual cruelty was a new note to the 1860s. It did not matter that there was no obscene word in the whole book, nor that the great reading public preoccupied with their 'Saturday trash' would understand one line in ten. The sheer venom of the attacks on *Poems and Ballads* is symptomatic not of the desire to preserve the innocence of those who might happen to come across the book but of alarm at finding one's own fantasies coming to life, even in esoteric verse form. 'In the darkness they murmured and mingled' struck too many chords. Ill-understood and misinterpreted, so did 'And in my flesh thy very flesh entombed'.

John Morley, who initiated the move against the book, was more of a politician than a man of letters. Created a viscount in 1908, his articles and speeches in favour of Home Rule for Ireland made him a conspicuous lackey of Gladstone. He wrote a biography in four volumes of Gladstone in which the curious habit the great statesman had of consorting and swapping notes with prostitutes was not mentioned. Like everyone else, apparently, he did an edition of Herrick for the Victorian public, and expurgated with the best of them. He was not a man to be attuned to the anguished sensuality of a man like Swinburne, but he was piqued by the presence of a man with gifts that made his own seem miniscule. Even as a smut-hunter he was in the second rank; he was editor for a time of the *Pall Mall Gazette*, but was superceded by W. T. Stead, a man who knew how to make exposures of sexual goings-on pornographic yet socially laudable. Morley was never able to do this.

A publisher far more unfortunate than Payne was Henry Vizetelly. Usually dismissed in a couple of sentences, Vizetelly was a martyr in the cause of freedom to publish and be damned. Born in 1820, the son of a printer, he was apprenticed as a wood engraver. Sparked off by the success of the *Illustrated London News*, the first weekly to be fully illustrated, Vizetelly helped start the *Pictorial Times*, and twelve years later the *Illustrated Times*. In 1865 he became Paris correspondent of the *Illustrated London News*, and whilst there he wrote several books, most of them based in France or free translations of French books.

When he started in publishing in 1887 he concentrated on publishing translations of French and German authors, and although expurgated these were regarded with suspicion. In 1888 Vizetelly was prosecuted by the National Vigilance Association formed two years earlier to promote 'social purity'. The book in question was Emile Zola's *La Terre*, the most indelicate passage of which dealt with a dairymaid bringing cow to bull at a farm. Nevertheless, a Liberal MP 'believed nothing more diabolical has ever been written by the pen of man'.

Vizetelly knew what he was doing. In a protest against the obscenity law of 1857 he asked the Attorney General, 'Is actual life to be no longer described in fiction simply because the withdrawing of the veil that shrouds it displays a state of things unadapted to the contemplation not of grown up men and women but of the "young person of fifteen" who has all the work of Mr Mudie's novelists to feast upon?' It was a pertinent question, not often

asked in the nineteenth century. Why should literature be tailored
to the intellectual capacity of a child?

La Terre, and with it the realistic French novel, was found
guilty, and Vizetelly was fined £100. *The Times* voiced the opinion
of what must be generously supposed to be educated man:

> It is not always easy to draw the line which separates what is
> permissible from what is not. But if the line is not to be drawn so
> as to exclude translations of such works of Zola as 'La Terre' and
> 'Pot Bouille' it is plain that it cannot be drawn at all. . . . We
> cannot but rejoice, therefore, that Mr Vizetelly has
> acknowledged his offence and been punished for it. In future,
> as the Solicitor-General intimated, anyone who published
> translations of Zola's novels and works of similar character will
> do so at his peril, and must not expect to escape so easily as Mr
> Vizetelly.

Vizetelly was a brave man, and had pointedly *not* acknowledged
his offence. To prove it, he reissued Zola's works the following
year. This time he was fined £200 and sent to prison for three
months. He was a man of nearly seventy, but this did not prevent
the establishment making an example of him. The establishment
was not the law, but the middle classes; they were the people who
decided what was permissible. *La Terre* dealt with real life, and
that was enough for that headless body, middle-class prejudice.

10

THE NAKED TRUTH

WHAT the Victorians permitted is as interesting and often as curious as what they refused to allow. The Bathing Question was perhaps the most typical anomaly, where, wrote the lawyer/gossip William Hardman in 1863, 'shameless Britons expose their persons to curious Britonesses. Contemplative among the Nereids he parades his immodest harmlessness in absolute freedom.' George Meredith reported to Hardman in 1870 from Eastbourne, where 'antique virgins spyglass in hand' watched naked men scampering out of their bathing machines with 'a glistening on the right cheek and the left'. Francis Kilvert, a country vicar with a taste for pretty girls, preferably under-age, noticed at Seaton bathers with 'shoes, stockings, and drawers off wading in the tide, holding up their clothes nearly to the waist and naked from the waist downwards'.

The seaside was an environment that existed in a pocket in time; courtship on the beach could be carried out with an enthusiasm that would have invited police interference elsewhere, and on the more secluded stretches of coast-line there was the 'air bath', a fashionable name for what was later called naturism. This was extremely respectable nudity, and voyeurs rarely found out where these English St Tropezes were.

Another place where nudity was open and unashamed was Burlington House, the home of the Royal Academy, and every year nudes rubbed shoulders with *Between Two Fires* and *Joyless Winter Day*. They were framed in gilt, were given fancy titles, but they were none the less nudes, and people who made an effort to look through the gay ladies in the Haymarket and averted their eyes from flies copulating in their drawing rooms willingly paid to look at them. It was high art, and therefore above reproach. The artists themselves lived exemplary lives, could earn £10,000 a year, and many of them had been knighted; the most diligent of the providers of high-class nudes, Lord Leighton, was eventually made a baron. There was nothing more qualified to ingratiate them with the picture-buying class than wealth and social position.

The privileged position of the Royal Academy nudes reflects the bemused and chaotic situation when the establishment supported something that by all the laws of probability should have been ousted. The status of the nude in art was safe because of the reverence for the Greeks, especially Greek sculpture. This was a by-product of the emphasis on the classics in the public school curriculum, and the upper classes had no intention of deferring to middle-class opinion on this matter. Most of the new middle classes had not had the benefit of a classical education, and they were therefore outsiders. The enthusiasm with which the Elgin Marbles were treated when they arrived in Britain in 1812 was a mystery; a frieze of broken statues did not deserve space on ships that would be better occupied in bringing raw materials to the workshop of the world.

The Royal Academy was a bastion of eighteenth-century aristocracy, even though most of the pictures on sale at the Summer Exhibition were painted with the middle-class buyer in mind. They bought the historical pictures, the pretty scenes of rustic life, and the multitude of pictures that told a story. They also bought the nudes, for they told a story as well – *Venus Disrobing for the Bath* (1867) was classical and therefore honourable, and if it was salacious as well so much the better.

There were rules to obey. The nudes had to be painted in a classical, historical, or mythological setting, they had to look like coloured photographs, and they had to be perfect specimens. There were to be no fat old women, as in Rembrandt, or plump apple-red bottoms, as in Renoir. Above all, there was to be no pubic hair. Thus depilated, the nudes were free to disport themselves in any manner, provided that they kept their thighs together or, if this was not possible in the context, were placed modestly in the background.

Mythology provided many handy subjects for the artist to indulge himself in expressing any fantasies that might be struggling to get an airing. The subject of Andromeda, painted by Lord Leighton in 1891, was ideal for spectators who liked to see a naked woman fastened with chains to a rock, and there were few of the practitioners of High Art who could resist portraying slave girls, bound and nude.

Although Burlington House had its rich visitors with cheque books out and pens poised, it also had the critics and those to whom a naked woman was a naked woman whether she was called Phryne or Ariadne. The Bishop of Carlisle was taken aback by a picture by Lawrence Alma-Tadema, one of the three most important artists of the genre (the others were Lord Leighton and Edward Poynter):

> My mind has been considerable exercised this season by the exhibition of Alma-Tadema's nude Venus. [There might] be artistic reasons which justify such public exposure of the female form ... In the case of the nude of an Old Master much allowance can be made, but for a living artist to exhibit a life-size, life-like, almost photographic representation of a beautiful naked woman strikes my inartistic mind as somewhat if not very mischievous.

He was writing to the portrait painter George Richmond in 1879, but four years earlier John Ruskin, the most powerful critic of the time, had expressed his displeasure over Poynter's *The Golden Age*, claiming that it savoured 'somewhat of adventitious gas-lighting', and that the aim of the painting was 'to show us like Michelangelo the adaptability of limbs to awkward positions, but he can only, by this anatomical science, interest his surgical spectators'.

Other critics were more guarded, and the 1867 exhibition provided a problem for the anonymous critic of the *Art Journal* when he came face to face with Leighton's *Venus Disrobing for the Bath*:

> A full-length, life-size Venus, not so much 'disrobing' as already undressed, is a little startling now-a-days. A figure like this, which braves prevailing prejudices, not to say principles, can only be justified by success. It either must be very good, or else it will be condemned as very bad, and altogether intolerable. That Mr Leighton's 'Venus' holds its ground, that the bold attempt

has been treated with respect, amount to a tacit admission that the artist has at any rate not failed . . . His picture is eminently chaste. The figure is, as she should be, unconscious of shame. The beauty of the form, too, has in it purity; somewhat perhaps of that higher beauty which, like truth, commands homage.

The reviewer goes on to say that he applauded the attempt, and that the colouring made it a refined picture – 'it has a pale silvery hue, not as white as marble, and not so life-glowing as flesh'. A painter does a good service to Art who 'reconciles the untutored English eye to the beauties of the unclothed figure'. He holds up a warning finger to the presumptuous: 'Only let it be remembered that to such a painter is committed a grave responsibility. He is bound to paint on the side of virtue, and so to exalt beauty as to silence passion.' He was less interested in G. D. Leslie's *Willow, Willow* with its 'gentle moody melancholy' and Mrs Robbinson's *Queen of the Tournament*, 'as gay as a bed of roses'. Whatever Leighton had done, he had made an impact; he was never short of buyers at a thousand guineas a picture.

The inhibitions under which the English exponents of High Art painted helped to give an added piquancy to their work. They did not have the unselfconsciousness of their predecessor, William Etty (1787-1849), who was compared, not to his disadvantage, with Titian. Celibate, introspective, Etty, whom I described in 1969 in *Worm in the Bud* as a great and underestimated painter, is only now being evaluated properly. In terms of cash, as the Victorians would have liked, he is now in the thousands bracket instead of the hundreds. He was a painter's painter, and was never more than modestly successful, supported by a brother for many years. He took pleasure in women's flesh, even if he never touched it; he painted real women, while Leighton, Poynter, and Alma-Tadema painted archetypes which were erotic in the same way as pornographic photographs were erotic. They were subtly saucy, flaunting themselves in their Roman or Greek stage settings.

Credit must be given to these painters, for the paradox is that it is not easy to make the naked erotic. Stark naked is no empty phrase. Pornography soon found out that complete nakedness was a bore, and the purveyors of dirty photographs soon discovered that the best sellers were not the women naked but the women nearly naked. This was instinctively understood by the hanging committee of the Royal Academy, and almost by the unnamed critic who had to write a half column on the 1867 Leighton picture. A woman wearing a garter or stockings, or a chemise reaching down to the waist, the favourite attire of the prostitute entertaining her guest, would have no chance of being shown on the hallowed walls even though, in terms of square inches, there would have been less flesh showing.

There was something of cold calculation in the personality of Lord Leighton. In 1856 Robert Browning, who had recently met Leighton, wrote to the American sculptress Harriet Hosmer.

> [Leighton] has a capital Pan enjoying himself in a dell, from a superb Italian model here, (the perfection of a man), and a Venus, very clever too; and designs for perhaps a dozen delicious pagan figures; a sudden taste that has possessed him.

He never put a foot wrong socially, and his mother's exhortations to be pure and her prayers for him to be 'preserved from moral evil' were superfluous. There was gossip. Some paintings he sent to America to sell were considered to go too far and were locked up in a cupboard. His friend and mentor the court jester Henry Greville advised him to turn his thoughts 'entirely to well-covered limbs, and paint no more *Venuses* for some time to come', and there was talk of some kind of dubious association with one of his male models, John Hanson Walker, and the three Misses Pullen, orphans used by Leighton as models. There were also rumours that Leighton was involved with the Oscar Wilde set, and during the trial of Wilde in 1895 Leighton was out of the country, allegedly for the benefit of his health, though he was a sick man and died the following year.

Alma-Tadema and Poynter were happily married. Alma-Tadema was Dutch-born and did not settle in Britain until he was in his late thirties. Edward Poynter, born in Paris of Hugenot ancestry, was accepted into the heart of the establishment despite his lurid and startling, almost sadistic, *Perseus and Andromeda*, which, with its unusual composition and dream-like imagery anticipates twentieth-century surrealism. Poynter became Slade professor of art at Oxford in 1871, director of art at what is now the Victoria and Albert Museum from 1876-81, culminating in his appointment in 1894 as director of the National Gallery, a post he held for more than a decade.

There were spectators who were activated by such paintings, though they rarely confessed it except in diaries not intended for public consumption. In 1872 the Rev. Francis Kilvert visited London and did the rounds of the galleries. One picture particularly excited him

> The beautiful girl stripped naked of her blue robe and stabbed in the side under the left breast is sailing through the air and reclines half standing, half lying back, supported tenderly in the arms of her lover who has been stabbed in the same place. They are passing over the fiery gulf. The naked girl is writhing and drawing up one of her legs in an agony – but her arms are thrown back and clasped passionately round her lover's neck. Her head lies upon his breast, her face is turned back up to his, and her eyes are looking into his eyes. She seems to look up to him and through him to another for comfort and help and strength and an example of suffering patience, and he looks down upon her with infinite pity and sadness and tenderness and love. The anguish of death is stamped upon her white and sharpening, yet still lovely features, but her soul is rapt above her pain in an ecstasy of love.

In 1873 Kilvert again went to London, and was again turned on by art:

> I went to Doré's Picture Gallery in New Bond Street. There was a new picture there, an Andromeda, a handsome graceful girl life size, well painted, the flesh tints very natural. The slender girlish form is bowed and shrinking from the monster, the white feet are washed by the lap of the green waves, the manacled hands and wrists are straining at the chain and the rich brown hair is blown wildly forward from the bowed back and beautiful shoulders across the horror-stricken face.

Although Kilvert did not specify it, the first picture was Doré's *The Tortured Lovers*, Dante's Paolo and Francesca. Painted in 1863, it was one of the best-known of Doré's works. Gustave Doré (1833-83) is probably most regarded today for the illustrations he did for Blanchard Jerrold's book on London, but in his own time he was immensely popular in France and England, so much so that the Doré Gallery was opened in New Bond Street to exhibit his melodramatic, theatrical, and grandiose works.

There was nothing subtle about Doré, but he was powerful, and whatever he illustrated, he imposed on it his own interpretation. He made a speciality of struggling, writhing, naked men and women, and fitted them in whether he was illustrating Tennyson, Dante, or the Bible. His technical skill and his mastery of stage-effects were seen at their best in his engravings, of which he did tens of thousands. He was obvious because he wanted to be obvious; he shouted when there was no need to shout. His Bible illustrations have all the delicacy of graffiti in a public lavatory, and although he appreciated mythological themes as well as the English High Art painters his attitude was very much different, except that if there was a chance to have a character naked he would have it so.

In his preface to the vast book of Doré engravings published by Cassell, Edmund Ollier discusses Doré's treatment of women, referring to the Francesca of *The Tortured Lovers* in terms that vie with Kilvert's luxuriant description:

> Here the beauty is allied with agony, with vehement passion, with mingled longing and remorse, with tortured memory and unrelieved despair.

He moves from the particular to the general:

> Other female figures might be pointed out in Doré's works which have either animal luxury or the splendour of strong emotion but they are rarely characterised by the gentleness and grace of the female character in its perfection of physical culture and moral loveliness. When M. Doré wishes to draw a woman of this description, he becomes tame or uncouth.

Like Leighton, Alma-Tadema, and Poynter, Doré was a success financially. Between 1850 and 1870 he earned £280,000. His female nudes did not have to have gentleness and grace; the public wanted them globe-breasted with long sensuous legs.

One of the most significant phrases in Ollier's panegyric is 'animal luxury'. This was rare in late Victorian art when it related to women, though Etty had had the ability to portray it, and Thomas Rowlandson (1756-1827) had revelled in it. The French had this talent, and British art critics regretted that the situation in Britain did not allow artists to express themselves fully and honestly. In the *Magazine of Art* for 1892 Bernard Hamilton wrote that 'the French school is not hampered like ours by pseudo-moral restrictions, and a free range is given to an earnest student of flesh-painting ... Over here there is a prejudice that not only cannot recognise the function the nude plays in art, but even blinds many to the intentions of those who have the moral courage to openly oppose the fanatics that decry the model as necessarily immodest.'

Hamilton went into raptures over 'the soft delicate flesh of Canabel's Venus rising from the foam', and commented: 'what refinement of colour and grace there is in Collin's nude girls dancing on the sand! How well Verdier has rendered 'Echoes' as nymphs who, while answering cries that reverberate through the glen, fade into thin air as they fly from the pursuer!'

In France, too, there was a middle class as hypocritical and censorious as that in Britain, but they were not so influential. The Paris Salon was not the Royal Academy, and whereas the Royal Academicians flirted with nudity, pretending to be historical, the French artists gloried in their freedom. P. Leroy's *The Bath* was openly erotic, but, wrote a critic in the 1898 *Magazine of Art*, 'it is sufficiently learned to secure its acquisition by the State; the coloration of the principal figure is doubtless admirable, yet the whole picture seems as coolly calculated as its arrangement, and in spite of the skill with which female modesty has been suggested, the work fails of complete success.' J. J. Henner's *Levite of Ephraim and Dead Wife* went much further than any Royal Academy entries in its thinly disguised necrophilia. A man, his intentions all too apparent, is gazing down at a naked woman prone on a slab. 'Effective and beautiful as it is', said the English critic, '[it] is a mere convention as regards true painting of flesh. The picture of a glistening white body lying upon its back is but a variation played by the painter upon his *Dead Christ*.'

The tribute paid in London to Dore can be seen as a breakthrough of French ideas in art, a success – as opposed to the failure of French literature, as represented by the prosecution on grounds of obscenity of Zola and Balzac in translation (Baudelaire and Gautier escaped because no one translated them and imported copies in the original could be read by the zealous).

It must not be supposed that there was any grand scheme behind Dore's freedom from prosecution in the very years – the 1860s and 1870s – when prurience was at its height. People had to take their nudes where they found them, thankful that something was getting through the mesh woven by the middle-class censors. A famous picture such as the *Rokeby Venus* by Velasquez could be reproduced in the pages of one of the art periodicals, but if it was used as the frontispiece of a pornographic book (as was done) it was reckoned obscene and the publisher could be prosecuted (if he could be found, which was not very likely). This absurdity was relished by Lord Lyndhurst when he opposed Lord Campbell's 1857 bill to put down pornography.

> Suppose now a man following the trade of an informer, or a policeman, sees in a window something which he conceives to be a licentious print. The officer then goes to the shop, and says to the shopkeeper, 'Let me look at that picture of Jupiter and Antiope (pronouncing it wrongly – Ant-i-ope with three syllables).' 'Jupiter and what?' says the shopkeeper. 'Jupiter and Antiope,' says the man. 'Oh, Jupiter and Antiope, you mean (he pronounces it Ant-i-op-e in four syllables),' says the shopkeeper; and hands him down the print. He sees the picture of a woman stark naked, lying down, and a satyr standing by her with an expression on his face which shows most distinctly what his feelings and what is his object. The informer tells the man he is going to seize the print, and to take him before a magistrate. 'Under what authority?' he asks; and is told – 'Under the authority of Lord Campbell's Act.' 'But,' says the man, 'don't you know that it is a copy from a picture of one of the most celebrated masters in Europe?' That does not matter; the informer seizes it as an obscene print. He asks if the shopkeeper has got any more prints like it. 'Oh, yes, I have got several others,' is the reply. Whereupon he searched the shop, and in doing so perhaps he stumbles upon a print of the story of Danae. There he sees a naked woman lifting her eyes to heaven, but standing in a very strange attitude, the shower of gold descending upon her, a little Cupid peeping over her shoulder pointing with his dart, and other circumstances which I will not describe. Well, is this print also to be brought before the magistrate? These prints come within the description in this Bill as much as any work you can conceive. And yet they are both celebrated pictures; the first is a copy of a famous Correggio which hangs in the large square room of the Louvre . . .'

Touché, though this marvellous sardonic summary of a ridiculous situation did not stop the Obscene Publications Act being passed.

Lord Campbell did not live to see the Royal Academy going permissive; he died in 1861.

Notwithstanding the success of the academical nudes, perhaps the most famous naked lady was not a picture but John Gibson's statue, *The Tinted Venus*. Gibson (1790-1866) was the quaintest of fellows, the son of a Welsh market gardener, an eccentric who always carried three packages around with him (the Greeks liked the quantity three). As a student he was so intent on the assimilation of anatomical knowledge that he did not hesitate to rob graves for bodies to dissect, as he admits in his autobiography.

In 1866 the *Art Journal* described Gibson as 'the most eminent British sculptor of modern times'. The first commission for a marble figure came in 1849, and while this was being executed an industrialist from Liverpool, Robert Preston, gave a repeat order. *The Tinted Venus* was five years in the making, from 1851 to 1856, and was one of the great hits of the International Exhibition held in London in 1862 (more extensive and all-embracing than the more famous one of 1851), shown off in a mock Grecian temple designed by Owen Jones, decorator, and author of influential books on ornament. The *Sculptor's Journal* of 1863 considered it 'one of the most beautiful and elaborate figures undertaken in modern times', though the *Athenaeum* was harsher; it had been executed with 'little insight and less artistic enthusiasm'.

The colouring was applied to the marble using a cloth and wax, and although Gibson maintained that his authority for tinting sculpture was Greek there were many who thought that imitating solid flesh was even more heinous than painting it in a picture. There seemed something subtly perverse, even illogical, about flesh that was really stone. In the twentieth century the surrealists did much the same thing, deliberately confusing appearance with reality, by cutting up small squares of marble and putting them in a setting that suggested that they were cubes of sugar.

Most reprehensible of all was that the Venus had the face of a typical Victorian girl. She was, declared Elizabeth Barrett Browning, 'more grisette than goddess'. Not for Gibson, though. 'As I sat before my Venus,' he related, 'alone and intent, she looked like a celestial spirit.' In 1971 the most famous, not to say notorious, sculpture of the nineteenth century sold at Sotheby's, Belgravia, for £2,400. It was no longer shocking, but still striking, and continued to have the ambiguity that upset the Victorians.

It was not completely nude; a kind of cloak obscured the loins, though the pert breasts were not particularly modest. Whatever Gibson thought of his creation, it lacked the chastity of Greek or Renaissance sculpture – they showed everything and it was not salacious. If part of the body is concealed, it draws attention to that very part.

Advanced educationalists of the nineteenth century thought that children should be presented at school with representations of the nude in ancient sculpture so that, as one writer put, they could become immunised. It was also suggested that photographs of nude models should be shown to schoolchildren, though this was more controversial, especially if, as mooted, such photographs were not touched up and the models remained undepilated. Pubic hair was once again the problem. In the magazine *Nineteenth Century* Frederic Harrison wrote about this in terms that must made many readers wonder what he was talking about. 'There is one convention so ancient, so necessary, so universal, that its deliberate defiance to-day may arouse the bile of the least squeamish of men and should make women withdraw at once.' It was not appreciated that the tradition of not showing pubic hair had its genesis not in prudery, but in the art of the east, where people were accustomed to shave it off.

The academicians had depicted the Ancient Greeks running around naked and taking part in activities in which, to say the least of it, clothing would have been advantageous. There is every evidence that the High Art painters were basing their fantasies on fact. The Romans put sin into nakedness, and combined with their arch-enemies the Christians to make the body disgusting. It has been said that nakedness was so reprehensible to Christianity because of a semantic mix-up over the word 'flesh'. The flesh (subjective) is evil, so the flesh (objective) must be hidden.

The matter of complete nudity was rarely discussed sanely, and there was controversy whether it aroused sexual passions or not. The French essayist Montaigne had no doubt. The 'skilfullest masters of amorous dalliance appoint for a remedy of venereous passions, a full survey of the body'. Prostitutes realised this, and so did anthropologists. In his *A Naturalist in Mid-Africa*, G. F. Scott Elliott wrote that he always found that chastity varied inversely as the amount of clothing. So did artists. A life class is one of the most antiseptic of all environments, and most professional models take off their dressing gown as soon as possible. No one would dream of disputing the claims of nudists that their behaviour *en masse* is irreproachable.

Nakedness dispels curiosity; without curiosity there is the acceptance of things as they are. Day-dreams have no place in an environment seething with nudity. Those Victorian males who saw nudes felt that they were specially privileged. And it usually cost them. There were nudes, often atrociously drawn, in pornography, and pornography was expensive (a slim volume of less than a hundred pages usually cost more than a pound). Prostitutes demanded more money if they gave their services naked. Wives often proclaimed with pride that their husbands had never seen them nude. *Tableaux vivants*, Victorian strip-tease, was not cheap and was usually a confidence trick, for when all the clothes were removed the stripper often wore a skin-tight flesh-coloured costume. There were photographic nudes in the print shops and dirty book shops (one dealer was caught with more than a hundred thousand obscene photographs on his premises), and there were photographic-seeming nudes in the galleries.

The latter cost little or nothing to see, and they caused no heavy breathing within the august precincts. If it was free, it was reasoned, it could not be very potent; Victorian capitalism nods across a hundred years.

11

APES AND ANGELS

MANY Victorians behaved in an ostensibly moral manner through fear, fear of social obloquy, fear of offending those to whom they owed their livelihood, and fear of God. God was all-knowing and all-seeing, could see a shop-assistant purloining change from the till and a respectable middle-class man playing, as it was called, High Life in London. As more and more people ceased to believe in God and vengeance from on high, an inhibition was removed. The stern exhortations to be pure were no more regarded than cracker mottoes.

The decline of religion as a governing force was regarded with unease, and was associated with the 'creeping Socialism' exemplified by the Reform Bills of 1832, 1867 and 1884, giving the vote to most householders. The historian Macaulay, who could look back objectively but at the present only in fear and trembling, regarded suffrage with 'dread and aversion'. The first thing that would happen in the new democracy would be that the masses would 'plunder every man in the kingdom who has a good coat on his back and a good roof over his head'.

There were many on whom the blame for the break-up of religion could be placed, but in particular there were the scientists who in their new cosmology showed that there was no place for a god. The geologist Charles Lyell despatched Biblical chronology to the world of myth, and it needed a great effort of will to believe that the world was created, as per schedule, in 4004 BC. In 1844 Charles Darwin wrote to his friend Joseph Hooker: 'I am almost convinced . . . that species are not (it is like confessing a murder) immutable . . . I think I have found out (here's presumption!) the simple way by which species become exquisitely adapted to various ends.'

Seemingly an innocuous sort of sentence, but in the coming years it was to initiate one of the most important books written in the century and herald in the theory of evolution. Darwin did valuable work on coral reefs, barnacles, and orchids, work that has not been out-dated since, but his contention that man had evolved from an ape-like creature stunned the thinking public, clergy and laymen alike. Nature was, indeed, red in tooth and claw, and only the best adapted survived. 'I have called this principle, by which each slight variation, if useful, is preserved, by the term of Natural Selection,' wrote Darwin in *The Origin of Species*.

The first casualties were Adam and Eve. Learned clerics had ceased to believe in them, but had kept their doubts·to themselves. In 1838 Charles Hennell published his *Inquiry Concerning the Origins of Christianity* in which cautious disbelief raised its head, in 1840 H. H. Milman published a *History of Christianity* that was modestly suspect, and in Germany in 1835 David Strauss, with his *Das Leben Jesu* had used the New Testament as a battering ram against traditional Christianity. Writers on theology had knocked Adam and Eve down; the scientists picked up the bits and put them under a microscope.

Darwin built up the argument relentlessly, drawing from observation extending over many years. Bertrand Russell remarked that Darwin's theory was typically Victorian in that it was 'an extension to the animal and vegetable world of laissez-faire economics'. Darwin was also typically Victorian in his enthusiasm for collecting facts. His scholarly readers liked facts, too, but they disliked the implications of the book. William Whewell, Vice-chancellor of Trinity College, Cambridge, refused to have *The Origin of Species* in the college library. The astronomer Sir John Herschel condemned it as 'the law of higgledy-piggledy', and the clergy ranted about folly, madness, and atheism. Adam Sedgwick, who had taught Darwin geology, warned that Darwin had plunged humanity 'into a lower grade of degradation'.

Even those scientists who agreed broadly with Darwin's ideas had reservations about mankind being fitted into the scheme. William Carpenter (1813-85), a biologist whose books on physiology remained standard works well into the twentieth century, admitted 'that all birds are from one progenitor, and probably all fishes and reptiles from another parent.' But the last mouthful chokes him. He can hardly admit all vertebrates from one parent.

Darwin, a nervous, shy, and ultra-modest man, was ill-equipped to cope with ecclesiastical and lay criticism, but he had an ally in T. H. Huxley who delighted in controversy and roundly set about those who attacked his friend. Huxley's own book, *Man's Place in Nature*, was a further brick in the edifice that would replace the church by science.

Both Darwin and Huxley made use of new discoveries by other scientists. As early as 1797 John Frere had described finding flint instruments in rock strata dating from a period that according to the Bible never happened. In 1848 an unusual skull was found on the Rock of Gibraltar. Although human-like, the brain cavity was shallow, the forehead disgustingly low, and there were heavy ridges over the eye sockets. A similar skull plus a skeleton were found in 1856 in the valley of the Neander in Germany, giving a name to Neanderthal man. Among scientists there was little doubt that these remains were those of some precursor of *homo sapiens*.

The impact of evolution theory and the concept of the survival of the fittest – a phrase lifted from the philosopher Herbert Spencer but soon applied to Darwin's work – created consternation. It took mankind down a number of pegs; it was not the lordly species of old, created in one fell swoop, but nothing more than an animal. In the common mind, evolution meant that man was descended from a monkey, and if people behaved like monkeys they could hardly be blamed. Those who should have known better seized on these misapprehensions as a platform to proclaim themselves above it all. In a speech at Oxford in 1864 Disraeli made his own attitude abundantly and inanely clear:

What is the question now placed before society with a glib assurance the most astounding? The question is that – Is man an ape or an angel? My Lord, I am on the side of the angels.

Disraeli, as was his wont, was making a cheap debating point, but others seized on the damage that evolutionary theories did to the traditional way of looking at things. The external world was no longer provided by God for the edification of man, and this seemed to Howard S. Pearson to be nothing short of scandalous:

It seems to be supposed that the researches of Darwin and others on the mutual relations of flowers, insects, and birds have thrown an entirely new light upon man's relations to the universe as a whole. We are forever being reminded that all our notions about God having made the flowers beautiful and sweet with any view to man's pleasure are pure sentiment. We may please ourselves, they say, whether we admire or not, but we may rest assured that the beauty – if beauty it be – was never intended to captivate our important eyes, and that colour, form, and perfume all alike address themselves – not to man's corrupt and jaded senses – but to the far finer aesthetic capacity of the bee and the butterfly. Speaking more correctly we should rather say that there was no beauty. The chalice of the lily is a trap and the perfume of the rose an advertisement. All is struggle for life, in the street or in the garden, and the splendour of the blossom and the cheap clothier's posting bill are just the same spirit working under different manifestations. But it seems to me that this doctrine pays, if I may say so, a very poor compliment to the Almighty.

This is worth quoting in full, not because Howard S. Pearson is anything more than a forgotten nobody, but because it shows Victorian self-opinionation at its most flatulent and flabby. Darwin was resented not because what he said was untrue, but because he had dared to strip off rose-coloured spectacles.

> In God's high garden the crimson flowers
> Flushed as he came
> (*John W. Taylor*)

They did not any more. If crimson flowers flushed they did it for a more mundane reason not wholly unconnected with propagation.

In 1871 Darwin published *The Descent of Man*, which further demoted man. Others were at the indelicate task of stripping sentiment from fact. In 1865 John McLennan had published *Primitive Marriage* which, to the unqualified (who naturally made the most hullaballoo), degraded marriage. It was not made in heaven, as previously thought by Tennyson and others, but had evolved from anarchy and sexual promiscuity through polyandry to monogamy and descent through the father. In 1869 Darwin's cousin, Francis Galton, published *Hereditary Genius*, showing that talent and genius, as well as moral attitudes, tend to be inherited. In the competition of civilised life sexual selection made for achievement;

clever people would look for other clever people to mate with. Engagements were not made in heaven, either. Young folk were, unknown to themselves, merely pawns in the hands of an uncaring Nature which was only concerned with the end product.

It might be supposed that this plethora of books seeking to establish a new role for man was of concern only to reviewers and other scientists. The reviewers did not think so. They saw implications that scientists, assumed to be living in ivory towers, did not. It seemed to J. H. Newman that the dethronement of man was also the signal for moral chaos:

> The lowest class, which is most numerous and is infidel, will rise up from the depths of the modern cities and will be the new scourges of God.

A more important issue was that of right and wrong. In the old days people behaved morally because there would be retribution if they did not. Now that man was nothing more than an updated ape, how could he be expected to appreciate the difference between right and wrong?

Of course, Newman and his fellow worriers were over-reacting. There was no rising up from the depths of modern cities in response to news that God was dead, or if not dead was not operating as he once was. But what did happen is that the literate classes were relieved of sexual guilt. *The Origin of Species* was a best-seller, and there were few who did not have some idea of what it was about, if only from reviews. If people behaved like animals, it was no more than their right.

The war between religion and science produced many casualties. The warriors on the side of religion were not in the same league as their opponents, whose sweet reason was not dented by threats of apocalyptic doom. In 1887 Huxley published an essay in the *Fortnightly*:

> Theological apologists who insist that morality will vanish if their dogmas are exploded, would do well to consider the fact that, in the matter of intellectual veracity, science is already a long way ahead of the Churches.

The triumph of science was a defeat of hypocrisy. It was no longer good enough to be told to behave oneself otherwise one would go to Hell. Those who took the middle path realised that science and religion were by no means mutually exclusive, but at the time many thought that there could be no compromise.

No one can say what effect the acceptance of evolution had on behaviour as distinct from thought, or whether the superior patronising of Christianity caused the Ten Commandments to be broken more often. The poet A. H. Clough put the situation nicely in his *Dipsychus* (1849):

> 'There is no God,' the wicked saith,
>   'And truly it's a blessing,
> For what he might have done with us
>   It's better only guessing.'

There was one aspect of evolution theory that had an important effect on sexual thought, and gave openings for hypocrisy. This was natural selection, the tendency of those best fitted to survive to dominate. This, over the millions of years, had been a trial and error process, but could selection now be guided? 'Evolution is a grand phantasmagoria,' admitted Francis Galton, 'but it assumes an infinitely more interesting aspect under the knowledge that the intelligent action of the human will is, in some small measure, capable of guiding its course.'

This meant that some people should be encouraged to propagate, and others discouraged, for the good of society. Thus the science of eugenics, a word first given currency in 1833, and made respectable by Galton. He pointed out that the active and the ambitious deferred marriage until they could afford it, and there was a permanent obstacle to the fecundity of the 'more elevated classes'. The improvident and the weak-willed were prolific, and in time this would lead to the deterioration of the species, and civilisation would crumble into barbarism.

To thinkers on the subject there was plenty of evidence that if the tendency of those unfitted to perpetuate themselves was left unchecked *homo sapiens* would lose the cognomen *sapiens*. *Homo stupidus* was already about in large numbers, born of the feeble-witted, the unemployed, and, of course, the working classes. It was logical to alter all this. In his *The Origin and Development of the Moral Ideas* Westermarck was optimistic: 'Future generations will probably with a kind of horror look back at a period when the most important, and in its consequences the most far-reaching, function which has fallen to the lot of man was entirely left to individual caprice and lust.'

Eugenics being a branch of science, it was only to be expected that the church was regarded as the chief barrier to the acceptance of its ideas. 'Be fruitful and multiply', stuck in the craw of eugenists, who pointed out that this command was uttered when there were only eight persons in the world and the instruction seemed reasonable. Things had changed. 'We have to remember,' Havelock Ellis wrote, 'that today humanity has spawned itself over the world in hundreds and even thousands of millions of creatures, a large proportion of whom, as is but too obvious, ought never to have been born at all.'

For the converted it was evident that the ancient Greeks had advocated eugenics. In his *Republic* Plato discussed the possibility of improving the species by letting warriors have the first pick of the maidens. Eugenics, the advocates maintained, was not selfish. It was, said Galton, 'a virile creed, full of hopefulness, and appealing to many of the noblest feelings of our natures'. He did not add that the eugenic movement was full of nuts, replete with sickly theorists who should be the last to be allowed to perpetuate themselves. One of the lunatic fringe, Vacher de Lapouge, proclaimed that love for the sake of sexual pleasure was an aberration comparable to sadism and sodomy. Results of this aberration should be dealt with through abortion or infanticide.

Eugenics was a subtly conducted class war. Those most fitted to survive were the rich and the powerful, and the members of the movement. The superman, the logical end of eugenics, was a six-foot-four lord with directorships in the City. Facts were conveniently ignored in the interests of promotion. One of the most telling was that the qualities most deplored by the eugenists were often seen in those traditional bastions of survival success, the county families. As they were whole-hearted supporters of eugenics, their high rate of insanity, largely due to in-breeding, was skated over.

One of the militants of the movement was Major Leonard Darwin, who horrified social reformers when he declared that the poor deserve to be poor. He pointed out that their ranks were constantly being added to by the descent of the unfit from the upper layers of society, but not that the middle classes were being enriched by members of the poor who were struggling upwards, members who had something to contribute to society but who would have been, if Major Darwin had had his way, sterilised by means of the 'harmless and painless' X-rays, first used in surgery in 1897. This was called 'negative eugenics'; encouragement to the 'superior' classes to breed was called 'positive eugenics'. Positive eugenics could be encouraged by subsidising likely candidates; big superior families needed big superior houses, and the government should help out with the rates (big inferior families did not own houses, so there could be no difficulty passing this bill through).

The high point of engenics was in the years leading up to World War I, and the movement never took off again in Britain though it had a lot to answer for in Germany, where class discrimination shaded into racial discrimination. Nevertheless, it enjoyed a wide measure of support in late-Victorian Britain among scientists, middle-class people, and sociologists. Charles Booth believed that industry could not work without an unemployed margin, 'but the margin in London today seems to be exaggerated in every department, and enormously so in the lowest class of labour'. He did not advocate sterilisation, but there were many of his well-meaning contemporaries who did. C. H. Hughes said that there were 'circumstances under which the propagation of a human life may be as gravely criminal as the taking of a life already begun'.

At its most selfish, eugenics expressed resentment, resentment that inferior folk, the *lumpen proletariat*, should indulge in sex as often as they wished without worrying about the consequences whereas the better-off were obliged to restrain themselves in the interests of society (and themselves). The poor were not interested in the concept of 'national regeneration' introduced by Miss J. H. Clapperton in 1885. A four-legged frolic, one of the many lower-class terms for copulation, was, to them, worth all the thousands of words spent trying to educate them (naturally for their own good).

The vogue for eugenics had its roots in the ability of science to strike out for itself in *The Origin of Species* and its confidence in its opposition to traditional Christianity. Nineteenth-century science was blunt and aggressive, and scientists laid down the law, not only regarding their own spheres but others in which they carried no authority. They still do it.

If eugenics had been logical, Charles Darwin himself would have found himself neutered. Sickly, neurotic, he begat more than ten children, many of whom inherited his constitutional defects. But eugenics was not logical, and members of the in-group would never have had cause to fear the snip-snap of surgical scissors about their private parts. Major Leonard Darwin, the doyen of the eugenists, was Charles Darwin's fourth son!

12

A QUESTION OF
MULTIPLICATION

THERE was no area so filled with muddle, dissention, prejudice, and misinformation as birth control. Birth control, being for no very clear reason an obscene term, was called Neo-Malthusianism, the name being taken from the obscure eighteenth-century clergyman Dr Thomas Malthus who pronounced that there was a natural tendency for populations to increase faster than the means of sustenance. He thought that people should exercise self-restraint; the people would not.

Malthus specifically denied that he advocated mechanical means to prevent conception. 'I should be extremely sorry to say anything which could be either directly or remotely construed unfavourably to the cause of virtue,' he wrote, 'I should always particularly reprobate any artificial and unnatural modes of checking population, both on account of their immorality and their tendency to remove a necessary stimulus to industry.' So from the first, birth control was associated with immorality.

Contraception was not new. 'Instruments of safety', 'bladder policies', and 'condoms' were known in the sixteenth century. They were simple linen sheaths, and later sheep's intestines and isinglass were used. The discovery of the vulcanisation of rubber by Goodyear and Hancock in 1843-4 led to the familiar contraceptive sheath to be found in their thousands on any English beach. The prostitutes of China and Japan used rounds of oiled silk paper to cover the mouth of the womb, but for many years the French letter, or the English cape or mantle (*capote anglaise* and *redingote anglaise*) were the favourite means of birth control (though birth control was the last thing the users were interested in).

They were used not to prevent conception, but to prevent being afflicted with pox. Thus their eighteenth-century name, instruments of safety. They were associated with sin, and this connection took a long time to live down. Casanova had used them and did not like them; he did not 'care to shut himself up in a piece of dead skin to prove that he was perfectly alive'.

During the nineteenth century the emphasis changed; birth control was the method by which those who wanted to better themselves could achieve this. A large family reduced the chance of getting on. Francis Place was a tailor with fifteen children, and in 1822 he published *The Principle of Population* in which he said, 'If, above all, it were once clearly understood that it was not disreputable for married persons to avail themselves of such precautionary means as would, without being injurious to health, or destructive of female delicacy, prevent conception, a sufficient check might at once be given to the increase of population beyond the means of subsistence.'

Place suggested the use of a sponge tied to a piece of ribbon or thread on the principle of a modern tampon. This, he maintained, was 'cleanly and not indelicate', and did not 'diminish the enjoyment of either party'. That women could enjoy sex was almost blasphemous. Place was vehemently attacked, but other books were produced, *Moral Physiology* by Robert Dale Owen in 1831, *Elements of Social Science* by George Drysdale in 1854.

It is interesting to note the ponderous titles. Pornography often hid behind similar titles, a leering facetiousness that convinced no one. But behind the ponderous titles of manuals on birth control was ponderous material, and those who were looking for cheap thrills were disappointed. Of the 600 pages of *Elements of Social Science*, in which Drysdale introduced the phrase 'preventive intercourse', there was nothing salacious, and little new. Although this book went through thirty-five editions by 1904, Drysdale had no magic message; he just went through the trusted methods – the contraceptive sheath, the douche, the sponge, and the utilisation of the safe period, which he reckoned at twelve days.

The sponge was later superceded by the soluble pessary, patented by W. J. Rendell in 1886, but even when the sponge was mentioned by Place in 1822 it had been in use for some time. People who wanted to limit their families were not fools, and were perfectly able to work out ways and means for themselves. It did not need a Newton or an Einstein to decide that a barrier was needed, whether it was in the form of the sheath, the oiled silk paper of the Oriental prostitutes or its later development, the Dutch cap. In 1840 the use of the sponge as a contraceptive device was mentioned in the *Town*. A mock news item stated that a certain visitor to London 'complains with some show of reason that since his arrival in England he has been much annoyed by the system of *spongeing* that has been adopted in some fashionable *circles*'.

Writers on birth control were aiming for a public that had not thought about limiting their families, and this public did not buy massive tomes. The improved but improvident working classes did not have the money for expensive books, and pamphlets met the case better. Millions of pamphlets were sold, and millions more were distributed free from door to door; the pamphlets reached their targets, as did the sixpenny booklets produced in quantity towards the end of the century. Many of these were published to advertise the wares of the writer, and because the intent was making money rather than taking the good news to the masses they were inaccurate and unreliable.

The methods could also be downright dangerous. An anonymous production of 1831, *Notes on the Population Question*, advised women to use corrosive sublimate, the popular name of the highly poisonous bichloride of mercury. Doctors with a cavalier attitude towards their patients used this as an antiseptic, not realising that it could be absorbed through the skin. The fatal dose when drunk, as it sometimes was, was five to eight grains. As recently as 1918 a woman died after inserting an 8.75-grain tablet into her vagina. Unscrupulous advisers eager to jump on the bandwaggon also suggested strychnine and iodine; no one will ever know how many fatal accidents occurred through misinformation.

Typical of the sixpenny booklets was Dr H. A. Allbutt's *The Wife's Handbook*, in which he warned readers that douching by itself was not sufficent, and that the so-called safe period was only 95 per cent reliable. Allbutt was struck off the medical register on account of this 'indecent publication', but he also erred in advertising himself – 'When any difficulty is experienced in introducing the "Soluble Pessary" as far as the mouth of the womb, I would advise the use of Dr. H. A. Allbutt's "introducer".'

Birth control books and pamphlets poured from the presses, though never in the quantities that the reformers would have wished. Some were dour, even mystical, and others were down to earth, even flippant. Advice could be ill-considered, but no more so than in medicine generally; prussic acid was in many medicine cabinets, used as a sedative, 'allaying pain, sickness, and nervous irritability' and mixed with lotions. If an overdose was taken, a recommended antidote was for the unfortunate person to be dashed with water. Or ammonia, swallowed.

The use of corrosive sublimate in tablet form as a prophylactic was one among many dangerous usages of mercury. As an agent to remove obstruction of the bowels in the form of quicksilver, it was administered in huge quantities, as much as a pound at a time. This method, as is clear from medical handbooks of the time, was considered quite acceptable as late as 1850. Blue pills for adults and grey powder for children were preparations containing mercury that were used for numerous purposes. Plummer's pills contained mercury and antimony, and were administered to sweat a patient. Birth control chemistry could be fatal, but so could most Victorian therapeutic methods.

Some of the birth control methods were frivolous, and may or may not have worked. *The Power and Duty of Parents to Limit the Number of their Children* (1868) suggested coughing, sneezing, jumping, and violent exercise after intercourse. Except for the purpose of creating ludicrous images in the mind of the reader such books were valueless, and might even have been published by the opponents of birth control.

These opponents were a mixed lot. They included those who were against birth control as unaesthetic and 'contrary to the purity of thought and manliness of life which are the characteristics of this nation' *(British Medical Journal)*. Michael Ryan in his *Philosophy of Marriage* (1837) stated that the use of 'various abominable means' to prevent conception is 'based upon a most presumptuous doubt in the conservative power of the Creator'. The interference with the course of Nature was one of the most frequently used arguments. Canon Knox Little saw cosmic implications in the widespread use of birth control: 'We find a state of society so terribly corrupt in some particulars, that it may be said to present some likeness to the state of things at the break up of the Roman Empire.'

'We do right in believing that the practice of Neo-Malthusianism is immoral,' declared Rev. R. Ussher in his *Neo-Malthusianism* (1897). 'It is strangling human life in its very source. The degrees between it, abortion, and infanticide are very slight.' Father Clarke, of the Society of Jesus, went further. The consequences of birth control would be 'to abolish the sanctity of human life, and to condone, or rather to sanction and approve, deliberate murder'. These are points of view expressed without hypocrisy. Although unstated, the crux of the matter for theologians is the point at which a soul is started. Has spermatozoa a soul before it fertilised the egg?

This was reasonable ground for the traducers of birth control to stamp over, but their motives could be less pure. They tried to augment their case by calumning those who used birth control, who 'barter and change the sacred possession of a child for a vile prostitution of flesh and bank-notes ... who revel in secret indulgence and vice.' They drew the attention of the British to what had happened to the French (well known to be as keen on birth control as the English, and who had begun to practise it earlier to judge by the significant decline in the French birthrate). The British readers nodded; if they did not grasp the other lines of argument, they did this, for the French were celebrated for their dirtiness and decadence.

If reviling did not work cajoling might. How happy were families with the little ones grinning over their Christmas pud, where sisters spoke unto brothers and all was harmony and good cheer! How different from the childless couples who spent their time sneering at each other! Statistics were dredged up to show that children of large families were brighter, happier, and more successful than singletons. The presence of children brought out the best traits of character in parents; it stimulated them to work for their sakes, and prevented wasteful extravagance.

'How many an evil desire,' asked the novelist Whyte Melville wistfully, 'how many an unkind thought, has been quenched at its birth by the pure, open gaze of a guileless child?' However, such speculations were irrelevant. They might appeal to the undecided who happened to be sentimental, but it was thought by the more acute anti-birth controllers that the ground could be cut from under the feet of Neo-Malthusianists by hacking at the founding father himself, the Rev. Mr. Malthus and his erroneous assumptions.

The main factor against Malthus was that he was not an optimistic Victorian but a pessimistic Georgian. He thought that as the population increased there would be less food to go round. This, said the Victorians arraigned against his successors, was not so; it was impossible for Malthus to anticipate the improvement in the production of food, and the means of bringing it to Britain (steam). Malthus was not to blame for his assumptions; when he was alive Britain was deliberately encouraging breeding to supply armies for the Napoleonic wars.

If sustenance was lacking for a nation, it was due to 'faulty social and economic laws, such as an unequal and unjust distribution of wealth, a lack of judicious emigration, a proper system of education, good marriage laws, a reformed mode of farming, tenure of land, and temperance'. Thus the ramblings of the Rev. R. Ussher. He did not seem to know that Britain had a goodly array of these, or if he did he ignored them for the sake of the argument. Not that he needed much of an argument; it was clear among the circles in which he moved that there was plenty of food to go round (though not in the poor quarters of London where more than half the population lived below the theoretical starvation level).

The opponents of birth control were not necessarily all hypocrites; they honestly believed what they were saying, though their judgments were clouded by selfishness. They were interested in themselves, not in others. The rest of the world was a willing provider of food and good things for Britain; that was its role, as ordained by God.

Economists entered the fray. Economists are not noted for their compassion, and take a perverse pride in pursuing their hobbyhorses no matter where they might gallop. Adam Smith (1723-90) considered that the object of building up a British Empire was to raise up 'a people of customers', and a good deal of bloody cruelty was complacently carried out with this precept in mind. Economists were not impressed by the speculations of Malthus. 'The increase of population, so far from being regarded as a calamity, is in reality one of the factors of progress,' wrote Minton in his *Capital and Wages*. A large community, other things being equal, is capable of producing more wealth, man for man, than is possible in a small community.

Naturally this only applied when the community was alert, active, organised, not when it was inert, idle, and largely unchristian, as in India. With an increasing population in a civilised country, there was more competition; people worked harder to obtain wealth. This was the quintessence of Victorian *laissez-faire*. It also meant that people worked harder not to obtain wealth but to keep their heads above water, and when they failed they gave in. Some, including Herbert Spencer, thought that this was no bad thing, and castigated legislators for feather-bedding such failures, or, as he preferred to put it, 'interfering with the beneficient operations of the pitiless discipline which kills off the unsuccessful members of society'.

Spencer was voicing the unspoken opinion of economists who were against birth control, and especially birth control for the masses. Victorian capitalism assumed a vast pool of untrained unskilled labour from which it could take its pick. When the supply of labour was less than the demands of industry, there would be competition among employers instead of competition among workers and they would either have to go labour-intensive, meaning capital investment on new machines, which could perhaps restore the *status quo*, reduce the scale of operations, or pay more (which in turn would mean that employers unable to pay the new rates would go under). In the late eighteenth century, the cotton industry had gone labour-intensive, but doing this to make more profit was a different thing to being forced to do it to survive.

Furthermore, a diminishing population would reduce the home market for products of industry, and if this reduced population was a thinking, calculating people it would not be fobbed off with rubbish. The use of birth control by the lower classes showed forethought, and this was the last quality wanted by industry. A man with a small family was better able to cope with the demands of life, and in the future there would be less factory-fodder, no uneducated hordes eager to do the dirty work.

There were no consolations from history. After the Black Death which reduced England's population by two-thirds agricultural workers enjoyed unprecedented prosperity. In Ireland in the 1840s there was a peasant population of eight million living in the most appalling poverty; famine and emigration brought the population down to four million and the bad days were over. Between 1700 and 1800 the population of Great Britain increased by 30 per cent; between 1800 and 1900 it increased by 300 per cent. If the opponents of birth control had been right, this would have meant joy and happiness all round, but only industry was really happy. The more compassionate tried to find a way to alleviate the hardships of millions of poor. Carlyle in *Latter-Day Pamphlets* (1850) and Charles Kingsley in *Alton Locke* thought that emigration would solve the problem of over-population; the cynical thought that disease and starvation would be Nature's answer; many did not want to think about it at all, satisfied in their own minds that the Poor Law and indiscriminate charity would wave their magic wands and solve the problem of the surplus population. Typical of these human ostriches was Dickens's Mr Podsnap:

> 'There is not,' said Mr Podsnap, flushing angrily, 'there is not a country in the world, Sir, where so noble a provision is made for the poor as in this country.'

Podsnap concludes with the words:

> It is not for *me* . . . to impugn the workings of Providence. I know better than that, I trust, and I have mentioned what the intentions of Providence are. Besides . . . the subject is a very disagreeable one. I will go so far as to say it is an odious one. It is not one to be introduced among our wives and young persons . . .

So much for the problem of the surplus population.

Most middle-class people did not have intimate contact with the poor. As with Mr Podsnap, it was a disagreeable subject, and many of them assumed that the Poor Law Amendment Act of 1834 had done all that needed to be done. The previous Poor Law had been based on an act passed in 1601, when it was assumed that it was the duty of the parish to see to their destitute. Money was doled out to the poor in their own homes, and if they earned some money, but not enough to keep them and their families alive, this was supplemented. Naturally enough, employers underpaid their employees, knowing that the parish would make up the wages to above starvation level.

This could only work in a predominantly rural society, and then not very well. The able but idle worker slacked, knowing that the parish would bail him out. The middle classes did not like this, aware that indirectly they were subsidising the poor. The administration of the old Poor Laws was investigated in 1833, and a report was published showing that the system as it stood was

> a check to industry, a reward for improvident marriages, a stimulant to population, and a blind to its effect on wages ... a natural institution for discountenancing the industrious and honest, and for protecting the idle, the improvident, and the vicious ... the destroyer of filial, parental and conjugal affection, a system for preventing the accumulation of capital, for destroying that which exists, and for reducing the ratepayer to pauperism.

The 1834 Poor Law put the poor into workhouses, made them work for their upkeep, separated wives from husbands, and mothers from children. It took the poor from their hovels and put them in prison-like barracks, known as the 'Poor Law Bastilles'. These were the utterly superfluous population, out of sight and out of mind. The passably superfluous, the unemployed who were not actually starving, the cat-meat sellers, the scavengers and the mud-larks, the dustmen and the labourers, did not read birth control literature. They could not read. The most persuasive of pamphlets was no good to people who did not care whether they had five children or fifteen children, who copulated when drunk or sober but as they were usually drunk, more often the former, or who were not interested in higher living standards. The girls began child-bearing at thirteen or fourteen and did not stop until the menopause or until they died. Perhaps some of the women had heard about birth control, and knew about the safe period, but it was not so easy to fight off a drunken husband determined to have his rights.

These were called the Perishing Classes. The least qualified to survive, the least likely to accept advice. Disease and starvation did thin their ranks, but not enough to satisfy their betters. The improved working classes did use birth control methods, though to what degree is impossible to say. Sidney Webb estimated that between a half and two-thirds of married people practised some form of birth control. That was in 1906. The census of 1911 showed that clergyman, those venomous opponents of birth control, were 30 per cent less fertile than the population as a whole. Between 1872 and 1894 the birth-rate in the United Kingdom dropped from 34.3 per thousand to 28.9.

Many family doctors were shocked when asked by their female patients about birth control methods. Dr Strahan wrote:

> Ask any medical man in practice among the middle and upper classes, and he will tell you that the married woman among his patients who is not fully alive to these practices is the *rara avis*. Some women have too high a sense of morality to sink to the level of their sisters in this respect; but assuredly these are in a minority, and in a minority which is decreasing daily.

Notwithstanding this tirade, the professional classes used birth control more than any other social group. How were they able to countenance it for themselves, and attack its use by other people? It was not difficult. The double standard was so widely accepted that it needed no great effort to decide that what was good for oneself was not necessarily good for others. There was also a comfortable ambiguity about what exactly was meant by birth control.

Birth control could mean no more than self-restraint. Even the most bitter of clergymen could find little to criticise in this as it was warmly recommended by the church. It could also mean *coitus interruptus*, withdrawing the penis without emission; a religious sect in America was founded on this. It could also mean all sexual activities that stopped short of penetration. including oral sex and sodomy. Sodomy between husband and wife was widely practised among coal-mining communities as a method of birth control. There was also the unmentionable practice of mutual masturbation. The supporters of birth control who were not concerned with the economics and sociology of the matter believed that these activities were more unnatural than intercourse; their argument, though it often had to be left unstated, was that intercourse using mechanical preventatives was not perverse.

Until the 1870s the distribution of literature on birth control was done surreptitiously, but in 1872 the *Malthusian Magazine* was started as the organ of the Malthusian League. It had a small

circulation and only appealed to the already converted. In 1876 a
Bristol bookseller named Cook was convicted for selling an
obscene work, Charles Knowlton's *Fruits of Philosophy: An Essay
on the Population Question*, which had been on sale in
Britain since it was first published in America in 1832. Nobody had
bothered before. Its British publisher, James Watson, had died, and
responsibility for it rested with Charles Watts, who had bought the
plates from James Watson's widow. Acting on advice, Watts went
to Bristol and declared himself the responsible publisher. He was
arrested on 8 January 1877, and four days later was committed for
trial at the Central Criminal Court. The trial was to be heard on 5
February, but in the meantime Watts changed his plea from not
guilty to guilty, having come to the conclusion that the book,
hardly more than a pamphlet, was indefensible.

He had been encouraged to act the martyr by Charles Bradlaugh,
social reformer, secularist and freethinker, one-time errand boy,
soldier, and now editor of the *National Reformer*. He was a full-
time trouble-maker who was now in his forties without having
accomplished very much, and he thought, rightly, that controversy
would put his name before the public. His lectures on the necessity
of atheism were not always well attended, and they were apt to end
in noisy humiliation. There was not much evidence that he cared
one way or the other about birth control; if the establishment was
against it, that was sufficient for him. The more indelicate and
embarrassing, the better.

He was associated with Annie Besant, whom he had met in 1874
at the Hall of Science, in Hoxton, London. He employed her on his
newspaper at a guinea a week, she lectured on women's rights and
free thought, and with her arrogant good looks and trim presence
she became the number one star of the atheist lecture circuit, to
Bradlaugh's chagrin. Both had shattered marriages, and he wanted
to marry her. Mrs Besant was more intent on her mission.

Bradlaugh was disappointed that Watts betrayed him by
pleading guilty. 'The Knowlton pamphlet is either decent or
indecent,' he declared. 'If decent, it ought to be defended; if indecent, it should never have been published ... I hold the work to be
defensible, and I deny the right of any one to interfere with the
full and free discussion of social questions affecting the happiness
of the nation.' Watts was found guilty, released on his own
recognisances of £500 to come up for judgment when called upon.

It was contended that it was unlawful to publish such physiological details as were found in Knowlton's book. Bradlaugh and Mrs Besant founded the Freethought Publishing Company to republish the book.

They did not believe in waiting for lightening to strike, but delivered the first copy of their edition to the chief clerk of the Guildhall, together with a notice that they would personally attend at a specific time on the next day to sell further copies. Similar notices were left with the police and at the office of the City Solicitor. On time they turned up, and plain-clothes detectives were among those brandishing their eager pennies. The pair were later arrested, Mrs Besant being searched in the process, and remanded until 17 April 1877. A defence committee was formed.

It was realised that this was not just an ordinary porn case, but that wider issues were at stake. The prosecution agreed to Bradlaugh's request to have the trial moved from the Old Bailey to the Court of Queen's Bench. It wished to do a deal, and professed willingness not to proceed against Mrs Besant, though Mrs Besant refused. Bradlaugh's recognisances for £400 were not high, and bail was allowed. He realised that the establishment was in a dilemma, and this belief was reinforced when he found that the Corporation of London refused to prosecute but left it to the police.

Bradlaugh's line-up of influential witnesses rather let him down. Professor Henry Fawcett and Charles Darwin were sub-poenaed, but cried off, though there were volunteers to make up for them, including H. G. Bohn, founder of Bohn's Library, a well-known publishing firm of the highest repute, and Dr Drysdale, who, as a writer of birth control books, had an interest in the outcome of the trial. Pending the trial, the Freethought Publishing Company was raided and dubious material was confiscated.

The verdict was 'guilty'. The jury were of the opinion that the book was 'calculated to deprave public morals' but the defendants were exonerated 'from any corrupt motives in publishing it'. The defendants were sentenced to six months' imprisonment, a fine of £200 each, and forced to enter into recognisances for £500 each for two years. Neither went to prison. They were released on bail pending appeal on a writ of error, and in February 1878 the appeal was allowed.

The trial did not directly affect Bradlaugh; he had made his presence felt, and that was sufficient. Mrs Besant was less fortunate. She was robbed of the custody of her child for ten years. Notwithstanding the notoriety she had won, she published her own book on the subject, *The Law of Population: its Consequences and Bearing on Human Conduct and Morals* which sold 200,000 copies. When she became a Theosophist in 1891 she withdrew it.

In later years, Charles Bradlaugh became the member of parliament for Northampton who could not take his seat because he would not take the requisite oath. It was six years before he was let in. The Bradlaugh and Besant trial was still remembered by some of his fellow members. An Irish Catholic named Corbet spoke of 'Mr Bradlaugh's Byzantine doctrines of morality' and another member, A. M. Sullivan, strove to exclude Bradlaugh from parliament on the score that 'his Malthusianism taken in conjunction with his Atheistic opinions, struck fatally at the foundation of civil society'.

The publicity given to the trial was as effective as ten million free pamphlets. Bradlaugh was not in prison, busy at treadmill and oakum-picking; extracts from Mrs Besant's little book were quoted in many respectable newspapers. Although publishing 'unlawful physiological details' remained risky, for the law had not changed, reformers were willing to take a gamble. There was a rule of thumb; if birth control literature had pictures it was obscene, if not, doubtful. No one was keen to give so much publicity again at the expense of the tax-payer.

13

HOLY WEDLOCK

ACCORDING to the Prayer Book, marriage was an 'admirable mystery'. According to *The History of Human Marriage* by Edward Westermarck, it was 'a more or less durable connection between male and female, lasting beyond the mere act of propagation till after the birth of the offspring'. In a narrower sense, it was a union regulated by custom and law, an institution rather than a method of regularising sexual intercourse. The Roman Catholic idea of marriage was a sacrament, the priest being present merely as a witness, and it involved something more than sex and children. Married love, wrote Coventry Patmore in *Religio Poetae*, bore 'the clearest marks of being nothing other than the rehearsal of a communion of a higher nature'.

The Protestant marriage was basically secular and romantic, based on exclusive and permanent love, and this was the form taken up by respectable Victorians. It was a shaky edifice built on the uncertain ground of inexperience, ignorance, and blue-eyed anticipation. Marriage was a magic word, an admirable mystery indeed, and even men and women who were sexually experienced expected something marvellous from it, as though the contract would transmute something in their own natures.

Men and women believed in the institution of marriage because it did not occur to them not to. Love was the essence of it, and the British looked askance at arranged marriages as practised on the continent. Marriage not based on love was a degradation of romantic ideals; this was promulgated by even those whose own marriages had failed, but who could not face up to this. In these cases hypocrisy flourished unchecked, not through faults in the unhappy parties but because they hád refused to be realistic. Realism meant to acknowledge that exclusive sexual love was not a compensation for lack of mutual interests, incompatibility of temperament, differences in intelligence, or monetary difficulties. Love might laugh at locksmiths, but it did not laugh at boredom, exasperation, contempt, or poverty.

Sensible people, finding that the first flush of excitement and joy was passing, made their own private readjustments, though even the most commonsensical were obliged by the fashion of the times to preserve the facade of the perfect union. Awareness that marriage had not lived up to expectations did not necessarily mean unhappiness; the man and woman could work out a *modus vivendi* suited to both. Hobbies, work, and children could channel the once so fervent adoration.

Some authorities, such as Count Keyserling in his *Book of Marriage*, maintained that unhappy marriages promoted self-development, leading to an inward happiness not experienced nor even understood by those who lived a perpetual honeymoon. Keyserling saw marriage partners as a unit, but a unit in which the man and the woman enjoyed a freedom and independence from each other. Coventry Patmore, though he seems here to contradict himself, referred to the chief end of rational marriage as 'contrasted personal consciousness'.

Many marriage difficulties stemmed from courtship. For many young women this was a state in itself, instead of a prelude, and the consideration that they found in a suitor was afterwards completely lacking in a husband. There were many handbooks on courtship concentrating on etiquette and how to learn about the loved one – calling on a fiancée without warning so that the young man can form an estimate of her neatness, domestic habits, and tidiness, or asking her to select a book for a sister to determine her taste. The courtship handbooks warned against taking a person from a different social level. *How to Woo and How to Win*, anonymously published in Glasgow in 1856, paints a vivid picture of the man who marries beneath himself:

> He may be obliged to admit those to his table whom a year ago he would have grudged sitting room in his hall. Strange outré-like apparitions, with sandy hair and moleskin small clothes, call him 'brother' and 'cousin', and plague his existence with

petitions for employment; and he almost dreads to take up a newspaper or police report lest he should stumble upon some tidings, not of the most flattering nature, connected with his new kith and kin.

The Rev. F. B. Meyer suggested in his *Love, Courtship and Marriage* (1899); that a man about to be married should consult the family doctor of the girl to see if there was any insanity in the family, though the man, if he had any guilty secrets, could ethically keep these to himself as a 'pure young girl . . . probably would not understand what he referred to'.

Above all, courtship handbooks stressed the awful consequences of having sex before marriage. A 'lady doctor' in E. B. Kirk's *Talk with Girls* declared: 'I have known a girl to be ruined because her betrothed told her that all engaged people had intercourse'. The percentage of engaged couples anticipating their marriage night was never mentioned; it was the rule rather than the exception among the poor, who married to escape from an overcrowded home, and was often suggested by the girl so that in the event of a pregnancy she had a hold over her lover. In his survey of the London poor Charles Booth quoted a doctor as saying that 'most young men are bounced into marriage' and a clergyman who maintained that it was 'always the woman who puts up the banns'.

The poor knew what to expect from marriage, and few had romantic illusions. A high proportion of them had sexual experience, often from the age of twelve or thirteen, and those who had not had had every opportunity to view copulation at close quarters in their homes. The segregation of the sexes was not possible and not understood among the poor, and parents did not bother to conceal their marital activities from their children.

Courtship can be seen as a curious ritual, an atavistic survival from primitive marriage that fitted badly into the pattern of Victorian life. It was not a chart for the future marriage, as many thought it might be. Men and women behaved in a manner that they afterwards considered ridiculous and acutely embarrassing. Women who were not suited to it played the coquette. There was the heroine in Elizabeth Barrett Browning's poem 'Amy's Cruelty':

Fair Amy of the terraced house,
  Assist me to discover
Why you who would not hurt a mouse,
  Can torture so your lover.

You give your coffee to the cat,
  You stroke the dog for coming,
And all your face grows kinder at
  The little brown bee's humming.

But when *he* haunts your door – the town
  Marks coming and marks going –
You seem to have stitched your eyelids down
  To that long piece of sewing!

You never give a look, not you,
  Nor drop him a 'Good morning,'
To keep his long day warm and blue,
  So fretted by your scorning.

Man as cringing mouse was described by Richard le Gallienne in his book *Attitudes and Avowals*:

How often has man, through the ages, girded himself and put on his whole armour of masculine complacency, and gone forth to defy this sunbeam. So strong, so determined to assert his supremacy and independence, – O so beautiful a front of impregnability! – to be shattered utterly, even comically abased, by a woman's smile.

These 'sunbeams' often turned out to be flickering light bulbs. They wanted a husband, and were uncertain how to go about it; any husband was better than none, even a wishy-washy curate. To be thirty and unmarried was to be on the shelf. In 1868 one of these unfortunates declared: 'The position of a single woman of thirty, in the middle class, is horrible. Her cares are to be properly dressed, to drive or walk or pay calls with Mamma; to work miracles of embroidery ... but for what? What we want is something to do, something to live for ...'

Young ladies in their early twenties were more interested in marriage as an escape from home; dread of spinsterdom had not yet arrived. Marian, a letter writer to the *Englishwoman's Domestic Magazine* poured out her woes in 1861, and the irony of the magazine's bleeding hearts specialist may or may not have helped her:

> Marian complains that happiness doesn't come; and, O wonder! happiness isn't with Marian another word for the Fairy Prince who has been expected ever so long. No! Marian complains that her parents talk about nothing but chairs, and tables, and carpets, and engravings, and pictures, and bronzes, and house-furniture, house art, housemaids, housemen, and house business in general. There is a lack of sympathy and kindness for herself and sisters which she most keenly feels. No one comes to see them, and she thinks it must be because her father and mother are such vulgar, disagreeable people ...

Such girls, snobbish as they were, were very vulnerable. In 1862 the same magazine replied to Mary Jane who had fallen 'desperately in love' with the '*beau ideal* of masculine grace and dignity'. She wanted to know how to get an introduction. Instead she was treated to a homily:

> There was a sentimental young lady who fell in love with an interesting creature with such a figure! and such an irresistible way of tying his neckcloth! She met him at a ball; permitted him to see how much she admired him; had private walks with him, and absolutely planned an elopement. On the night previous to this romantic adventure, her papa – who knew all about it – invited her to take a walk, led her to the Old Kent-road, down a narrow turning, to a penny barber's shop – there at the door, stood Apollo, ventilating his bibbed apron, and looking out for customers who wanted to be shaved! The romance faded away rapidly as the prismatic lustre of the barber's soap-bubbles.

Upper-class daughters, wrote Lord Ernest Hamilton, 'were reared like Pekinese pups for the market. ... It was by no means uncommon for girls to be led to the altar straight from the schoolroom. ... The idea was to keep daughters very conspicuously under glass cases as exhibits for eligible young peers, or eldest sons of peers, to examine and approve and select from, in full knowledge that what they selected always had been kept under a glass case.'

The results were achieved at a very heavy sacrifice, for it made maiden life dull, and the maidens themselves duller. Their destiny was settled, and the knowledge knocked all spontaneity out of them. Some of them recovered, but some did not. A good example of the genus was furnished in *Mrs. Brown's Match*, a pot-boiling novel by Chandos Fulton serialised in the satirical weekly the *Hornet* in 1874:

> Adele as a girl had enjoyed dancing and the gaieties of the ball-room; but with the change of purpose and disposition came a spirit of resignation and passiveness that rendered her indifferent to almost everything that she did not deem her duty. It was her duty now to love her husband, and she determined to do so, and thought she did.

Chandos Fulton defined courtship:

> Courtship is a bye-path near the highway of life. It runs through romantic depths of the forest, down into dales where flowers grow, and all is enchanting – but it soon returns to the highway, which is broad and full of ruts, and hard travelling to a good many.

Jane Welsh Carlyle shared Fulton's opinion. In 1859 she was writing to a friend, Miss Barnes of Chelsea:

> And you are actually going to get married! you! already! And you expect me to congratulate you! or 'perhaps not'. I admire the judiciousness of that 'perhaps not'. Frankly, my dear, I wish you all happiness in the new life that is opening to you; and you are marrying under good auspices, since your father approves the marriage. But congratulation on such occasions seems to me a tempting of Providence.

Mrs Carlyle reproached herself for writing as a raven might if it had been taught, but this did not stop her turning the screw:

> But of your father? Who is to cheer his toilsome life, and make home bright for him? His companion through half a lifetime gone! his dear 'bit of rubbish' gone too, though in a different sense. Oh, little girl! little girl! do you know the blank you will make to him?

Her account of her own courtship was crisp and succinct:

> Just because, in virtue of his being *the least unlikeable* man in

the place, I let him dance attendance on my young person . . . I came to *need* him – all the same as my slippers to go to a ball in, or my bonnet to go out to walk. When I finally agreed to marry him, I cried excessively and felt excessively shocked – but if I had then said *no* he would have left me – and how could I dispense with what was equivalent to my slippers or bonnet?

Peter Quennell described the Carlyle match as 'the gloom and sulphur-smoke of an almost modern purgatory'. It has also been speculated that it was a good thing that Thomas Carlyle married Jane Welsh, as by doing so only two people were made unhappy instead of four.

There were some who were drawn into marriage by a magnet, not particularly wanting it but feeling that it was expected of them. Edward Fitzgerald married Miss Barton, and immediately regretted it. 'Had good sense and experience prevailed,' he wrote, 'it would never have been completed! You know my opinion of a "Man of Taste", never so dangerous as when tied down to daily Life Companionhood!'

He blamed himself for it failing, putting it down to 'want of courageous principle in not making the best of it when taken'. Only later did he fully realise that his love objects were men, and that his marriage had not only been foolish but meaningless. Mrs Fitzgerald *née* Barton vanished from the scene, her vision of happy marriage in ruins, her suitor a thing of straw.

In his novel *John Inglesant* (1881), J. H. Shorthouse portrayed the suitor as he, for millions of girls, should have been:

Mary, you know me better than I know myself; I am ignorant and sinful and wordly; you are holy as a saint of God. Do with me what you will, if there is anything in me worthy of you, take me and make me worthy; if not, let me go: either way I am yours – my life belongs to you – neither life nor death is anything to me except as it may advantage you.

In his letters to Fanny Brawne, John Keats commented acidly: 'I have met with women whom I really think would like to be married to a Poem, and to be given away by a Novel'.

Few disagreed that marriage was a serious business (excepting always the poor and the aristocracy, whose morals and attitudes were marvellously similar). All the poets said it was, though their refreshing innocence might well have been ignored in favour of Francis Bacon's pithy axiom: 'He that hath a wife and children hath given hostages to fortune; for they are impediments to great enterprise, either of virtue or mischief'. He also gave hostages to society, for marriage was the basis of Victorian life. That was the first principle, and those who defied it did so at their peril.

There is no difficulty in seeing why marriage was elevated to such a state; it and the family spelled out stability and order. It has often been said that Queen Victoria made marriage respectable after the excesses of her Hanoverian predecessors, but her influence has been much exaggerated. Marriage was recognised intuitively as a still centre in a whirlpool of change. The importance of the institution of marriage, irrespective of its merits as a way of regulating sex, meant that it had to be supported. Marriage was defective, but there was nothing better available, though many candidates were pushed forward, and the legitimation League was evolved to work out some civilised alternative.

If anything was sacred in Victorian Britain, it was the family. This point of view was put by John Bright (1811-89), leading member of the Anti-Corn-Law League formed in 1839, Free-trader, opponent of the Crimean War, and a key figure in the passing of the Reform Act of 1867:

> Crowns, coronets, mitres, military display, the pomp of war, wide colonies, and a huge empire are, in my view, all trifles, light as air, and not worth considering, unless with them you can have a fair share of comfort, contentment, and happiness among the body of the people. Palaces, baronial castles, great halls, stately mansions, do not make a nation. The nation in every country dwells in the cottage.

It did not, of course; John Bright was making political noises. The nation dwelt in villa and park, in the tree-lined avenues of Camberwell, the gabled monstrosities on the outskirts of Manchester, in exclusive seaside towns, or in the fashionable Birmingham district of Edgbaston. The middle classes were the firm base on which Victorian prosperity rested, and the middle-class family was the microcosm of the state, with a settled hierarchy, a code of conduct that must seem to be above reproach, and a head that seemed to know what he was doing. If the family was tainted then so was the society. Only when the mystique that surrounded the family is appreciated does the prejudice and virulence with which apparent threats to the organisation were treated make sense, whether these threats were from birth control, women's emancipation, alternatives to marriage, or, demonstrably, homosexuality.

Middle-class morality was something of a closed shop. It was tacit, and it did not need to be formulated. It did not bear too close a scrutiny, and its apologists could appear uncertain because they were not certain how much to reveal. Fortunately they were addressing a middle-class audience, and their assumptions are as significant as their message. Newly married members of the middle class joined a kind of freemasonry of kindred spirits, a club from which they would be ejected if they disobeyed the unwritten laws – not to do openly what was better done in private, and if they did it, not to tell.

There was no typical middle-class man, though W. L. Sergeant painted a picture of a convincing industrial archetype:

> Intelligent, but rather narrow: that he is favourable to school instruction, but justly estimates still more highly that industrial education which gives skill, steadiness, and a pride of independence: that his mind is not overstrained by pecuniary speculations, because he knows that in the long run he is secure of success through his good and careful management: that he is temperate and domestic; being too intent on his affairs to lose time and health in excesses, and too busy to be driven by ennui into vice: that he is inelegant and careless of aesthetical considerations, but free from those pretences which are the worst of vulgarities: that he is firm and self-reliant; a little dogmatical and impatient of contradiction, and when very successful apt to run into pursepride ... sturdy, self-reliant, industrious, enterprising, greedy of success, patriotic, a lover of peace, but a greater lover of the honour of his nation.

A formidable creature, perhaps with too many high-lights. Smug can be substituted for 'secure of success', and churlish and self-opinionated for other flowery phrases. Such a man would perhaps take a mistress, but in the strictest secrecy; he would be a tyrant to his work force, a terror to his servants in the home, a tiresome husband but a doting father to girls. Sons would be frightened of him. A sense of inferiority would make him

truculent with those of superior birth who did not have something
to offer him; he often married someone of gentler birth to give him
the social graces that he himself lacked.

The industrial middle classes paid their respects to religion,
usually one of the Nonconformist sects which bolstered up their
instinctive beliefs in the demon drink, in original sin, and in
recompense in the hereafter for a good job well done. What was not
specified was inferred – such as the virtues of thrift:

> Who strives to get, and strives to save,
> In ten years time will riches have.

The words are by W. Hutton, the historian of Birmingham, and
the sentiments were shared nationally, by Scrooge in *The Christmas Carol* as well as by the singer of self-help, Samuel Smiles.
Striving to get was a sanctified operation, and whether it was accomplished at the expense of the lower classes was immaterial.
Fergus O'Connor, the Chartist leader, editor of *The Northern Star*,
circulation 50,000, told the pioneers of the Labour movement:
'Your employers are quaffing your sweat, gnawing your bones,
drinking the blood of your infants'. And he was right.

The middle classes supported moral uplift provided that it fitted
in with the acquisition of money. In Leeds in the mid century there
were societies for every form of human betterment – choral, floral,
madrigal, anti-monopoly, anti-slavery, temperance, a Society for
Promoting Permanent Universal Peace (manufacturers were
suspicious of this one – war helped trade), a Benevolent Strangers
Aid Society, and a Guardian Society for Females Who Have
Departed from the Paths of Virtue.

Whatever their differences, the middle classes and the aristocracy
shared one important feature – they were property owners.
Friedrich Engels (*The Condition of the Working Class in
England*, 1845) was not taken in by the veneer of respectability of
what he preferred to call the bourgeoisie. 'They are so degraded by
selfishness and moral depravity as to be quite incapable of salvation ... they really believe that all human beings (themselves excluded) and indeed all living things and inanimate objects have a
real existence only if they make money or help to make it. Their
sole happiness is derived from gaining a quick profit. They feel
pain only if they suffer a financial loss.'

The industrial middle classes rated their contemporaries on

how much money they had (how much is he *worth?* tells us this) and although the Commissioners of Inland Revenue have now stopped this innocent pastime there was no secrecy about Victorian cash flow, nor about religious affiliations. Private life was a different matter. In his autobiography Samuel Smiles referred to his married life with commendable brevity: 'These are things over which we draw the curtain'.

Business men and manufacturers found that running a marriage was not the same as running an office or a factory. Wives were not necessarily down-trodden creatures who welcomed totalitarianism in the home. They also had quaint altruistic ideals. Mrs George Cadbury, wife of the Quaker chocolate and cocoa tycoon, thought that 'the greatest need of England today is the revival of spiritual life. ... Do we not feel at times that our spiritual life is sluggish, that our lamps are burning dim, that our eyes are heavy, the vision far away?' George Cadbury, model employer and pioneer of the garden city, might have agreed, but others were appalled. What did the spiritual life ever earn for anybody?

The wives of the middle classes exerted a profound influence on Victorian society. They were more intent on stability than were their husbands. Stability meant that their position was safe and that their standards of living could be kept up. It was they who were most vocal in attacking all phenomena that threatened the comfortable life; the freemasonry of middle-class wives was as strong as that of their husbands. When danger threatened they closed ranks.

Their very real power was based on bluff. Only by combining could they represent public opinion. They were second-class citizens, not allowed the vote, technically property of their husbands. Not until the 1836 Marriage Act was a religious ceremony in a Roman Catholic or nonconformist place of worship legally binding, not until the Married Women's Property Act of 1870 (improved in 1882) was she anything but an appendage of her husband. The act had two main aims, to allow a woman to own property, and permit her to make out a will. Until then, she had no property to leave; savings from her housekeeping legally belonged to the husband. 'Why she be allowed to have money in her pocket to deal with as she thinks fit I cannot understand,' argued Lord Fraser in 1881.

Her sexual role was as an inferior. She was obliged to accede to all her husband's demands and the double standard of morality – she could not commit adultery but her husband could. This was enshrined in the controversial Matrimonial Causes Act of 1857. The *Saturday Review* put the male point of view in 1869:

> Whether women can understand it or not, as long as society exists, incontinence on man's part will be compared with incontinence on woman's part, not as a matter solely of personal right, which here means personal wrong, but as a matter of public policy. On ethical grounds it is the same in one case as the other: on social consideration, the adultery of the wife is, and always will be, a more serious matter than the infidelity of the husband.

Not until 1878 was it permitted for a magistrate to grant a separation order and maintenance to a wife on the ground of aggravated assault. Just chastisement, however, was still permitted:

> She must kneel down at his bidding –
> From his feet his shoes unbind,
> Even if his whip descendeth
> On her head, she must not mind –
> *(anonymous manuscript in the
> library of the Society of Friends)*

Middle-class Victorian women were tougher than they have been supposed. They were shrewd operators, manipulating the penal laws against their sex to their own advantage. The sensible ones did not complain about not having the vote, but left that to unfortunate spinsters who had not succeeded in the only profession that women were suitable for – marriage.

14

A GROUNDING IN HYPOCRISY

L EADING girls from the schoolroom to the altar might have been shocking to outsiders, but the unsentimental realised that the sweet innocent child might well have acquired a knowledge of the facts of life that her parents would have envied. It was a good grounding in hypocrisy to behave in a manner that one knows is false, to simper detachedly and assume an adorable coyness. However, the shock of marriage as it was could be as overwhelming to a girl nourished on boarding-school fantasy as one who was unaware that there was a physical side to the match.

Boys usually enjoyed a period of freedom between school days and marriage, especially if they belonged to the middle or upper reaches of society. University would intervene for the latter, and a middle-class parent would frown on an entanglement that might stop a son of whom much was expected from 'getting on'. The years between school and marriage might enable a boy to get himself straight, to find out for himself about life instead of having it smuttily imparted by his better-informed fellows, and perhaps forget a traumatic school life.

Girls were often educated at home. This usually guaranteed innocence. Boys were sent to boarding school if they belonged to one of the privileged orders, and there they were obliged to suffer in silence, living a life that could shame them throughout their entire span. A year or two at a boarding school could twist their natures in a disturbing manner.

Swinburne became a flagellant due directly to his experiences at Eton, where flogging was regarded as hardly more punishment than writing a hundred lines and was resorted to for minor infringements. Most schoolboys suffered the punishment phlegmatically, but others it sexually stimulated. Flogging was a token that one belonged to a class which enjoyed special privileges; criminals and miscreants of all descriptions were flogged across the shoulders, but public school pupils were flogged on the buttocks. The weals were the symbol of superiority.

Flagellation was merely one aspect of public school life, with its filth, fagging and frugality. A gently brought up boy found himself in a hell on earth, with no one to tell him how to cope. A father who had previously served his time at Eton or Harrow had conveniently forgotten his own days, or thought that it was a necessary phase for every adolescent to pass through. Parents were the most unsympathetic when a boy decided to run away from school.

In her *Records of Later Life*, Fanny Kemble (1800-93) remembers a conversation at a country house where the subject was discussed:

> In speaking of the education of young English boys at our great public schools, the whole system pursued in those institutions was condemned as bad; but on all sides, nevertheless, admitted to be better (at any rate, for the sons of noblemen) than the incessant, base, excessive complaisance and flattery of their servants and dependents, from which, they all said, that it was impossible to screen them in their own homes, and equally impossible that the should not suffer serious moral evil. Lord Francis said that for a lad like his newphew, the Marquis of Stafford, there was but one thing worse than being educated at Eton, and that was, being educated at home; therefore, concluded they all in chorus, we send our boys to our public schools. So the children are sent away lest they should be corrupted by the obsequious servants, and luxurious habits and general mode of life of their parents.

Although there were far more boys' schools than girls' schools, M. Betham-Edwards in her *Reminiscences* (1898) spoke feelingly of the 'contamination' of her time at her school, and vices with which girls 'ought to have been absolutely unfamiliar were openly discussed and in a languaeateegoured of the gutter'. Boys and girls not only talked about forbidden things, but they practised them. In the appendices of his *Studies in the Psychology of Sex*, Havelock Ellis includes case histories that show that more was assimilated at school than the three Rs.

C.D. was a clergyman, age 34, slightly built, myopic, who remembered his lurid pre-school fantasies of being chastised by a young and beautiful woman. He also practised masturbation, and when he went to school at ten he found it 'extensively practised, both at that school and at the two others I afterward attended . . . I heard no arguments advanced sufficiently cogent to make me see the necessity for a real moral effort against the habit'. After he had left school, weighed down with shame and guilt, he was preoccupied with 'a struggle for chastity, morbid fears and regrets about the past, efforts to cope with the neurasthenia, and a haunting dread of coming insanity [through having continuously masturbated through puberty]'.

A.B.'s sexual memories began at the age of seven or eight, when he and his sister played mothers and fathers, but a form of mothers and fathers in which they pretended to relieve themselves at the WC. The father's groom told him the facts of life, a nursemaid told him that at her last place the boy had copulated with his sister, and when A.B. went to school he was more or less informed. He asked another boy if he could see his penis, which the boy did. On holiday his father's footman masturbated him, and he fell into the habit, indulging at his new boarding school in mutual masturbation and perhaps group masturbation. At home he tried intercrural intercourse with a young brother, aged five. Intercrural intercourse is the use of the folds of the thigh as a surrogate for the vagina.

He continued these activities at the large public school he later attended, but they were momentarily checked by his housemaster, who had walked through the boy's cubicle and noticed a stain on the sheet. Confessing to masturbation, A.B. was told that he would injure his heart or go mad, and, alarmed, he promised not to do it again, relapsed, and was expelled for having an indecent French photograph in his study.

E.T. was initiated by a servant, and went to boarding school at ten, where 'he learned the vulgar phrases for sexual organs and sexual acts, and acquired the habit of moderate masturbation. Coarse talk and indecent jests about the opposite sex were common amusements of the playroom and dormitories'. B. and another boy at his school used to beat each other with a cricket bat upon the bare buttocks, and practise mutual masturbation. A surgeon aged forty related his sexual experiences at school:

> I attracted the attention of one of the big boys who slept in the same room with me; he came into my bed and began to play with my member, saying that it was the usual thing to do and would give me pleasure. I did not feel any pleasure, but I liked the attention, and rather enjoyed playing with his member, which was of large size, and surrounded by thick pubic hair. After I had played with him for some time I was surprised at his having an emission of sticky matter. Afterwards he rubbed me again, saying that if I let him do it long enough he would produce the same substance from me. This he failed to do, however, though he rubbed me long and frequently, on that and many other occasions.

A similar narrative comes from G.R., an army officer, whose earliest sexual recollection was putting his hand down his trousers and playing with his penis. At school 'I was initiated, and used to handle the penis of the boy who told me. On several occasions I did *fellatio* for him, and liked it, but he never offered to do the same for me, and I don't think he got much satisfaction out if it.' G.R. later went to a large public school. 'I believe,' he wrote, 'the tone of my house, if not of the whole school, was exceptionally bad; though it may only be that I saw more of it because I was attracted by it, and that other schools are the same really. Things involving certain expulsion if found out were done more or less in public, and I have myself openly got into bed with or masturbated other boys, and on more than one occasion have helped forcibly to masturbate small boys or hold them while others had connection with them.'

G.R. was disgusted by what he called *paedicatio* (sodomy), mainly because it would deprive him of the pleasure of lying face to face and stomach to stomach, his method having, as he put it, 'connection' with the other boys. G.R. also practised buggery with animals, particularly cows and mares. Looking back from the age of thirty-five he admitted that he had given this up for ten years, but would have no objection to doing it again. G.D. began masturbating at seven, under instruction from an older brother, and 'decency demanded secrecy in the gratification of what soon became an imperious desire, and the preliminary operations included, almost from the first, mutual *fellatio* and approximation of the excited organs'.

Many of the boys, experienced as they were in homosexuality, were not aware of the facts of sex until their teens. G.D. had read about the clitoris, but did not know what it was until he visited an anatomical museum in the Haymarket. Another of Ellis's subjects, A.N., was instructed by a girl of his own age when he was ten years old, inculcated into masturbation and homosexual behaviour about fifteen, married at twenty-six. As with many other boys, A.N. believed that masturbation was a natural instinct as it was performed by so many of his fellows with whom he went to school or came into contact. He accepted that it was 'dirty', but not 'morally reprehensible'.

Although Havelock Ellis's subjects have one thing in common that might throw doubt on their reliability – their willingness to reveal all – there can be little doubt that they shared a common experience, and more recent researches particularly by Kinsey and company confirm the general truth of their statements, that many boys were initiated by servants, relatives (usually cousins or uncles), that mutual masturbation was commonplace at school, and that they were undisturbed by guilt until the message was brought home to them that they could be injuring their health (false), that their hearts would be affected (false), that they would become impotent (usually false), or go mad (false). Shame at having indulged in what were afterwards seen as disgusting habits meant that all mention of the subject must be forbidden, and memories erased if possible. Juvenile sexual antics were a massive base for adult sexual hypocrisy. Even those who had not been involved felt shame at association with those who had; in a day school it was possible to be innocent of what was going on, but hardly in a boarding school, whether it was a prep school, a crammers' establishment, or one of the prestigious public schools. Wherever there was dormitory life there was no way not to notice nocturnal pursuits of the kind vividly portrayed by Havelock Ellis's subjects.

Not surprisingly schoolboys built up a fictitious picture of their schooldays, for themselves and for others. Anything was better than the reality, though the more obvious unpleasant features of school life – the bullying, the dreariness, or the dreadful masters – could be accommodated better than the unspeakable. Leslie Stephen, scholar and father of Virginia Woolf, spoke of men dwelling more fondly upon their schooldays in proportion to the remoteness of their memory; to Leslie Stephen's brother, James Fitzjames, Eton school life was a state of war.

The homosexuality and the cult of masturbation that thrived in boarding schools was known to the masters, and, indeed, the roll call of teachers of many famous public schools contains more than a statistically predictable proportion of homosexuals, though few became headmasters, as Dr Vaughan of Harrow did. Masters had their pet boys, just as the older boys had their 'bitches'. The official biographers of the famous lay stress on their subjects' purity and avoidance of all suspect activities. According to John Morley, Gladstone 'rigidly refused any part in boyish indecorums'.

The newer schools were no better than the old established public schools, and although Rugby was formed by Dr Arnold with the express purpose of forming pure upright Christian young gentlemen it was only marginally freer from vice and corruption than the others. Lancing was typical of the newer schools. The Rev. C. Chambers described life in the Lancing of 1872:

> The School House room was a scene of much trial to small boys: about ninety of us lived together: the fire was at one end. A group of older boys used to surround this and none others had much chance of seeing it ... a common amusement was to get an unfortunate kid into the middle of a group and throw him from one to another. Making small boys kiss one another was a form of torment.

Two years later matters were much the same. Lieutenant Colonel S. F. Bayley looked back at his experiences without enthusiasm:

> Owing to the bullying which went on in the House room I (being a weakly little boy and not very brave) spent a lot of my time in the cold cloisters, rather than run the chance of getting 'roasted' if I went inside. 'Roasting' consisted in making a boy stand close in front of the House room fire with his trousers stretched very tight and holding him there till he yelled.

The consideration by John Percival, headmaster 1887-95, later Bishop of Hereford, that Rugby 'was a fine, strong, healthy, rough and vigorous, self-centred and completely self-confident society' could have been disputed by other one-time scholars. Writing from

Winchester in 1849, and not looking back in sentimental hindsight, James Lee Warner declared: 'Stealing here is not uncommon
and they alter the eighth commandment to "Thou shalt steal
nothing except ..." '

A favourite amusement at Winchester was 'bolstering matches'
between the younger boys, in which the object was to take the skin
off one's opponent's nose. At Harrow a monitor gave a younger
boy thirty-one cuts with a cane, disfiguring him and injuring him
so much that he had to be removed from school. At Eton, said the
historian Sir Edward Creasy, 'the lads underwent privations that
might have broken down a cabin-boy'.

By being a 'bitch' of an older boy, a timid youngster could avoid
some of the trials and tribulations. He had a protector, just as
prostitutes had bullies. Acceding to homosexual propositions
was self-defence. Knowing that one had been morally weak was
another cause of shame, and it was no consolation to those who
had given in to know that others had put physical safety as a first
priority.

They were victims of the system. The appointment of prefects
and monitors guaranteed a tyranny of the strong over the weak,
and the acceptance and promotion of the fagging institution by the
masters meant that there was a trade in favours. A Royal Commission report of 1864 did not look kindly on fagging, especially
fagging outside the school premises. At Rugby, 'fagging at games
seems almost to have resolved itself into a peculiar method of
making physical education compulsory'.

To whom could a boy turn? Hardly the masters. Although John
Percival, headmaster of Rugby, had an 'unerring eye for the un-
wholesome boy' he had the traditional schoolmaster's distaste for
the sneak. Most masters were too busy with internecine feuding to
bother with the complaints of small boys. Public schools always
had a clergyman or two about the place, and he would be the
person most often approached and the most likely to create guilt by
promising divine retribution if the boy did not cease to behave in
an 'unmanly' manner.

Childhood sexual experiences could also colour an adult attitude towards sex among girls, though they rarely had to cope
with an environment as savage as the boys' schools. One of
Havelock Ellis's female correspondents went to boarding school at
fourteen. 'During the three years I stayed there I never heard a

word the strictest mother would have objected to. One or two of the older girls were occasionally a little sentimental, but on no occasion did I hear the physical side of things touched upon.' Other correspondents, however, testified to the continuous discussion of the mysteries of life, and the attachments between girls, known as 'raves', 'spoons' and 'flames'.

> 'Raves' on teachers are far commoner than between two girls. In this case the girl makes no secret of her attachment, constantly talking of it and describing her feelings to any who care to listen and writing long letters to her friends about the same. In the case of two girls there is more likely to be a sexual element, great pleasure being taken in close contact with one another and frequent kissing and hugging. . . . I imagine that there is seldom any actual inversion, and on growing up the 'raves' generally cease.

Although memories of raves, spoons and flames were no doubt embarrassing they were not so charged with guilt and shame as boys' recollections. However, the discovery of masturbation could be no less disturbing than in the case of boys, and there were always relatives and servants to encourage such activities. Unquestionably girls' boarding schools were more 'select' than boys'; there were fewer of them and because they were competing in a very small market their standards were higher, there was more emphasis on cleanliness, and they were not atrociously understaffed. Understaffing made the appointment of prefects and monitors essential. At Eton, the headmaster Keate was forced to teach the fifth and sixth forms together, a total of 170 boys.

At the start of the Victorian period there were seven large boarding schools, Winchester, Eton, Westminster, Charterhouse, Harrow, Rugby, and Shrewsbury, with two important day schools, St Paul's, and Merchant Taylor's. During the next seventy-five years this list became greatly extended to cope with the huge number of middle-class boys whose parents were anxious to raise them in the social scale. There were the private schools, varying from the Dame schools which were no more than baby-minding establishments to quite good institutions, and there were the academies. The academies were originally started as Noncomformist rivals to the public schools and were highly successful. Many of the rising industrial middle classes were Nonconformists of one shade or another who would not countenance the Church of England instruction imparted at the public schools. To give some idea of the strength of Nonconformism, there were 11,514 Methodist churches in England and Wales in 1883 against 14,573 Church of England.

Academies were usually much smaller than the public schools, included a wider range of subjects (such as bookkeeping, navigation, and science), and were good, bad, and indifferent, ranging from the type of school described by Dickens (Dotheboys Hall) to the excellent Heath Academy near Wakefield, staffed by nine masters. The nineteenth-century grammar schools were under-endowed and were mainly day schools. It was the boarding school, whether it was called a public school, a private school, or an academy, where sexual habits that could colour a life were grounded.

Not all parents looked back wistfully at their schooldays; some who were expected as a matter of course to send their sons to Eton or Harrow pointedly did not, even though this could be a crippling handicap socially. Others took houses nearby, so that sons could go as day boys.

As early as 1785 William Cowper in his poem *Tirocinium* had issued a warning about public schools:

> Would you your son should be a sot or dunce,
> Lascivious, headstrong, or all these at once;
> Train him in public with a mob of boys,
> Childish in mischief only and in noise,
> Else of a mannish growth, and five in ten
> In infidelity and lewdness men.

As a formative influence in the establishment of a sense of guilt about sex the boarding schools of the nineteenth century were high on the list; sexual shame shared was not halved but doubled. The wealthy and the comfortably off sent their sons to boarding schools; even the academies, whose fees could be as low as a few pounds a term, did not take the poor. Consequently the poor escaped the guilt that led to hypocrisy on sexual matters, and only when the better off (who were also, of course, the most powerful and the instigators of public opinion) forced their hypocrisy on the poor did shame about sex infiltrate through society. The 'improved' poor believed that their betters were better informed than they were, and if sex was nasty then so it was.

If schools provided a grounding in hypocrisy, so did the universities. There were eleven in the United Kingdom (which then included Ireland), with a total student population in 1876 of 13,400. Oxford had 1,860 students, and Cambridge 1,920. The United States, with a population of 50 million compared with that of 34 million for the United Kingdom, had 360 universities with a student population of 69,400. The boys who went to a British university were therefore a tiny percentage, but what they lacked in numbers they made up for in importance; they were the future prime ministers and legislators (Gladstone, Lord Salisbury, Peel, and Lord Rosebery went to Christ Church, Palmerston went to Edinburgh, and Lord Melbourne went to Trinity College, Cambridge).

Schools had established guilt about sex, a guilt that had to be concealed, but the universities were more concerned with social hypocrisy, though traits that were acquired at public school often blossomed. Homosexuality flourished at the colleges, though there was none of the random, vicious buggery and sadism that were such a feature of the boarding school. Social and sexual hypocrisy often fused until their victims were activated by they knew not what. Because of their importance in the establishment, graduates had a large part to play in laying down guide lines for society to follow. They were responsible for legislation on sexual matters, and because of remembered shame they had a tendency to over-react.

Life in Oxford, said Benjamin Jowett, the influential Master of Balliol College, Oxford, was like 'living in a hot-house' and when there was 'an outbreak of abnormal immorality among a few of the young men in Oxford' his 'wonderful reticence and refinement coupled with sternness and *swift, decided action*' were considered sufficient to quash this inconvenient epidemic. However, the problem of closed societies, whether they be boarding schools, universities, prisons, or nunneries, was too much for the patient endeavours of one man, however capable. Most of the principals, professors, fellows, and scholars who constituted the teaching machine were too involved in their own affairs to worry overmuch about the morals of their charges. They were, in Hilaire Belloc's phrase, remote and ineffectual.

University education was a farce. In the early years of Queen

Victoria's reign there were no entrance examinations. Anyone could get an ordinary degree, there were few subjects, professors often lectured in empty rooms, and medieval statutes blocked those few who were anxious to reform. Reform was a dirty word. Lord Melbourne noted cynically that 'universities never reformed themselves; everyone knew that' – everyone knew there was too much competition and jealousy, too many and varied motives constantly in play to produce the desired effect.

Hypocritical behaviour was encouraged, and the orders given to undergraduates regarding religious observance were openly flouted. Not until 1842 was it decided that masters, fellows, and undergraduates no longer need recite a set form of prayer on rising in the morning and going to bed at night. This instruction had been in force since the days of Queen Elizabeth, but few took any notice of it. Non-attendance at chapel, however, resulted in a fine. Undergraduates (and the staff) had to give the impression of being God-fearing creatures; the appearance was more important than the reality.

The heads of colleges were laws unto themselves, and would take orders from nobody. In 1850 Professor Corrie, formerly Master of Jesus College, Cambridge, and now Vice Chancellor, refused to answer questions regarding finances and degree courses. He considered that it was no one's business except his. When a commission was formed to look into the whole question of universities, the Master of Caius College, Dr Chapman, maintained that the commission was not constitutional or legal, and placed every obstacle in its way. No one blocked a parliamentary commission – except Dr Chapman. It was only under the most intense pressure that King's College, Cambridge, surrendered the right of scholars to proceed to BA without taking an examination of any kind.

The universities had the power to hold their own kangaroo courts, and could arrest and imprison prostitutes. The proctors were the marshals of university law, and they had their own prison inside the university. In 1860 a number of prostitutes were sentenced to fourteen days imprisonment, and although the case went to the Court of Common Pleas, the university triumphed. The university was more than a closed society; it was a mini-state, a kind of Rhodesia that had declared unilateral independence.

Disillusion set in among those undergraduates who had arrived at Oxford and Cambridge with high ideals. 'You will remember two reverend gentlemen who were high in college office when I was an undergraduate,' wrote Macaulay to William Whewell, Master of Trinity College, Cambridge, in 1854. 'One of them never opened his mouth without an oath, and the other killed his man.' Dons drank like fishes, and the distinguished Anglo-Saxon scholar John Kemble (1807-57) was often 'so drunk that he could hardly speak or stand', though this did not stop him becoming Examiner of Plays, the theatre's censor. The establishment looked after its own, drunk or sober.

Undergraduates were always aware of the hypocrisy and selfishness of the dons. The dons were strictly speaking clergymen, but this did not make any difference to their lives. F. H. Bowring, a one-time undergraduate, wrote in his diary that 'the average Dons were not High Church or Low Church, Broad Church or Nonconformist, but easily accepted the current opinions of the time. Enthusiasm was not in them.' Instruction was so bad that undergraduates were forced to use private tutors, at their own expense, to learn anything. In 1840 undergraduates of just one Cambridge college (Trinity) paid £10,000 a year in private tuition fees. At least the tutors did something for their money (£14-£20 per term per student) but they were no less corrupt. The most sought-after tutors sent their pupils to tradesmen of their choice, and obtained a cut of the profits; it was one of the conditions of their taking the pupil.

Impressionable young men took on the tone of the universities. It was clear that the dons were only interested in doing the minimum possible for their salaries, and would willingly subscribe to the conventions while cynically controverting them if it suited them. Degrees were not a product of hard work and diligence, but a token that the recipient had joined the clan and could carry its ethos into public life; a degree was a visible sign that one had succumbed. 'A man may get the highest honours in mathematics and natural philosophy,' commented J. M. Wilson in his *Addresses on Morality in Public Schools* (1887), 'and have never seen a crystal, a lens, an air pump, or a thermometer.' And this was after widely publicised reforms were carried out following the Oxford University Act of 1854 and the Cambridge University Act of 1856, and the more far-reaching Oxford and Cambridge Act of 1877.

Universities demonstrated that hypocrisy paid; it was more important to seem to conform than actually conform; it was easier to accept the inestimable social advantage of a degree than protest that one did not deserve it. Hypocrisy in learning at school was epitomised by the universal use of the 'crib'. No gentleman need use a crib at university; it was a vulgar tool, and, besides, unnecessary.

15

THE REBELS

EVERY age has had its outsiders, men and women who refuse to accept the rules of their period and go their own way regardless of the consequences. There is, however, a difference between those who consciously swim against the stream, and those who do not know what the rules are, so in the nineteenth century there were those who opposed marriage because it was a gimcrack and ridiculous institution and those who did not marry because there did not seem any cause to. There were also those who were physiologically or psychologically unsuited to marriage, a heterogeneous group that included homosexuals, male and female, and those who suffered from some sexual aberration.

It is reckoned that 5 per cent of the population is homosexual, and so in the nineteenth century there were more than a million men and women outside the pale. Women were more fortunate than men; Lesbianism was not a crime, and was not incorporated into the 1885 Criminal Law Amendment Act because no one had thought of a way female homosexuality could be explained to Queen Victoria. Passionate friendships between women were therefore beyond the reach of the law.

Male homosexuals were a different matter, and throughout the period they were subject to persecution, often organised by those who had themselves been homosexual but had 'reformed'. They were easily identified scapegoats, and those who had other quirks managed to concentrate the acrimony of society on to homosexuals. Swinburne wrote in 1879 of his one-time friend Simeon Solomon as 'a thing unmentionable alike by men and women, as equally abhorrent to either – nay, to the very beasts'. There was a reason for this treachery. Solomon had been 'raising money by the sale of my letters to him in past years, which must doubtless contain much foolish burlesque and now regrettable nonsense never meant for any stranger's eye who would not understand the mere childishness of the silly chaff indulged in long ago.' Solomon, who died in a workhouse in 1905, had candidly confessed that his 'affections are divided between the boy and the birch' and had whimsically attacked those 'who find a delight in visiting casinos, and other dull, disreputable resorts of the like nature, and an amusement, nay, a satisfaction in copulating with vulgar and often diseased persons of the opposite sex.'

Most homosexuals preferred to keep their predilections quiet, or use a cover. At a time when it was considered a good thing for gentlemen to encourage self-improvement among working men, an association between a man and a boy friend could be glossed over. Oscar Browning, a master at Eton who was dismissed on account of his 'sinister influence' and who then moved to King's College, Cambridge, filled his rooms with sailors, stable-boys, and other low life, without reproof. He also took favourites home to meet his mother. Continually passed over when he applied for prestigious jobs, he eventually became head of a teachers' training college, from which he was asked to resign.

Roden Noel, son of the first Earl of Gainsborough, dilettante poet, and Groom of the Privy Chamber to Queen Victoria 1867-71, 'long laboured among the children of the lower classes and bidden successfully for their love'. So rhapsodised his biographer, but Noel was more interested in older specimens of the genus and was known by fellow homosexuals as 'the Centaur'. His happy-go-lucky approach was envied by friends transfixed with guilt and fear. Noel was a good patron of male prostitutes, soldiers wishing to supplement their miserly income, and cynical working men who did not see why a toff should not stump up for his peculiar pleasures.

One of Noel's friends was J. A. Symonds, who had once had Dr Vaughan dismissed from his headmastership of Harrow by sneaking on him. Symonds (1840-93) spent much of his life abroad where his activities did not come under the scrutiny they would have encouraged at home. Swinburne referred to him scathingly as a 'platonic amorist of blue-breeched gondoliers', and when

Symonds came to England in 1892 he brought one with him, a Venetian named Angelo who had capitalised on Symonds' infatuation with him by supporting a mistress and two sons on Symonds' money.

Symonds announced the presence of Angelo by declaring him 'an old peasant (who) has been with me for ten years and is a very good fellow. Just now I am really dependent on him while travelling'. Angelo was a well set-up man of thirty-three, a nicely preserved example of the type. Symonds considered that man was the 'higher organization of human form, infinitely richer in variety of lovely qualities, and is incomparably nobler in its capacities of energetic action.' He was a leader in the move to make homosexuality respectable, whether under the name of homogenic love or something else, and he collaborated with Havelock Ellis in the first volume of the latter's *Studies in the Psychology of Sex* dealing with sexual inversion.

This pursuit was not welcomed by those who preferred to keep their secrets, and to them Symonds and his crusade was an additional burden to bear as few wanted another eruption of the middle-class wrath that ensued when any particularly juicy homosexual case broke surface. The Symonds method was to tabulate all the famous homosexuals of the past from Michaelangelo onwards and try to encourage those of latterday to confess and be counted. Although they did not know it, this was tantamount to wide publicity, even when they were guarded. It was Symonds who exposed Edmund Goose as homosexual when to everyone he was a pillar (leaning crookedly because of his blunders of scholarship) of the literary establishment.

'I know of all you speak,' declared Gosse in a letter to Symonds, 'the solitude, the rebellion, the despair . . . the wild beast dies. He is not dead, but tamer; I understand him and the trick of his claws.' It is traditional to sneer at Edmund Gosse, 'poor old Gosse', but most of his detractors have not read him. The son of a zoologist and half-crazed Plymouth Brother, Gosse spent his life in the service of English Literature, an arbiter of literary taste, lauding authors in print and attacking them in private, a busybody and a social crawler, but a man who went out of his way to encourage young authors. So far as the public was concerned, Gosse was happily married, and he did his utmost to perpetuate his normality. His uneasiness, his fear of attack, his desperation when critics mauled his work – how far do these stem from dread of exposure of his secret, a secret only suspected by those who had spotted one or two indiscreet phrases in an early volume of poetry?

Henry James had a great respect for Gosse, irrespective of whether or not he knew the truth about him. Henry James was also under suspicion. Had he not contributed to the notorious *Yellow Book*, symbol of decadence? But James was amused and sardonic about homosexuality and the efforts to make it respectable. If Symonds 'has, or gathers, a band of the emulous we may look for some capital sport', he wrote.

Anxious for his own reputation, Gosse was willing to cover up those of others. He could write of Edward Fitzgerald without mentioning Fitzgerald's fisherman friend, Joseph Fletcher, known as Posh, 'of the finest Saxon type with a complexion *vif, male et flamboyant*, blue eyes, a nose less than Roman, more than Greek, and strictly auburn hair, which any woman might sigh to possess'. Retiring, melancholy, Fitzgerald attracted nothing more than amiable laughter in rustic Norfolk when he walked out with his sturdy sailor. What in London was termed unnatural vice was not recognised in the country; country people made their own sexual adjustments, and it was in rural parts that perversions were most horrendous, with incest considered of no consequence and buggery with animals commonplace. At any one time there were hundreds of men in prison convicted of buggery, and for every person caught there were twenty or more who had committed it without being apprehended. In almost every village there was an authentic village idiot, the result of in-breeding.

The clothing of the Victorian men offered no clues as to whether they were hetero- or homosexual. It was a protective uniform. Simeon Solomon dressed in a seemly high-buttoned jacket with fashionable small lapels, and only with Oscar Wilde did the apparel proclaim the man. A man who appeared to be dressed in an effeminate manner could merely be a hang-over from the Regency. Clothing told an observer what one did and one's place in the social hierarchy, not what one was.

Nor was appearance a revelation. J. A. Symonds looked like a gangster in a B-movie, Oscar Browning had the appearance of a television pundit, Gosse resembled a walrus, and Solomon looked like a meek and modest rabbi. It might be supposed that the use of make-up was a give-away, but not so. In a letter Disraeli wrote to Lady Bradford he described an encounter with Lord Malmesbury:

> I took a little walk this morning, but it was an easterly wind. I met Malmesbury, walking very well, and looking very well tho' he says he has the Roman fever which has knocked him up again ... M. was skilfully rouged. People say that resource is effeminate. M. is manly enough, and the two most manly persons I ever knew, Palmerston and Lyndhurst, both rouged. So one must not trust too much to general observations.

Sexual nonconformists were only brought to book when the conditions were auspicious. The crusade against homosexuality could be embarrassing; it could bring the chickens home to roost. After the Oscar Wilde trials W. T. Stead wrote in the *Review of Reviews*: 'Should everyone found guilty of Oscar Wilde's crime be imprisoned, there would be a very surprising emigration from Eton, Harrow, Rugby and Winchester to the jails of Pentonville and Holloway'. The law could be reluctant in beginning a witch hunt, for no one knew whom it would bring in; the middle classes might enjoy a sensational trial, but not those who were operating the mechanism. They might speak out against sodomy, just as a public analyst today might take a strong line against chlorination of water, but they did not expect much to be done about it, trusting that if they made the right noises that would be sufficient.

Unquestionably there was a conspiracy of silence. There were homosexuals in parliament, homosexuals in the legal profession, and homosexual aristocrats. Admittedly it had been a long time since an avowed homosexual had held high office in parliament (as distinct from adulterers and debauchees); one had to look back to Canning (born 1770) for that, though Disraeli was not exempt from all suspicion. Homosexuals did receive rough justice if they fell foul of the law, but this did not happen too often, even after the 1885 act which sent Oscar Wilde to Reading Gaol for two years. Wilde was a self-selected victim, wrapped up like a parcel waiting for the chop. There were many who advised him to jump the country, willing to pay his fare; they were not necessarily homosexual themselves, but anticipated the fuss the trial would cause; but Wilde was an Artist, and did not mind the world knowing that he was associating with office boys (Edward Shelley), arty working-class poets (John Gray), billiard-markers (Frederick Atkins), and the brothers Parker (valet and groom), as well as Lord Alfred Douglas ('Bosie').

The London homosexual scene of the 1890s was termed 'feasting with panthers', and Wilde was in the middle of it, taking his roughs to grand restaurants and glorifying in the squalor of low life, beset by blackmailers ('Uncle Burton') and all the passing trade that grew up around homosexuality. Wilde existed in a world of the picturesque and seedy. The romance of the streets was no empty phrase. He thought that he could sort it out in the courtroom, delivering the *coup de grace* to the impertinent prosecuting counsel, but unfortunately for him real life started when he mounted the dock. To be arrogant and self-confident was, in the circumstances, not the best way to win friends and influence people. Edmund Gosse was odd, but by being circumspect he obtained a knighthood and a string of honorary degrees; Edward Fitzgerald was odd, but he lived in a part of England where no one was concerned about his handsome young chum and now he is known solely for his *Omar Khayyam*. He did not, as he put it, need to fling 'the Winter Garment of Repentance'.

Keeping a low profile was easy if one set one's mind to it. One could be as camp as a row of tents if one behaved with decorum, as Edward Lefroy did, a clergyman who only betrayed himself in writing sonnets about sportsmen with 'crisp hair, frank eyes, and honest English skin'. In a letter Lefroy speculated that 'some folk would say it was a mark of sickly or diseased sentimentalism to admire any but feminine flesh. But that only proves how base is the carnality which is now reckoned the only legitimate form.' Carnality had no place in the mute adoration of Edward Lear for Franklin Lushington.

There were certain forms of homosexual behaviour which were difficult to reconcile with secrecy. Transvestism was often associated with display; a man who dressed in women's clothes would have the urge to go out into the streets to see whether he was convincing. He often was, and many transvestites were picked up by other men who believed them to be women. There are three types of transvestism – men wearing women's clothes, women wearing men's clothes, and both sexes adopting the garb of childhood. There was nothing offensive in women wearing men's clothes, and the uniform of horse-riding was one of the first of the unisex costumes. Women dressing up as men was a hallowed tradition, as we see in the plays of Shakespeare and his contemporaries. Men dressing up as women had also been allowed in the past; on the early stage all feminine parts had been played by men.

The revulsion against men dressing as women that reached a peak in the nineteenth century was partly due to a sense of the ridiculous and a realisation that Victorian fashions that looked absurd on women looked even worse on men. There was no objection to men wearing women's clothes when there was a reason, as in plays such as *Charley's Aunt*, one of the longest running of farces, in school or amateur dramatics, or in home charades. The Victorians had a coarse sense of fun at times, and such forms of transvestism were desexualised and therefore permissible.

Havelock Ellis coined the term Eonism for transvestism, and he and his contemporaries investigated the phenomenon searchingly. In-built transvestism could be caused by uncertainty about one's role in life, or could be a kind of narcissism. Young children were clothed the same way whether they were boys or girls, and boys could miss the dresses when they reached the age to adopt more masculine garb. Dresses were associated with a happy childhood. Parents could be blamed for instilling uncertainty about sexual roles; mothers who wanted a girl often dressed their sons as daughters long after they should have gone into trousers, though the reverse, daughters dressed like boys, was more uncommon. On the other hand, female tomboys resented the fact that they were girls, and deliberately cut their hair short and wore form-concealing clothes when they arrived at the age of puberty.

One of Ellis's male correspondents 'came across a lot of prettily trimmed underclothing, and was seized with a desire to put it on. I did so – and from that moment I date what I term my change of sex. I cannot describe to you the pleasure I felt when thus dressing myself for the first time in female garments. It was exquisite, delicious, intoxicating, far and away transcending anything I had before experienced, and when, after some trouble, I was completely attired as a girl, and placed myself in front of the glass, it was a positive revelation.' The man built up a collection of women's clothes, gloated over illustrations of 'sweet chemises, dainty drawers and charming corsets' in women's periodicals, and from walking in the garden he progressed to traversing country lanes in drag, dressing as a girl in a railway carriage, and the summation, a nocturnal prowl in a London square, 'clad in a charming combination of evening and young girl's dress, with a sleeveless bodice cut low to the last possible inch, and with the shortest possible skirts and petticoats, in which the delicious nudity of my bosom, and the naked exposure of part of my thighs between the tops of my elaborately gartered openwork silk stockings, was exquisitely exciting and in delightful contrast to the compression of my body in my tightly laced corsets.'

Another correspondent, disliked by his mother because he was not a girl, was fascinated by corsets, high-heeled and high-legged boots, combinations, and earrings. From the age of thirteen he wore clothing abstracted from his mother, and after he married he wore his wife's underclothing when she was not in the house. He obtained great pleasure from tattooing, and especially from the figure of a butterfly on the upper side of his penis. He also pierced his nipples and placed earrings in them, but this did not please him, so he sewed on pearl buttons instead. Although an extreme case, the man found girls, as well as his wife, willing to co-operate. The last addition to the tattooing was 'a fully-worded inscription of a sexual nature' on his stomach, which he was terrified of his wife seeing.

Although it was annoying to those who preferred the clear categories of male and female, and liked to know whom or what they were addressing, transvestism does not appear to have done anybody any harm. When transvestites were flaunting themselves at the music hall or the theatre they were tiresome to the law in exactly the way gaudy prostitutes were. If found out, they took the consequences; they had disobeyed the unwritten law: not to be found out.

The most celebrated transvestism case was that relating to Boulton and Park in 1871. It received much publicity, but the case itself was a shambles for there was strictly speaking no law against wearing drag, much to the displeasure of Lord Chief Justice Cockburn. Ernest Boulton and Frederick Park had dressed up as women, had frequented the Alhambra and the Surrey Theatre, had picked up men, and had involved minor members of the aristocracy in their high jinks. The police surgeon had examined their bottoms for evidence of penetration without permission from a magistrate, and in every possible manner the police had overstepped the mark. The jury brought in a verdict of not guilty, despite the summing-up of Cockburn, who found it 'impossible to speak in terms of sufficient reprobation of indecent conduct of this description. No one can doubt it is an outrage not only of public morality but also of decency.'

Transvestites did not have any conscious contempt for institutions; they acted according to their impulses, and did not set out to prove anything by appearing in public in drag (only their skill at dissimulation). They carried on in their own way, with only an outside chance of being apprehended on some charge or other. They were less vulnerable than the homosexuals who loitered at the Serpentine in Hyde Park looking at the male bathers, or who hovered around the army barracks (many homosexual brothels were located near Kensington barracks).

There were others too who, though heterosexually inclined, went their own way regardless of consequences. The Bohemian set saw no reason to abide by the rules; the middle classes were not awesome censors but a bunch of Philistines to be exploited, whose peculiar views on the sanctity of marriage were no concern of theirs. There was often a social purpose behind their work; they sought to express their horror at the ruthless organisation of modern society.

There were Bohemians of every shade, from the artists and writers who had studied and worked in France and had acquired Parisian ways, through the egocentric Pre-Raphaelites, the Aesthetes of the Oscar Wilde period, on to the Decadents of the 1880s and 1890s. The most influential of the Pre-Raphaelites were Rossetti and William Morris, greatly different in personality as they were. Dante Gabriel Rossetti, described by Ruskin as the 'great Italian lost in the Inferno of London' went from woman to woman as the mood took him, from the ailing sickly Elizabeth Siddal to the big lusty Fanny Cornforth, known to him as 'Elephant'. Eventually he seduced William Morris's wife. Rossetti, said John Henry Middleton, a Cambridge don and a friend of both Rossetti and Morris, was 'addicted to loves of the most material kind both before and after his marriage, with women, generally models, without other soul than beauty'. The marital affairs of Rossetti's associate William Bell Scott were equally bemusing. John Millais, later to be one of the stalwarts of the Royal Academy, stole John Ruskin's wife off him (although Millais was knighted, Queen Victoria never received his wife, the former Mrs Ruskin).

The Pre-Raphaelites were not particularly immoral, but they were unorthodox and free. They were not censorious, and people behaved as they felt. The glowing social ideas, of creating a new Jerusalem, were lost, but habits persisted. The Aesthetes rebelled against middle-class ugliness, and made Life into an Art Form. Its philosopher was Walter Pater, a Brasenose College don. When asked by one of his neophytes, 'But why should we be good, Mr Pater?' he replied, 'Because it is so beautiful.' Not because it would be convenient. It was also beautiful to be bad, and right and wrong were concepts that could be bounced around as it took the fancy. The Pre-Raphaelites were indifferent to Victorian morality; the Aesthetes were contemptuous. They had their own scale of values, and the more conventional, striving to bring these strange people to order and make them conform, found themselves grappling with smoke-like wraiths. Standards of acceptability were turned upside down. The middle classes had circumscribed ideas on religion; it was good for one, in some unspecified manner. The Aesthetes rated religion on its aesthetic quality. The 'starveling ceremonies of the Low Church are not worth witnessing', dismissed Pater, and that was enough for him, not interested whether the Low Church represented the virtues of English Christianity as opposed to the Popish devilry of the High Church.

At a time when censorship was producing a string of court cases on grounds of obscenity Walter Pater despatched the whole matter into triviality: 'It does not matter what is said provided it is said beautifully', he announced. It was an age of Culture. When Goering heard the word he reached for his revolver; the middle classes would have liked to have applied to a magistrtate for a search warrant. Pater was satirised by W. H. Mallock in his *The New Republic* (1877). Mallock was not liked by the Aesthetes, nor their successors a decade or more on. He was, said Henry James, 'a most disagreeable and unsympathetic youth, with natural bad manners increased by the odious London affectation of none'.

Pater appears in Mallock's book as Mr Rose, who 'always speaks in an undertone and his two topics are self-indulgence and art'. What does successful life consist of? 'Simply in the consciousness of exquisite living,' replies Mr Rose.

The Pre-Raphaelites and the Aesthetes intermingled, and what they represented was synthesised in the Decadence, in which the young lived out the parlour game of Walter Pater. The symptoms of what was considered by many to be a disease showed itself in a variety of ways. Oscar Wilde's *A Picture of Dorian Grey* (1891) is one of its holy relics. That it was published at all illustrates the slackening grip of Victorianism; it might even have sounded the death knell of it.

The Aesthetic age was self-conscious, gently cuckoo, but the Decadence was demoniacal. 'No, I do not seek Happiness,' said Oscar Wilde, 'but Pleasure, which is much more tragic.' The old order was dying with the old queen, and the supporters of the *status quo* put up their shutters, occasionally emerging in a screaming horde when they scented blood, as when Oscar Wilde came up for trial in 1895. When they were sated, they went back; it had been the last sortie of an ancient warrior clan.

The key figures of the 1890s were both tragic and comical, often at the same time. They went in search of scarlet sins, but were often too drunk to do anything about them when they found them. Aubrey Beardsley penned his malodorous fantasies, but was too ill to act them out. A new race of publishers arose, such as Leonard Smithers, who published Beardsley and his like. There was a fashion for grotesque perversity, impish hermaphrodites, and tall fiendish women with small heads. An untouched naked photograph of a simpering whore was old hat.

'The disposition of the times is curiously confused,' wrote Max Nordau in his *Degeneration*, 'a compound of feverish restlessness and blunted discouragement, of fearful presage and hang-dog renunciation.' Richard le Gallienne saw it differently: 'A New Spirit of Pleasure is abroad amongst us, and one that blows from no mere coteries of hedonistic philosophers, but comes on the four winds.' The height of bliss for women, wrote the novelist Grant Allen, author of the novel *The Woman Who Did*, was 'to be educated, to be emancipated, to be free, to be beautiful'. It was difficult to be all four but they tried.

A New Spirit of Pleasure sounds like middle-aged people wife-swapping in Wimbledon, but it meant much less than that. Max Beerbohm spoke sardonically of the 'lurid verses written by young men who, in real life know no haunt more lurid than a literary public house'. The pursuit of sin was followed with the utmost decorum; eventually when the novelty wore off, the wordy wits of the Decadence married and settled down, boring anyone they could collar with their reminiscences of the Naughty Nineties.

They were proud to call themselves outsiders, a harmless affectation that bothered no one. The women called themselves emancipationists, and were a problem to almost everyone. If any group conquered Victorian hypocrisy it was this scornful and often dedicated band. These women were often at odds with themselves, and would have accomplished more had they not been victims of their own doubt. They hurled themselves at male bastions; sometimes they were bruised by impact with crass stupidity and reaction, but on other occasions these ramparts were made of cardboard and succumbed to assault.

The emancipation movement, or, as it was called, the Cause, began years before Queen Victoria was summoned to the throne, when an attempt was made to give women some kind of equity with men, to get a fairer deal if not a completely fair deal. The women got no help from Victoria. In 1852 she complained that 'We women are not made for governing – and if we are good women we must dislike these masculine occupations.' She hated the campaign for Women's Rights, and said that the ringleaders ought to be whipped.

As the age went on, women obtained more and more of men's perquisites. In 1865 John Stuart Mill had been elected to Parliament on the emancipationist ticket and tried to get 'man' replaced by 'person' in the Reform Act of 1867, hopefully anticipating women getting the vote. He was more sanguine than they were; as in many things, women were more practical. As William Hazlitt suggested half a century earlier, they do not stop to reason about things that are obvious. 'If the house is on fire, they will at once proceed to put water on the flames, whatever the etiquette of the occasion may demand.'

Unwillingly, women were allowed into medicine, but not into law or the church. They did not get the vote until World War I, but they managed to work it so that they went out without chaperones, rode bicycles, went on walking holidays with whomever they pleased, and took jobs outside the home. When this happened, their situation changed dramatically. They were valued members of the consumer society, and had to be catered for. They even ceased to be patronised by the humorous papers.

In 1848 *Punch* had taken a jaundiced look at Women's Rights, and anticipated a Woman's Club with its own rules:

1 Woman naturally is superior to man. The rule of the husband by the wife is in the order of nature.
2 The wife is the natural guardian of her husband's secrets.
3 To the wife belongs the absolute control of her own milliners' bills.
4 The extreme age of woman is thirty years. She may be below this age, but cannot pass beyond it.
5 Woman has a right to her opinions. It is an odious tyranny which enforces the reasons of them.

This shows a typical male view of woman, as some kind of retarded child. 'Be good, sweet maid, and let who can be clever,' prattled Charles Kingsley. 'Man is the hunter, woman is the game,' mused Tennyson. Too often women took themselves at man's valuation; sometimes they pretended to. In the cant phrase, they boxed clever, and male domination began to come apart at the seams. In one sense, women were as hypocritical as men, but they acted so to redress unquestionable wrongs.

That woman was not the preconditioned object of legend became evident in the 1870s. In 1871 the masculine tastes of slang and cigarettes were adopted. Girls were 'awfully jolly' and young men were addressed by their girl friends as 'dear boys', while parents were 'too awfully dreadful'. In 1885 old-fashioned fuddy-duddies were shocked to read that

During the last few years there has been a decided improvement among girls of the well-to-do class in the direction of sport; two out of three play tennis all the summer; there are no bread-and-butter Misses now; there are no Girls; they are all Young Women. Far from them is all idea of schoolroom ignorance and innocence, farther still all notion of submitting to parental authority. Their Mother is a person whom it is their first duty to get rid of as soon as possible. The Young Woman nowadays marries herself not to the man she likes but to the man she can manage. She knows everything; she reads everything from French novels to the evening papers. For a wager she will dive head-first off a boat or run you a race round Belgrave Square in the middle of the night.

In *Side-Lights on English Society* (1881) E. C. Grenville-Murray surveyed the scene with interest not unmixed with hysteria:

The ambition of the modern woman is to show herself everywhere. She is no longer content with the drawing-room, the ballroom, and theatre; she must reign in the open air; and sports have been invented – croquet, skating, and lawn tennis – in which she can mix with men and dwarf them.

A glance at *Whitaker's Almanack* shows that in 1888 women were well represented in competitive sport. A Miss Cox did well against men in yachting, Mr and Mrs J. T. Smith created a new tandem tricycle record, and in tennis at the Covered Court Championship in Hyde Park women were much in evidence, with Mrs Hillyard the Ladies' Singles Champion. Yet women were still wearing bustles.

Women may not have got the vote, but they had freedom. They were like Jack-in-the-Boxes; someone had unhooked the lid, and now that they were out there was no chance of getting them back again. Being free from domestic tyranny and the awful necessity of marriage was not the end of it. In *The Pictorial World* of 1887 Lady Harberton was making proposals that might well have caused paterfamilias to curl up with apoplexy:

Women have an equal right with men to use the limbs that God gave them. . . . Petticoats are exhausting, unhealthy, dirty, and dangerous. The trouser is not only more comfortable, healthy and clean, but also more decent, as less liable to derangement.

The writer Gertrude Atherton was more alarming still when she declared in *The Lady's Realm* of 1899 that marriage was a trap for the Artist. 'If you have a love affair,' she said, 'the man can die, or transfer his affections, or *you* tire – which is more tragic still . . .' Lady Troubridge dismissed to oblivion 'the man who, being somewhat of a fool himself, is haunted by the uneasy dread of being only known as the husband of that clever Mrs. So-and-So.' Mrs Wynne speculated that a woman's love, 'even for an unworthy object, might elevate him, and must develop her own character.'

Smug in his superiority, it is doubtful whether the average family man understood the revolution that was taking place. Those who did waited complacently for the moral chaos that would come, the crash of broken commandments that would echo through the state. It did not come. Middle-class morality, after all, had not accomplished much. Even in the 1860s when its influence had been at its peak, adulterers had continued to commit adultery, prostitutes had found clients, aristocratic hostesses had distributed their house guests according to their amorous inclinations, and female servants had, in time-honoured custom, given themselves to the budding masters of the house.

Middle-class morality was not missed; it had made people unhappy by making them feel guilt. It had forced them to lie to themselves, to wear the mask of compliance. But by removing the guilt, emancipation had helped remove half the pleasure, and it gradually dawned on the lease-holders of the new age that the forbidden fruit had not been an idle phrase after all. Stealing a solitary apple in the Garden of Eden was a challenge; it was not like being offered an orchard-full of Cox's Orange Pippins. It was as if a steeplechaser had found that someone, with the best of intentions, had removed the hurdles, and the race had become something of a bore.

POSTCRIPT

THE Victorians did not invent sexual hypocrisy – they inherited it. Gentility and the consideration of what was proper, what was respectable, had long been codified. Jane Austen's *Pride and Prejudice* was a typical Victorian novel – except that it was begun in 1796. In its characters we can see many of the qualities held up for emulation by middle-class Victorians. Unseemliness is avoided by the simple expedient of pretending that it does not exist.

A distinction must always be made between sexual hypocrisy and sexual ignorance, and it must be remembered that many well-meaning and worthy men and women acted in a hypocritical manner for the best of motives. The striving for a code of behaviour implies the belief that such a code is good, or, at worst, useful. For many, the stability of society was considered to rest on the stability of the family. The family was not an open-ended concept with room for its various components to make their own personal adjustments, but a microcosm of the state, with a set hierarchy and laws to guarantee that it did not fall apart through anarchy. That was the theory, and that it was faulty lay in the inability of men and women to realise their own limitations or appreciate that their needs might not be compatible with family structure.

Throughout the period marriage was increasingly secularised; this did not make it less but more rigid. A particular marriage was not the concern of the church, and its representative the local vicar, but of everybody. Marriage meant a family, not two people marrying to cater in a convenient way for their sexual needs. A family did not necessarily pray together any more; it was more important for it to stay together, and anything that seemed to threaten to disrupt the system was frowned upon. In 1857 laws were passed which regularised divorce, making it possible without a special act through Parliament for each dissenting couple that wanted a judicial severance. In no year did the number of divorces exceed 1,000; in each year between 1861 and 1880 7.63 marriages per 1,000 took place. With a United Kingdom population in 1881 of 35 million, this meant that for every 280 marriages there was less than one divorce.

Because of the structure of society, the Victorians were obliged to make the best of a bad job. People do not change much in a hundred years, and no doubt the percentage of bad marriages was as high then as it is now. When there is no way out of such a match, men and women make their own adjustments, while pretending that everything is fine. This could be ruinous, though the final expose of the ghastliness of tyrannical family life was not made until 1903 with the publication of Samuel Butler's *The Way of All Flesh*.

The forces that made marriage permanent have to be considered every time one inclines to be patronising about Victorian sexual thought and behaviour. For the young couple venturing to the altar 'till death us do part' meant precisely that. No wonder that events made it often an inconceivably bad bargain.

Had there been information available that suggested that marriage was a convenience rather than a mystical union, then many more marriages would have been tolerable rather than sexually disastrous and personally destructive, and as the century drew to its close the troubled and the mystified did begin to appreciate that their problems were shared by thousands, maybe millions, of others, and that all the reactionary prattle of doctors and the clergy acted as a smoke-screen. More to the point, they observed that certain classes of society were not obeying the rules that they themselves were striving so hard to keep (and if they did not keep them they did at least conduct themselves with discretion).

Sensational journalism played a part in showing how life was really lived, in particular high life. Scandals brought down politicians, and the antics of the Prince of Wales, delicately hinted at, shocked and irritated. Shocked deliciously or irritated agonisingly, for the Prince of Wales was following the inclinations he shared with many of his future subjects. Such exposures created rancour. Sexual freedom was envied as much as deplored, and explosions of righteous indignation punctuate the last two decades of the nineteenth century, culminating in the persecution of Oscar Wilde who was not only sexually uninhibited but abnormally sexually uninhibited at that.

It is only human nature for those who have made an effort to conform to the rules to expect their children to follow suit, irrespective of changing social conditions, and it takes several generations for this to work itself out of society. A guardian of morals can easily be seen as a spoil sport, laying down codes of conduct that have no relevance to life as it is lived, codes of conduct that have been taken over from parents, sometimes discarded at adolescence but adopted again when it becomes time for the person to marry and conform, and take arms on behalf of the institution of the family.

Victorianism did not end with the death of the old queen, and flashes of it illuminate the 1920s and 1930s when those who were born in the morbid and gaudy 1860s were entering a bitter and rancorous old age, deploring the sexual freedom of the flappers and the Bright Young Things just as their parents had poured scorn on the aesthetes. At its most obvious, this can be seen as resenting the young having the pleasures that were forbidden to them, but it also expresses bewilderment that behaviour patterns should be so different. Or seemingly different. But what people do is often in striking contrast to what they say they do.

How the Victorians really behaved is open to conjecture. From the evidence of the newspapers they did not behave very differently to people today, except that there were probably more battered wives and babies, a direct result of the repressions brought on by insoluble unions. They did their best to accommodate themselves to the situation. This meant that there were 80,000 prostitutes in London, their clientele largely made up of respectable married men whose wives failed to give them the satisfaction they had expected. There were thousands of child prostitutes to cater for virgin-hunters. There were many homosexual brothels, strip-tease joints, flagellation establishments, even brothels catering for married women whose husbands had not come up to the mark. The law of supply and demand ensured that they were all used; the temper of the time guaranteed that few would mention their guilty patronage.

APPENDIX A

CHOICE MORSELS

THE Bible was too sacrosanct to be meddled with by the censors and the expurgators. This was a cause of amusement, and a list was drawn up of all the dubious references in the Bible, eventually published in a pamphlet entitled *Is the Bible Indictable?* These are the passages, searched for by school children, pondered over by those anxious for instruction in the facts of life:

Genesis IV, 1, 17, 25; VI, 4; IX, 20-5; XVI, 1-5; XVII, 10-14, 23-7; XIX, 4-9, 30-8; XXV, 21-6; XXVI, 8; XXIX, 21-35; XXX; XXXIV; XXXV, 22; XXXVIII, 8-10, 13-30; XXXIX, 7-18.

Exodus I, 15-19; IV, 24-6; XXII, 16-17, 19.

Leviticus V, 3; XII; XV; XVIII, 6-23; XX, 20-1; XXII, 3-5.

Numbers V, 12-29; XXV, 6-8; XXXI, 17-18.

Deuteronomy XXI, 10-14; XXII, 13-21; XXIII, 1, 10-11; XXV, 11-12; XXVII, 20, 22-3; XXVIII, 57.

Joshua V, 2-8.

Judges III, 15-25; XIX.

Ruth III, 3-14

1 Samuel II, 22; V, 9; XVIII, 25-7; XXI, 4-5; XXV, 23, 34.

2 Samuel VI, 14, 16, 20; X, 4; XI, 2-13; XII, 11-12; XIII, 1-22; XVI, 21-2.

1 Kings I, 1-4; XIV, 10, 24.

2 Kings IX, 8; XVIII, 27.

1 Chronicles XIX, 4.

Esther I, 11; II, 2, 4; 12-17; VII, 8.

Job III, 2.

Psalms XXXVIII, 5, 7.

Proverbs V, 17-20; VI, 24-32; VII, 5-22.

Ecclesiastes XI, 5.

Song of Solomon I, 2, 13; II, 4-6, 17; III, 1-4; IV, 5-6, 11; V, 2-4, 8, 14-16; VII, 2-3, 6-10, 12; VIII, 1-3, 8-10.

Isaiah III, 17; XX, 2, 4; XXVI, 17-18; XXXII, 11-12; XXXVI, 12; LVII, 8-9; LXVI, 7-12.

Jeremiah I, 5; LL, 20; III, 1-3, 6-9; V, 7-8; XI, 15; XIII, 26-7; XX, 17-18.

Lamentations I, 8, 9, 17.

Ezekiel IV, 12-15; VI, 9; XVI, 4-9, 15, 17, 25-6, 33-4, 37, 39; XVIII, 6, 11, 15; XXII, 8-11; XXIII, 6-9, 14-21, 29, 41-44.

Hosea I, 2; II, 2-13; III, 1-3; IV, 10-18; V, 3-4, 7; VI, 9-10; VII, 4; VIII, 9; IX, 1-11, 14, 16; XII, 3; XIII, 13.

Matthew I, 18-25.

Romans I, 24-7

1 Corinthians V, 1: VI, 9, 15-16, 18; VII.

1 Thessalonians IV, 3-7.

Hebrews XIII, 4.

2 Peter II, 10-18

Revelations II, 20-2; XVII, 1-4.

In 1888 Vizetelly, being prosecuted for publishing a translation of Zola's *La Terre*, prepared a list of English classics which logically should be suppressed on the grounds of obscenity. There are curious omissions, such as Shakespeare's *The Rape of Lucrece*, and the plays of Webster and Tourneur, Shadwell and Farquhar. It is therefore not a systematic list, but it is a fascinating precis.

SHAKESPEARE: *Troilus and Cressida* Act I, sc. 2; Act III, sc. 2; Act IV, sc. 1, 2; Act V, sc. 1. *Romeo and Juliet* Act I, sc. 3; Act II, sc. 4. *King Lear:* Act IV, sc. 6. *Antony and Cleopatra* Act II, sc. 5. *Two Gentlemen of Verona* Act II, sc. 7. *Measure for Measure* Act II, sc. 1; Act III, sc. 1. *Much Ado About Nothing* Act III, sc. 3. *Taming of the Shrew* Act II, sc. 1. *As You Like It* Act III, sc. 2. *The Winter's Tale* Act I, sc. 2; Act IV, sc. 3. *Henry VIII* Act V, sc. 3. *Pericles of Athens* Act IV, sc. 6. *Venus and Adonis* entire. [No mention of *Henry IV* and the bawdy Doll Tearsheet or the double-talk of Falstaff's chums. And no *Hamlet!*]

BEAUMONT AND FLETCHER: (Eleven volumes edited Dyce, 1843) [It would have been more consistent for Vizetelly to refer to acts and scenes.] *The Maid's Tragedy* Vol I, pp 342-3, 349, 352-3, 356, 361, 363-5. *Thierry and Theodoret* Vol I, pp 115, 143. *The*

Knight of the Burning Pestle Vol II, p 222. *A King and No King* Vol II, pp 325, 328. *Cupid's Revenge* Vol II, pp 403, 440. *The Custom of the Country* Vol IV, pp 408, 441, 443, 465, 472. *Valentinian* Vol V, p 273. *The Wild Goose Chase* Vol VIII, pp 137-8. *The Spanish Curate* Vol VIII, p 464. *The Night Walker* Vol XI, pp 151-2, 212. *The Two Noble Kinsmen* Vol XI, pp 368-9, 405.

BEN JONSON: *The Alchemist* Act II, sc. 1; Act III, sc. 2; Act V, sc. 1.

PHILIP MASSINGER: *A New Way to Pay Old Debts* Act II, sc. 1; Act III, sc. 2; Act IV, sc. 3. *The Maid of Honour* Act III, sc. 1; Act IV, sc. 1. *The City Madam* Act II, sc. 2; Act IV, sc. 2.

JOHN FORD: *'Tis Pity She's a Whore* Act II, sc. 1; Act IV, sc. 3.

THOMAS CAREWE: *Poems, Songs and Sonnets* (1772) 'A Rapture', 'On the Marriage of T.K. and C.C.', 'The Compliment', 'The Second Rapture', 'Love's Courtship'.

GEORGE ETHEREGE: *Love in a Tub* Act II, sc. 3; Act IV, s.c. 4; Act V, sc. 5. *She Would If She Could* Act II, sc. 2; Act III, sc. 2. *The Man of Mode* Act I, sc. 1. *The Imperfect Enjoyment* pp 398-9 [Vizetelly refers to the 1888 edition, no doubt throughly expurgated by the editor, A. W. Veriteg.]

JOHN DRYDEN *Sir Martin Marall* Vol III, p 43. *The Mock Astrologer* Vol III, pp 267, 292. [Vizetelly refers to the 1882 edition edited by George Saintsbury. Saintsbury was a diligent expurgator, and this may account for the limited amount of smut Vizetelly found therein.]

WILLIAM WYCHERLEY: *The Country Wife* Act I, sc. 1; Act II, sc. 1; Act III, sc. 2; Act IV, sc. 2, 3, 4; Act V, sc. 1, 4. [That Wycherley should only be represented by one play is extraordinary. His coarseness still affronts the more squeamish exponents of Eng Lit.]

WILLIAM CONGREVE: *The Old Bachelor* Act III, sc. 10; Act IV, sc. 18, 19, 21, 22; Act V, sc. 7, 8. *The Double Dealer* Act II, sc. 5; Act III, sc 4; Act IV, sc. 9. *Love for Love* Act I, sc. 5; Act II, sc. 3, 5, 11; Act III, sc. 9, 15; Act V, sc. 6 *The Way of the World* Act I, sc. 9.

JOHN VANBRUGH: *The Provoked Wife* Act I, sc. 1; Act II, sc. 1; Act III, sc. 1, 3; Act IV, sc. 3; Act V, sc. 6. *The Confederacy* Act III, sc. 2. *The Relapse* Prologue; Act I, sc. 3; Act II, sc. 1; Act IV, sc. 1, 3; Act V, sc. 1, 3; Epilogue.

THOMAS OTWAY: *The Soldier's Fortune* Act I, sc. 1; Act II, sc. 1; Act IV, sc. 2.

THOMAS HEYWOOD: *The Rape of Lucrece* Act III, sc. 5; Act IV, sc. 6.

DANIEL DEFOE: *Moll Flanders* Title page and pages 15, 19, 21, 29, 42, 44, 68, 73-4, 89-91, 94, 130, 135-6, 147, 165, 183-5. [Vizetelly used Bohn's edition of 1887.]

MATTHEW PRIOR: *Poetical Works* (1779): 'Paulo Purganti and His Wife', 'Hans Carvel', 'A True Maid', 'A Sailor's Wife', 'Chaste Florimel'.

JONATHAN SWIFT 'The Problem', 'Corinna', 'The Lady's Dressing Room', 'Strephon and Chloe'. [Vizetelly does not specify which edition. Obviously he did a very brief skip through, merely looked at a page or two.]

HENRY FIELDING *Tom Jones* pp 44, 55, 73, 76-7, 85-6, 96-7, 130, 139-40, 147, 173, 218-20, 244, 255, 268, 272-3. *Jonathan Wilde* pp 541, 545, 570-1, 585. [Vizetelly used 1840 edition.]

TOBIAS SMOLLETT *Roderick Random* 12-13, 21, 37, 39, 48, 82, 89, 101, 106. *Peregrine Pickle* 227, 229, 246, 258, 261. [Vizetelly used Bohn's 1858 edition. Why no mention of *Humphrey Clinker?*]

LAURENCE STERNE: *Tristram Shandy* pp 1-2, 30, 46, 90-1, 107, 109, 145, 165, 175, 183, 185-6. *A Sentimental Journey* pp 21, 28, 31, 42. [A Routledge edition is referred to, but no date is specified.]

LORD BYRON: *Don Juan* Canto I, II, V, VI, VIII. [For some obscure reason Vizetelly selects a 'people's edition' of 1884, a sure indication that the material has already been gone through with a tooth-comb.]

D. G. ROSSETTI: *Poems* (1870) 'Eden Bower', 'Jenny', 'The House of Life', Sonnets 2, 4, 5, 39.

A. C. SWINBURNE: *Poems and Ballads* (1878) pp 21, 26, 34, 172, 191, 197, 310. A very ramshackle selection, obviously compiled in haste. Any schoolgirl taking A levels in English Literature would have done better.

APPENDIX B

QUESTION TIME FOR
YOUNG LADIES

WE have a very full picture of the Victorian period; it was the last great age of written and printed communication before the arrival of the telephone. The Victorians put things down in black and white, whether it was a cooking recipe, their thoughts about God, or instructions to the butcher. They were always asking questions; they wanted to know how to cure acne, what the highest mountain in Ireland was, and whether Malta was Christian or not. They also asked questions about etiquette and sexual matters.

Young women, and perhaps women not so young, directed their enquiries at magazines such as the *Girl's Own Paper*, and answers to correspondents reveal more than one might imagine. They demonstrate aspects of life rarely touched elsewhere; they show the prevalence of worry. And worry was one of the ingredients that constituted hypocrisy. In reading through this selection we have to work out the questions, but this is not difficult. It is worth the effort, for it can give us insight into the problems that *really* perplexed young women (and young men), not the ones thought up for them by professional writers, who, as always, tended to live a shielded life without the mundane perplexities of the common herd.

FLIP – Whatever error may be committed by a parent, you have no right to regard yourself as either a judge, or as absolved from your own obligations as a daughter. You cannot help seeing or feeling, but your words and conduct should be filial and respectful, and you have a debt of gratitude to pay for years of care and support.

N EARNEST INQUIRER – We fear we cannot help you, save to advise the use of plenty of exercise and cold water.

MOTHER'S OWN GIRL – It must be a matter for each conscience to decide for itself. If such things lead to wrong-doing or wrong-thinking, they are evil for that particular person.

TRAFFORD – There is no relationship between you and your step-mother's brother, and it is not a connection named within the degrees of forbidden marriages in the Table which you will find in the Book of Common Prayer. We are glad to hear that our paper has been a help to you in striving after 'a nobler life'.

BROWN BETSY – We think you had better tell your friend, whenever you have an opportunity, that your mother says the correspondence must cease, as you are both too old now for any such child's play. This will explain the change, and should he really care for you he will make it known; if not, you could not wish to continue trifling with your own feelings by further inter-course. In any case, you should abide by your mother's wishes.

ENGLISH GIRL – It is gratifying to us to hear that you 'feel better after reading our book, mentally and physically', 'influencing its readers to lead nobler and purer lives'. This is exactly our principal aim. Yes, a 'thoroughly respectable girl' could take the situation you name and adorn it; but you must select the house carefully, and ascertain the duties required of you.

KATHLEEN – You ought to lay the case before your parents. Tell your mother, and let them obtain an explanation from your intended husband. If he be dishonourable and wish to draw off from his engagement, be assured you have been spared much misery in the future as his wife. Better to have a clear under-standing on the question of his attachment to you at once, and let him go freely, if he desires it, and there be no just cause for a change on his part with which you could be blamed.

KATHERINE – The whole subject has been carefully treated in 'The Fairy of the Family'[!] in vol. iv.

R.M.C.C. – Young girls should not go out in the evenings without some older person's escort, and certainly not without the entire approval of their mothers.

UNHAPPY FLO – Do not mind about 'feelings'. Tell the person who thus annoys you that his conduct is ungentlemanly and rude in forcing himself upon you, and that if he continues it you shall be obliged to ask your father to interfere.

GEMSTA – We think that you may keep the little gift, if one to be regarded as merely that of friendship. You must know best the terms on which you meet, with which we are unacquainted.

BUTTERCUP – We do not think it safe for ladies to ride their tricycles in the crowded streets of a town, nor does it look well for them to do so.

CALCUTTA – We think that it is right for the bride and bridegroom to consult their own feelings and position in life; they are by no means forced to take a wedding tour.

TROTTIE – The defect of showing the veins at the back of the hand is not one to be cured. We suppose that you are thin. Try to fatten yourself.

JEAN H. – We are only told that love is wrong when we make idols of those we love and allow them to stand in God's place. Take a concordance, and look out all the texts in the New Testament on love. Alas! little Jean, we fear you will come to the conclusion that we all of us love too little—not too much!

A THORN IN THE FLESH – Your letter shows a sad and unhealthy state of mind and body. Take more exercise – sea bathing, if possible – and get the doctor to give you a tonic. Begin to think of other people, and how you can minister to their comfort. Read your Bible, and learn each day some verses of good poetry by heart, so that you may strengthen your mind. Pray earnestly for help to resist wandering and unhappy thoughts.

TOPSY – Unless you were previously acquainted, he was impertinent and intrusive in bowing to you.

YOUNG AND SIMPLE – We do not think that any good man, or one who respected you, would ask you to perform any act of impropriety. Ask your father and mother; there should be perfect confidence between you.

LILY OF THE VALLEY – We do not understand your letter. If always 'so courteous and kind to you', and you 'meet him often', how can you inquire 'whether you may speak to him?' You must speak to him very often, and he must know you well, if you also 'know that he esteems you as well as loves you'. Consult your near relatives, if you have any, whose good sense and kindliness may be relied on.

PATIENCE – If only a slight though dark down, or little more, do not trouble yourself at all about it, but leave it alone. Sometimes it gives an individuality and expression to the face that is by no means unpleasing.

KID – We do not choose to reply to you under a name selected in such bad taste; discreditable to those who advised its adoption.

TOLLORA – Excepting for medicinal purposes, such as in cases of asthma, it is at least un-English to smoke cigarettes, a habit introduced among us by certain continental countries. The highest classes smoke amongst the latter, but not so, as a rule, in this country.

HAROLD – If to an intimate friend, begin, 'My dear Mr Smith'. It would make no difference whether he were a clergyman or not.

REGULAR GUMMIDGE – We think your general health is at fault. Take a tepid bath every morning, and walk after breakfast with your husband to his office; then rest, and arrange your day with intervals of rest, work, and reading. Do not be idle, either in mind or body. Take some simple tonic, such as those recommended by 'Medicus'. Probably one of your troubles is that you do not realise the constant beauty and sweetness of service. 'Ye do serve the Lord Christ.' If needful, do your needlework on the sofa, and do not cry more than you can help; crying is a peculiarly useless occupation.

ENGAGED – We do not think twenty-one is too early for a young woman to be engaged or married; but we should prefer, for her future husband's sake, that her spelling and writing should be better than yours. There are five faults of spelling in your short note.

A.M.S. – Mark your trousseau after you are married, not before.

MIN – We fear we cannot accept your offer of a white rat, nor can we tell you what to do with the others.

D. MAUD – A little schoolgirl of fifteen years of age might certainly be very warm-hearted, and of as affectionate a nature as a grown person, but the term you employ must be unsuitable in such a case.

TINY TIDDLEY – Much depends on the degree of intimacy and affection hitherto demonstrated. Why not inquire 'whether anything had happened to interrupt the previous relations between you?' Certainly you should not resort to the rudeness of what is commonly called a 'cut'.

AN ORGANIST – Persons of the upper ranks of society never say 'good afternoon' among each other. It would be considered vulgar.

UGLY MUG – Your friend is in an unhealthy condition, or she would not eat dry tea-leaves.

YOUNG GIRL – At your early age (fifteen years) the less you read in the way of novels the better. Better be satisfied with history and travels.

COLUMBUS – We have rarely read such a disgraceful confession! Talk of the young married woman being a 'friend', and yet you acknowledge that, owing to your conduct with reference to her husband – of which you give a shameful account – she 'is really very jealous', though 'she does not say anything!' What do we advise you to do? Humble yourself on your knees before God, and never be in the man's society alone again. At eighteen you have no excuse for your ill-conduct.

STABLE BOY – We do not see that it is any affair of yours, or of ours either, whether a lady wear a wig or not, and whether she has lost her hair through illness; there is no need for making any excuses about it. Do not make personal remarks about anyone, and avoid puerile gossip. We think that smoking is a horrible practice for women.

OSMOND – Try to exercise a little strength of mind and steadfastness of purpose in shaking off so silly and degrading an infatuation about a strange man. Where are your good sense and self-respect? Even a poor Indian squaw needs to be wooed and won. And if this wretched fancy – unjustified by long intimate intellectual intercourse – prove a hindrance to your prayers, and stand between you and your God (as you say), the sooner you begin to keep out of sight of the man the better.

ELSIE GWENDOLINE and LIONESS – Why should not the man 'serving' at lawn tennis collect the balls for himself? It is better not to be officiously attentive where men are concerned.

A FEARFUL NIGHT – The two girls must have known it to be a disgraceful proceeding to receive two young men into the house, and encourage them to remain there till late, unknown to their parents; otherwise, they would not have concealed it from them. No blessing could rest on such clandestine meetings. Nay, their characters are already tarnished in the opinion of anyone who may have heard of it; and they must also hold a very low place for dignity and maidenly propriety in the estimation of the young men themselves.

FUZZIEBACK – The slang term 'spooning', as connected either with love-making or its base counterfeit, flirtation, is derived from a sea-term. A ship, when unable in a storm to bear the strain of the sail she carries, is said to 'spoon' or dip too low under the water; and so a man, when he has given way, under too strong a pressure brought to bear on him, intentionally or otherwise, by a woman he admires, is said to 'spoon'.

PUZZLED GIRL – If you be unable to make your choice between your two admirers, you had better lay the problem before your parents, who will, doubtless, solve it for you. We see no reason for flight. If you have no special regard and affection for either suitor, they (your parents or guardians) will make your decision known to them in as delicate and friendly a way as may be possible. They will not lament very long when they know the tepid milk-and-water condition of your feelings towards them.

VIOLET – Amidst a heap of letters we find one thus signed, complaining that, 'not being gifted with talkative powers', and 'having met with a gentleman, been out three times, and does not seem to give satisfaction in the way of conversing with him, he has written to say that he will discontinue to meet her' until such a date a month later. We confess we have no experience in such circumstances and arrangements. If your parents approve of your engagement to any man, go out for a walk with him. Not otherwise. And if you be dull and uninteresting, read some nice book on natural history, or missionary travels and adventures; and tell him some stories if you fear his finding you 'heavy on hand'. Make an effort to be agreeable.

MAJOR GENERAL'S DARLING has an odd idea of her life, its duties and pleasures, if she thinks she ought to 'let anyone understand she dislikes them'. She actually wants us to instruct her how to do so. The very idea of such ungracious thoughts and unkind and rude manners has set all our grammar astray.

MARGARET BLANCHE – You should take no notice of the man's waiting for you. Remain at home at that time until he be gone.

SPIDER – We are glad that you have the desire to read the Bible to one unable to do so. It is a first step in the right direction. Your fear of dishonouring Christ by so doing, considering your own unworthiness, is another good sign.

CHERIE – However 'brotherly' and 'sisterly' a man and woman who are not engaged to be married may feel towards each other, it is inexpedient to give and accept presents from each other, and should not be done.

DISTRESSED MAIDEN – We have no cure to offer for holes in the skin of the face by picking at it with a needle.

VIOLET – Of course you should have the politeness to bow, in passing, to any man in your own position in life who is engaged with you in your Sunday-school teaching and church decorating, and to whom you are accustomed to speak on those occasions.

ONE IN TROUBLE – The laws of England do not sanction nor permit any marriage formed under coercion. Were a girl forcibly dragged to the altar, and the ceremony begun, she always has it in her power to say: 'No; I refuse my consent'. Never marry a man whom you 'positively dislike' and cannot love, or could not respect, even if you personally liked him.

Girl's Own Paper   1883-7

A SELECT BIBLIOGRAPHY

Acton, William, *A Practical Treatise on Diseases of the Urinary and Generative Organs* (1841); *Prostitution, considered in its Moral, Social and Sanitary Aspects* (2nd ed 1870)

Adamson, J. W. *English Education 1789-1902* (1930)

Adderley, James, *In Slums and Society* (1916)

Altick, Richard D. *The English Common Reader 1800-1900* (1957)

Anon. *Annals of Fashionable Gallantry* (1885); *The Battles of Venus* (c. 1850-60); *Beauty and How to Keep It* (n.d.); *The Confessional Unmasked* (1851); *Courtship As It Is and As It Ought to Be* (1877); *Curiosities of Flagellation* (1875); *Etiquette of Courtship and Marriage* (1844); *Etiquette of Courtship* (1852); *Habits of Good Society* (1855); *Handbook of the Toilet* (1841); *Health and Beauty* (n.d.); *How to Woo and How to Win* (1856); *Ladies' Pocket Book of Etiquette* (1840); *My Secret Life* (c. 1888); *Sins of the Cities of the Plains* (1881); *Sylvia's Book of the Toilet* (1881); *The Toilet* (1839); *Yokels' Preceptor* (c. 1840); Excluded are the large number of anonymous pornographic works of fiction.

Armitage, Gilbert, *Banned in England* (1932)

Ashbee, H. S. *Index Liborum Prohibitorum* (1877); *Centuria Liborum Absconditorum* (1879); *Catena Liborum Tacendorum* (1885)

Bartlett, D. V. G. *London by Day and Night* (1852)

Bayard, Mme, *Toilet Hints* (n.d.)

Beale, Dorothea, *Reports on the Education of Girls* (1870)

Best, Geoffrey, *Mid-Victorian Britain* (1971)

Bevan, J. O. *Wooing and Wedding* (1910)

Bigg, G. S. *Face and Figure* (1899)

Bloch, Iwan, *Sexual Life in England Past and Present* (tr. 1938)

Booth, Charles, *Life and Labour of the People in London* (1891-1903)

Bremner, C. S. *Education of Girls and Women in Great Britain* (1897)

Brown, Baldwin, *Young Men and Maidens* (1871)

Brown, J. B. *The Home* (1883)

Browning, H. Ellen, *Beauty Culture* (1898)

Buckley, Jerome H. *The Victorian Temper* (1971)

Burn, W. L. *The Age of Equipoise* (1961)

Campbell, James, *Amatory Experiences of a Surgeon* (1881)

Carlyle, Thomas, *Chartism* (1839); *Past and Present* (1843)

Carpenter, Edward, *Love's Coming of Age* (1896); *The Intermediate Sex* (1908)

Chandos, John (ed.), *To Deprave and Corrupt* (1962)

Chesney, Kellow, *Victorian Underworld* (1970)

Cole, G. D. H. and Postgage, Raymond, *The Common People* (1938)

Cooper, W. M. *History of the Rod* (1870)

Craig, Alec, *The Banned Books of England* (1962)

Croft-Cooke, Rupert, *Feasting With Panthers* (1967)

Cruse, Amy, *The Victorians and their Books* (1935)

Cunnington, C. W. *Feminine Attitudes in the Nineteenth Century* (1935); *The Perfect Lady* (1948)

Curtis, S. J. and Boultwood, M. E. A. *History of English Education Since 1800* (1960)

Davenport, John, *Aphrodisiacs and Anti-Aphrodisiacs* (c. 1873); *Curiositates Eroticae Physiologiae* (1875)

Dawes, C. R. *History of English Erotic Literature* (1934)

Decker, C. R. *The Victorian Conscience* (1952)

Dicey, A. V. *Law and Public Opinion in England* (1914)

Dingwall, E. J. *Male Infibulation* (1925)

Dodds, J. W. *The Age of Paradox* (1953)

Dunbar, Jane, *Early Victorian Woman* (1953)

Ellis, Havelock, *Man and Woman* (1894); *Studies in the Psychology of Sex* (1897-1928)

Ellis, Ida, *The Essentials of Conception* (1891)

Ellis, Sara, *The Wives of England* (1843)

Epton, Nina, *Milord and Milady* (1962)

Ernest, Morris L. and Seagle, W. *To the Pure* (1929)

Fay, C. R. *Life and Labour in the Nineteenth Century* (1935)

Fenn, John, *The School Master's Legacy and Family Monitor* (1843)

Fere, C. *The Sexual Instinct* (1900)

Flack, Isaac Harvey, *Eternal Eve* (1950)

Flugel, J. C. *Man Morals and Society* (1945)

Fryer, Peter, *Mrs. Grundy* (1963)

Gallichan, W. M. *The Great Unmarried* (1916); *The Poison of Prudery* (1929)

Gaunt, William, *The Pre-Raphaelite Tragedy* (1942); *The Aesthetic Adventure* (1945); *Victorian Olympus* (1952)

Geary, W. N. *Law of Marriage* (1892)

Godwin, G. *London Shadows* (1854); *Town Swamps* (1859)

Goodwin, Michael (ed.) *Nineteenth Century Opinion* (1951)

Graham, T. S. *Modern Domestic Medicine* (1837)

Greenwood, James, *Curiosities of Savage Life* (1863); *Unsentimental Journey* (1867); *The Seven Curses of London* (1869); *Wilds of London* (1874); *Low Life Deeps* (1876)

Gretton, R. H. *The English Middle Class* (1917)

Grisewood, H. (ed.) *Ideas and Beliefs of the Victorians* (1949)

Hackwood, F. W. *Notes of Lessons on Moral Subjects* (1885)

Halevy, Elite, *A History of the English People in the Nineteenth Century* (1924-48)

Hallis, F. *The Law and Obscenity* (1932)

Hamilton, Ernest, *The Halcyon Era* (1933)

Hammond, J. L. and B. *The Age of the Chartists* (1930)

Harper, C. G. *Revolted Woman* (1896)

Harrison, J. F. C. *The Early Victorians 1832-51* (1971)

Haynes, E. S. P. *The Decline of Liberty in England* (1916)

Himes, N. E. *Medical History of Contraception* (1936)

Hogg, James, *The Habits of Good Society* (1860)

Home, C. S. *Nonconformity in the Nineteenth Century* (1907)

Houghton, W. E. *The Victorian Frame of Mind* (1957)

House, Humphrey, *The Dickens World* (1942)

Howe, J. W. *Excessive Venery, Masturbation and Continence* (1883)

Hyde, H. Montgomery, *History of Pornography* (1964)

Inge, Dean, *Christian Mysticism* (1899)

Inglis, K. *Churches and the Working Classes in Victorian England* (1963)

Irvine, William, *Apes Angels and Victorians* (1955)

Jackson, Holbrook, *The Eighteen-Nineties* (1913)

Jacollicot, L. *Medico-Legal Examination of the Abuses of Genital Sense* (1900)

Jay, A. O. *Life in Darkest London* (1891); *The Social Problem* (1893)

Jerrold, Blanchard, *A London Pilgrimage* (1872)

Johnston, G. *England As It Is* (1851)

Jones, Harry, *Courtship and Marriage* (1890)

Kingsley, Charles, *Health and Education* (1874)

Kirk, E. B. *Talk with Girls* (1905)

Krafft-Ebing, E. von, *Psychopathia Sexualis* (1925 ed)

Laver, James, *The Age of Optimism* (1966)

Legman, G. *The Horn Book* (1964)

Lewis, D. *In a Nutshell* (1883)

Linton, Mrs L. *The Girl of the Period* (1883)

Macfadden, Bernard, *The Power and Beauty of Superb Womanhood* (1901)

Mack, E. C. *Public Schools and British Opinion* (1930-41)

Marcus, Stephen, *The Other Victorians* (1964)

Narkun, Leo, *Mrs. Grundy* (1930)

May, Geoffrey, *Social Control of Sex Expression* (1930)

Mayhew, H. *London Labour and the London Poor* (1851-62)

McGregor, O. R. *Divorce in England* (1957)

Meyer, F. B. *Love, Courtship and Marriage* (1899)

Milligan, J. G. *Curiosities of Medical Experience* (1839)

Nadel, E. S. *Impressions of English Social Life* (1875)

Neff, W. F. *Victorian Working Women* (1929)

Newman, F. *Remedies for the Great Social Evil* (1889)

Newsome, David, *Godliness and Good Learning* (1961)

Nordau, Max, *Degeneration* (1895)

Paget, E. *The Spirit of Discipline* (1891)

Pare, W. *A Plan for the Suppression of the Predatory Classes* (1862)

Partridge, Eric, *Dictionary of Slang and Unconventional English* (1961)

Pearl, Cyril, *The Girl with the Swansdown Seat* (1955)

Pearsall, Ronald, *Worm in the Bud* (1969); *Night's Black Angels* (1975)

Peel, Mrs. C. S. *A Hundred Wonderful Years* (1926)

Perrin, Noel, *Dr. Bowdler's Legacy* (1970)

Pratt, E. A. *Pioneer Women of Victoria's Reign* (1897)

Praz, Mario, *The Romantic Agony* (1933)

Quennell, Peter, *Victorian Panorama* (1937)

Reiss, E. *The Rights and Duties of Englishwomen* (1934)

Rohnson, Victor (ed.) *Encyclopaedia Sexualis* (1936 New York)

Rose, Alfred, *Registrum Librorum Eroticorum* (1936)

Roughhead, William, *Bad Companions* (1930)

Ryan, Michael, *Philosophy of Marriage* (1837)

Schlesinger, Max, *Saunterings In and About London* (1853)

Shirreff, A. E. *Moral Training* (1892)

Smith, B. L. *Brief Summary of the Most Important Laws Concerning Women* (1854)

Stekel, W. *Sadism and Masochism* (1935)

Stock, St. George H. *Romance of Chastisement* (1866)

Strachey, Ray, *The Cause* (1928)

Taine, H. *Notes on England* (1872)

Tait, Lawson, *Diseases of Women* (1889)

Talbot, J. B. *Miseries of Prostitution* (1844)

Taylor, Isaac, *Home Education* (1838)

Thompson, E. P. *The Making of the English Working Class* (1964)

Thompson, F. M. *English Landed Society in the Nineteenth Century* (1963)

Thomson, David, *England in the Nineteenth Century* (1950)

Tonna, C. *The Wrongs of Women* (1844)
Turner, E. S. *History of Courting* (1954)
Ussher, R. *Neo-Malthusianism* (1897)
Walker, Mrs, *Female Beauty* (1837)
Watkins, O. D. *Holy Matrimony* (1895)
West, A. W. *A Blessing to Womankind* (1890)
Westermarck, E. A. *History of Human Marriage* (1891)
Wey, Francis, *A Frenchman Sees the English in the Fifties* (1935)
Wilkinson, J. *Popular Education* (1852)
Wilson, J. M. *Addresses on Morality in Public Schools* (1887)
Worth, Augustus, *The Confessional* (1882)
Wright, Thomas, *The Great Unwashed* (1868)
Young, G. M. (ed.), *Early Victorian England* (1934)

This is the tip of an iceberg, and a complete bibliography would overwhelm the text. There is therefore no mention of the dozens of splendid biographies dealing with key Victorian figures, such as Phyllis Grosskurth on J. A. Symonds, James Pope-Hennessy on Richard Monckton Milnes, Joan Evans on Ruskin, Susan Chitty on Charles Kingsley, Malcolm Muggeridge on Samuel Butler, or Roy Jenkins on Charles Dilke. American scholarship has produced *The Swinburne Letters* (1962), edited by Cecil Y. Lang, one of the great achievements of the decade. It is also superfluous to mention the vast number of nineteenth-century novels that illuminate the subject of this book.

The above list is representative, some good, some good in parts. That sterling contribution to pre-war understanding of the Victorians, *Early Victorian England*, in two massive volumes, has some appalling chapters. There are a number of general books on the nineteenth century to give background. J. W. Dodds' *The Age of Paradox* (1953) is about the best.

Rich as material is on the subject of this book, it is to be found rather in parliamentary investigations, newspaper reports, and articles in the general and specialised periodical press. The following list of newspapers, periodicals, and magazines is as important, perhaps more important, than the bibliography of books.

All the Year Round
Annual Register

Bird o'Freedom
Blackwood's
Boudoir
British Medical Journal

Cassell's Family Magazine
Chambers's Journal
Cremorne

Daily Telegraph
Day and Night
The Day's Work

INDEX